PENGUIN PLAYS

CAT ON A HOT TIN ROOF

THE MILK TRAIN DOESN'T STOP HERE ANYMORE

THE NIGHT OF THE IGUANA

Tennessee Williams was born in 1914 in Columbus, Missouri, where his grandfather was the episcopal clergyman. In 1926 his father, who was a travelling salesman, moved with his family to St Louis, and both he and his sister found it impossible to settle down to city life. He entered college during the depression and left after a couple of years to take a clerical job in a shoe company. He stayed there for two years, spending the evenings writing. He entered the University of Iowa in 1938 and completed his course, at the same time holding a large number of part-time jobs of great diversity. He received a Rockefeller fellowship in 1940 for his play *Battle of Angels*, and he won the Pulitzer Prize in 1948 and 1955. Among his other plays, *The Glass Menagerie* (1944), *A Streetcar Named Desire* (1947), *The Rose Tattoo* (1951), *Camino Real* (1953), *Baby Doll* (1957), *Orpheus Descending* (1957), *Something Unspoken* (1958), *Suddenly Last Summer* (1958), *Sweet Bird of Youth* (1959), and *The Night of the Iguana* (1961) have been published in Penguins.

His most recent plays are *The Roman Spring of Mrs Stone* (1969), *Small Craft Warnings* (1972) and *Eight Mortal Ladies Possessed* (1974). Tennessee Williams' *Memoirs* and a novel, *Moïse and the World of Reason*, were both published in 1975.

TENNESSEE WILLIAMS

CAT ON A
HOT TIN ROOF

THE MILK TRAIN DOESN'T
STOP HERE ANYMORE

THE NIGHT OF THE
IGUANA

PENGUIN BOOKS

In association with Martin Secker & Warburg

Penguin Books Ltd, Harmondsworth, Middlesex, England
Penguin Books, 625 Madison Avenue, New York, New York 10022, U.S.A.
Penguin Books Australia Ltd, Ringwood, Victoria, Australia
Penguin Books Canada Ltd, 2801 John Street, Markham, Ontario, Canada L3R 1B4
Penguin Books (N.Z.) Ltd, 182–190 Wairau Road, Auckland 10, New Zealand

—

Made and printed in Great Britain by
Richard Clay (The Chaucer Press) Ltd, Bungay, Suffolk
Set in Monotype Garamond

Cat on a Hot Tin Roof

To
AUDREY WOOD

PERSON – TO – PERSON

Of course it is a pity that so much of all creative work is so closely related to the personality of the one who does it.

It is sad and embarrassing and unattractive that those emotions that stir him deeply enough to demand expression, and to charge their expression with some measure of light and power, are nearly all rooted, however changed in their surface, in the particular and sometimes peculiar concerns of the artist himself, that special world, the passions and images of it that each of us weaves about him from birth to death, a web of monstrous complexity, spun forth at a speed that is incalculable to a length beyond measure, from the spider mouth of his own singular perceptions.

It is a lonely idea, a lonely condition, so terrifying to think of that we usually don't. And so we talk to each other, write and wire each other, call each other short and long distance across land and sea, clasp hands with each other at meeting and at parting, fight each other and even destroy each other because of this always somewhat thwarted effort to break through walls to each other. As a character in a play once said, 'We're all of us sentenced to solitary confinement inside our own skins.'

Personal lyricism is the outcry of prisoner to prisoner from the cell in solitary where each is confined for the duration of his life.

I once saw a group of little girls on a Mississippi sidewalk, all dolled up in their mothers' and sisters' cast-off finery, old raggedy ball gowns and plumed hats and high-heeled slippers, enacting a meeting of ladies in a parlour with a perfect mimicry of polite Southern gush and simper. But one child was not satisfied with the attention paid her enraptured performance by the others, they were too involved in their own performances to suit her, so she stretched out her skinny arms and threw back her skinny neck and shrieked to the deaf heavens and her equally oblivious playmates, 'Look at me, look at me, look at me!'

And then her mother's high-heeled slippers threw her off balance and she fell to the sidewalk in a great howling tangle of soiled white satin and torn pink net, and still nobody looked at her. *Having theatrical; affected*

I wonder if she is not, now, a Southern writer.

Of course it is not only Southern writers, of lyrical bent, who engage in such histrionics and shout, 'Look at me!' *Allegory story with a moral lesson* Perhaps it is a parable of all artists. And not always do we topple over and land in a tangle of trappings that don't fit us. However, it is well to be aware of that peril, and not to content yourself with a demand for attention, to know that out of your personal lyricism, your sidewalk histrionics, something has to be created that will not only attract observers but participants in the performance. *language of own personal emotion*

I try very hard to do that.

The fact that I want you to observe what I do for your possible pleasure and to give you knowledge of things that I feel I may know better than you, because my world is different from yours, as different as every man's world is from the world of others, is not enough excuse for a personal lyricism that has not yet mastered its necessary trick of rising above the singular to the plural concern, from personal to general import. But for years and years now, which may have passed like a dream because of this obsession, I have been trying to learn how to perform this trick and make it truthful, and sometimes I feel that I am able to do it. Sometimes, when the enraptured street-corner performer in me cries out 'Look at me!', I feel that my hazardous footwear and fantastic regalia may not quite throw me off balance. Then, suddenly, you fellow-performers in the sidewalk show may turn to give me your attention and allow me to hold it, at least for the interval between 8.40 and 11 something P.M.

Eleven years ago this month of March, when I was far closer than I knew, only nine months away from that long-delayed, but always expected, something that I lived for, the time when I would first catch and hold an audience's attention, I wrote my first preface to a long play. The final paragraph went like this:

'There is too much to say and not enough time to say it. Nor is there power enough. I am not a good writer. Sometimes I am a very bad writer indeed. There is hardly a successful writer in the field who cannot write circles around me ... but I think of writing as something more organic than words, something closer to being and action. I want to work more and more with a more plastic theatre than the one I have (worked with) before. I have never for one moment doubted that there are people – millions! – to say things to. We come to each other, gradually, but with love. It is the short reach of my arms that hinders, not the length and multiplicity of theirs. With love and with honesty, the embrace is inevitable.'

This characteristically emotional, if not rhetorical, statement of mine at that time seems to suggest that I thought of myself as having a highly personal, even intimate relationship with people who go to see plays. I did and I still do. A morbid shyness once prevented me from having much direct communication with people, and possibly that is why I began to write to them plays and stories. But even now when that tongue-locking, face-flushing, silent and crouching timidity has worn off with the passage of the troublesome youth that it sprang from, I still find it somehow easier to 'level with' crowds of strangers in the hushed twilight of orchestra and balcony sections of theatres than with individuals across a table from me. Their being strangers somehow makes them more familiar and more approachable, easier to talk to.

Of course I know that I have sometimes presumed too much upon corresponding sympathies and interest in those to whom I talk boldly, and this has led to rejections that were painful and costly enough to inspire more prudence. But when I weigh one thing against another, an easy liking against a hard respect, the balance always tips the same way, and whatever the risk of being turned a cold shoulder, I still don't want to talk to people only about the surface aspects of their lives, the sort of things that acquaintances laugh and chatter about on ordinary social occasions.

I feel that they get plenty of that, and heaven knows so do I, before and after the little interval of time in which I have their attention and say what I have to say to them. The discretion of social conversation, even among friends, is exceeded only by the discretion of 'the deep six', that grave wherein nothing is mentioned at all. Emily Dickinson, that lyrical spinster of Amherst, Massachusetts, who wore a strict and savage heart on a taffeta sleeve, commented wryly on that kind of posthumous discourse among friends in these lines:

> *I died for beauty, but was scarce*
> *Adjusted in the tomb,*
> *When one who died for truth was lain*
> *In an adjoining room.*
>
> *He questioned softly why I failed?*
> *'For beauty,' I replied.*
> *'And I for truth, – the two are one,*
> *We brethren are,' he said.*
>
> *And so, as kinsmen met a night,*
> *We talked between the rooms,*
> *Until the moss had reached our lips,*
> *And covered up our names.*

Meanwhile! – I want to go on talking to you as freely and intimately about what we live and die for as if I knew you better than anyone else whom you know.

TENNESSEE WILLIAMS

CHARACTERS OF THE PLAY

MARGARET

BRICK

MAE, sometimes called Sister Woman

BIG MAMA

DIXIE, a little girl

BIG DADDY

REVEREND TOOKER

GOOPER, sometimes called Brother Man

DOCTOR BAUGH, pronounced 'Baw'

LACEY, a Negro servant

SOOKEY, another

Another little girl and two small boys

(The playing script of Act Three also includes
TRIXIE, another little girl, also DAISY, BRIGHTIE,
and SMALL, servants.)

Cat On A Hot Tin Roof was presented at the Morosco Theatre in New York on 24 March 1955 by The Playwrights' Company. It was directed by Elia Kazan, with the following cast:

LACEY	*Maxwell Glanville*
SOOKEY	*Musa Williams*
MARGARET	*Barbara Bel Geddes*
BRICK	*Ben Gazzara*
MAE	*Madeleine Sherwood*
GOOPER	*Pat Hingle*
BIG MAMA	*Mildred Dunnock*
DIXIE	*Pauline Hahn*
BUSTER	*Darryl Richard*
SONNY	*Seth Edwards*
TRIXIE	*Janice Dunn*
BIG DADDY	*Burl Ives*
REVEREND TOOKER	*Fred Stewart*
DOCTOR BAUGH	*R. G. Armstrong*
DAISY	*Eva Vaughan Smith*
BRIGHTIE	*Brownie McGhee*
SMALL	*Sonny Terry*

NOTES FOR THE DESIGNER

THE set is the bed-sitting-room of a plantation home in the Mississippi Delta. It is along an upstairs gallery which probably runs around the entire house; it has two pairs of very wide doors opening on to the gallery, showing white balustrades against a fair summer sky that fades into dusk and night during the course of the play, which occupies precisely the time of its performance, excepting, of course, the fifteen minutes of intermission.

Perhaps the style of the room is not what you would expect in the home of the Delta's biggest cotton-planter. It is Victorian with a touch of the Far East. It hasn't changed much since it was occupied by the original owners of the place, Jack Straw and Peter Ochello, a pair of old bachelors who shared this room all their lives together. In other words, the room must evoke some ghosts; it is gently and poetically haunted by a relationship that must have involved a tenderness which was uncommon. This may be irrelevant or unnecessary, but I once saw a reproduction of a faded photograph of the veranda of Robert Louis Stevenson's home on that Samoan Island where he spent his last years, and there was a quality of tender light on weathered wood, such as porch furniture made of bamboo and wicker, exposed to tropical suns and tropical rains, which came to mind when I thought about the set for this play, bringing also to mind the grace and comfort of light, the reassurance it gives, on a late and fair afternoon in summer, the way that no matter what, even dread of death, is gently touched and soothed by it. For the set is the background for a play that deals with human extremities of emotion, and it needs that softness behind it.

The bathroom door, showing only pale-blue tile and silver towel racks, is in one side wall; the hall door in the opposite wall. Two articles of furniture need mention: a big double bed which staging should make a functional part of the set as often as suitable, the surface of which should be slightly raked to make figures on it seen more easily; and against the wall space between the two huge double doors upstage: a monumental monstrosity peculiar to our times, a *huge* console combination of radio-phonograph (Hi-Fi with three speakers) TV set *and* liquor cabinet, bearing and containing many glasses and bottles, all in one piece, which is a composition of muted silver tones, and the opalescent tones of reflecting glass, a chromatic link, this thing, between the sepia (tawny gold) tones of the interior and the cool (white and blue) tones of the gallery and sky. This piece of furniture (?!), this monument, is a very complete and compact little shrine to virtually all the comforts and illusions behind which we hide from such things as the characters in the play are faced with. . . .

The set should be far less realistic than I have so far implied in this description of it. I think the walls below the ceiling should dissolve mysteriously into air; the set should be roofed by the sky; stars and moon suggested by traces of milky pallor, as if they were observed through a telescope lens out of focus.

Anything else I can think of ? Oh, yes, fanlights (transoms shaped like an open glass fan) above all the doors in the set, with panes of blue and amber, and above all, the designer should take as many pains to give the actors room to move about freely (to show their restlessness, their passion for breaking out) as if it were a set for a ballet.

An evening in summer. The action is continuous, with two intermissions.

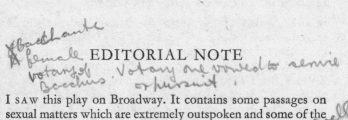

EDITORIAL NOTE

I SAW this play on Broadway. It contains some passages on sexual matters which are extremely outspoken and some of the audience of which I was a member indulged in Bacchanalian laughter; appropriately, these Maenads were female. This was the only source of embarrassment in the evening; the play itself caused none, for its harshness and crudities are an authentic part of its life. Tennessee Williams does for his country and generation something of what J. M. Synge did for Ireland. Here is life in the raw, the springs of vitality revealed at once in their animalism and in their poetry. To an Englishman, he opens a vision of the size of America, the huge fertility which can place apparently inexhaustible power in a man's hands ... 'twenty-eight thousand acres of the richest land this side of the valley Nile'. Big Daddy is a patriarch: he reminds one of a character in Genesis (perhaps from the less frequently quoted chapters); he has the same warmth of the soil in him. The best poetry of the play is in his speeches, which distil the wisdom of primitive human nature.

Brick and his Cat, the centres of the drama, vibrate in their desperation with the heat of the South. The family is clothed with the atmosphere of the South as with a garment. It is caged in the hot, thin-walled house, a prison amid the vast, rich lands around it. Tennessee Williams' use of repetition to create a prison of words is extraordinarily skilful: words beat like a tattoo on the heart, yet the beat is subtly changed at each hearing. This evocative quality of rhythm again reminds one of Synge. Perhaps it is no accident that in both writers the quality springs from a sad soil. ...

American drama, as it comes to maturity, enlarges the horizons of the theatre.

E. MARTIN BROWNE

New York,
October 1956

ACT ONE

At the rise of the curtain someone is taking a shower in the bathroom, the door of which is half open. A pretty young woman, with anxious lines in her face, enters the bedroom and crosses to the bathroom door.

MARGARET [*shouting above roar of water*]: One of those no-neck monsters hit me with a hot buttered biscuit so I have t'change!

[*Margaret's voice is both rapid and drawling. In her long speeches she has the vocal tricks of a priest delivering a liturgical chant, the lines are almost sung, always continuing a little beyond her breath so she has to gasp for another. Sometimes she intersperses the lines with a little wordless singing, such as 'Da-da-daaaa!'*

Water turns off and Brick calls out to her, but is still unseen. A tone of politely feigned interest, masking indifference, or worse, is characteristic of his speech with Margaret.]

BRICK: Wha'd you say, Maggie? Water was on s' loud I couldn't hearya. . . .

MARGARET: Well, I! – just remarked that! – one of th' no-neck monsters messed up m' lovely lace dress so I got t' – cha-a-ange. . . .

[*She opens and kicks shut drawers of the dresser.*]

BRICK: Why d'ya call Gooper's kiddies no-neck monsters?

MARGARET: Because they've got no necks! Isn't that a good enough reason?

BRICK: Don't they have any necks?

MARGARET: None visible. Their fat little heads are set on their fat little bodies without a bit of connexion.

BRICK: That's too bad.

MARGARET: Yes, it's too bad because you can't wring their necks if they've got no necks to wring! Isn't that right, honey?

[*She steps out of her dress, stands in a slip of ivory satin and lace.*]

Yep, they're no-neck monsters, all no-neck people are monsters . . .

[*Children shriek downstairs.*]

Hear them? Hear them screaming? I don't know where their voice-boxes are located since they don't have necks. I tell you I got so nervous at that table tonight I thought I would throw back my head and utter a scream you could hear across the Arkansas border an' parts of Louisiana an' Tennessee. I said to your charming sister-in-law, Mae, honey, couldn't you feed those precious little things at a separate table with an oilcloth cover? They make such a mess an' the lace cloth looks *so* pretty! She made enormous eyes at me and said, 'Ohhh, noooooo! On Big Daddy's birthday? Why, he would never forgive me!' Well, I want you to know, Big Daddy hadn't been at the table two minutes with those five no-neck monsters slobbering and drooling over their food before he threw down his fork an' shouted, 'Fo' God's sake, Gooper, why don't you put them pigs at a trough in th' kitchen?' – Well, I swear, I simply could have di-ieed!

Think of it, Brick, they've got five of them and number six is coming. They've brought the whole bunch down here like animals to display at a county fair. Why, they have those children doin' tricks all the time! 'Junior, show Big Daddy how you do this, show Big Daddy how you do that, say your little piece fo' Big Daddy, Sister. Show your dimples, Sugar. Brother, show Big Daddy how you stand on your head!' – It goes on all the time, along with constant little remarks and innuendoes about the fact that you and I have not produced any children, are totally childless and therefore totally useless! – Of course it's comical but it's also disgusting since it's so obvious what they're up to!

BRICK [*without interest*]: What are they up to, Maggie?

MARGARET: Why, you know what they're up to!

BRICK [*appearing*]: No, I don't know what they're up to.

[*He stands there in the bathroom doorway drying his hair with a towel and hanging on to the towel rack because one ankle is broken, plastered and bound. He is still slim and firm as a boy.*

His liquor hasn't started tearing him down outside. He has the additional charm of that cool air of detachment that people have who have given up the struggle. But now and then, when disturbed, something flashes behind it, like lightning in a fair sky, which shows that at some deeper level he is far from peaceful. Perhaps in a stronger light he would show some signs of de-liquescence, but the fading, still warm, light from the gallery treats him gently.]

MARGARET: I'll tell you what they're up to, boy of mine! –
They're up to cutting you out of your father's estate, and –
[She freezes momentarily before her next remark. Her voice drops as if it were somehow a personally embarrassing ad-mission.]

– Now we know that Big Daddy's dyin' of – *cancer....*
[There are voices on the lawn below: long-drawn calls across distance. Margaret raises her lovely bare arms and powders her armpits with a light sigh.

She adjusts the angle of a magnifying mirror to straighten an eyelash, then rises fretfully saying:]
There's so much light in the room it –

BRICK *[softly but sharply]*: Do we?

MARGARET: Do we what?

BRICK: Know Big Daddy's dyin' of cancer?

MARGARET: Got the report today.

BRICK: Oh...

MARGARET *[letting down bamboo blinds which cast long, gold-fretted shadows over the room]*: Yep, got th' report just now ... it didn't surprise me, Baby....
[Her voice has range, and music; sometimes it drops low as a boy's and you have a sudden image of her playing boy's games as a child.]

I recognized the symptoms soon's we got here last spring and I'm willin' to bet you that Brother Man and his wife were pretty sure of it, too. That more than likely explains why their usual summer migration to the coolness of the Great Smokies was passed up this summer in favour of – hustlin' down here ev'ry whipstitch with their whole screamin' tribe! And why so many allusions have been made to Rainbow Hill lately. You know what Rainbow

Hill is? Place that's famous for treatin' alcoholics an' dope fiends in the movies!

BRICK: I'm not in the movies.

MARGARET: No, and you don't take dope. Otherwise you're a perfect candidate for Rainbow Hill, Baby, and that's where they aim to ship you – over my dead body! Yep, over my dead body they'll ship you there, but nothing would please them better. Then Brother Man could get a-hold of the purse strings and dole out remittances to us, maybe get power-of-attorney and sign cheques for us and cut off our credit wherever, whenever he wanted! Son-of-a-bitch! – How'd you like that, Baby? – Well, you've been doin' just about ev'rything in your power to bring it about, you've just been doin' ev'rything you can think of to aid and abet them in this scheme of theirs! Quittin' work, devoting yourself to the occupation of drinkin'! – Breakin' your ankle last night on the high school athletic field: doin' what? Jumpin' hurdles? At two or three in the morning? Just fantastic! Got in the paper. *Clarksdale Register* carried a nice little item about it, human interest story about a well-known former athlete stagin' a one-man track meet on the Glorious Hill High School athletic field last night, but was slightly out of condition and didn't clear the first hurdle! Brother Man Gooper claims he exercised his influence t' keep it from goin' out over AP or UP or every goddam 'P'.

But, Brick? You still have one big advantage!

[*During the above swift flood of words, Brick has reclined with contrapuntal leisure on the snowy surface of the bed and has rolled over carefully on his side or belly.*]

BRICK [*wryly*]: Did you *say* something, Maggie?

MARGARET: Big Daddy dotes on you, honey. And he can't stand Brother Man and Brother Man's wife, that monster of fertility, Mae; she's downright odious to him! Know how I know? By little expressions that flicker over his face when that woman is holding fo'th on one of her choice topics such as – how she refused twilight sleep! – when the twins were delivered! Because she feels motherhood's an experience that a woman ought to experience fully! – in

order to fully appreciate the wonder and beauty of it!
HAH!

[*This loud 'HAH!' is accompanied by a violent action such
as slamming a drawer shut.*]

– and how she made Brother Man come in an' stand beside
her in the delivery room so he would not miss out on the
'wonder and beauty' of it either! – producin' those no-neck
monsters. . . .

[*A speech of this kind would be antipathetic from almost anybody but Margaret; she makes it oddly funny, because her eyes
constantly twinkle and her voice shakes with laughter which is
basically indulgent.*]

– Big Daddy shares my attitude toward those two! As for
me, well – I give him a laugh now and then and he tolerates
me. In fact! – I sometimes suspect that Big Daddy harbours
a little unconscious 'lech' fo' me. . . .

BRICK: What makes you think that Big Daddy has a lech
for you, Maggie?

MARGARET: Way he always drops his eyes down my body
when I'm talkin' to him, drops his eyes to my boobs an'
licks his old chops! Ha ha!

BRICK: That kind of talk is disgusting.

MARGARET: Did anyone ever tell you that you're an ass-
aching Puritan, Brick?

I think it's mighty fine that that ole fellow, on the door-
step of death, still takes in my shape with what I think is
deserved appreciation!

And you wanta know something else? Big Daddy didn't
know how many little Maes and Goopers had been produced! 'How many kids have you got?' he asked at the
table, just like Brother Man and his wife were new acquaintances to him! Big Mama said he was jokin', but that ole
boy wasn't jokin', Lord, no!

And when they infawmed him that they had five already
and were turning out number six! – the news seemed to
come as a sort of unpleasant surprise . . .

[*Children yell below.*]
Scream, monsters!

[*Turns to Brick with a sudden, gay, charming smile which*

*fades as she notices that he is not looking at her but into fading
gold space with a troubled expression.*

It is constant rejection that makes her humour 'bitchy'.]

Yes, you should of been at that supper-table, Baby.

[*Whenever she calls him 'baby' the word is a soft caress.*]

Y'know, Big Daddy, bless his ole sweet soul, he's the
dearest ole thing in the world, but he does hunch over his
food as if he preferred not to notice anything else. Well,
Mae an' Gooper were side by side at the table, direckly
across from Big Daddy, watchin' his face like hawks while
they jawed an' jabbered about the cuteness an' brilliance
of th' no-neck monsters!

[*She giggles with a hand fluttering at her throat and her breast
and her long throat arched.*

*She comes downstage and recreates the scene with voice and
gesture.*]

And the no-neck monsters were ranged around the table,
some in high chairs and some on th' *Books of Knowledge,* all
in fancy little paper caps in honour of Big Daddy's birthday,
and all through dinner, well, I want you to know that
Brother Man an' his partner never once, for one moment,
stopped exchanging pokes an' pinches an' kicks an' signs
an' signals! – Why, they were like a couple of cardsharps
fleecing a sucker. – Even Big Mama, bless her ole sweet
soul, she isn't th' quickest an' brightest thing in the world,
she finally noticed, at last, an' said to Gooper, 'Gooper,
what are you an' Mae makin' all these signs at each other
about?' – I swear t' goodness, I nearly choked on my
chicken!

[*Margaret, back at the dressing-table, still doesn't see Brick.
He is watching her with a look that is not quite definable.–
Amused? shocked? contemptuous? – part of those and part of
something else.*]

Y'know – your brother Gooper still cherishes the illusion
he took a giant step up on the social ladder when he married
Miss Mae Flynn of the Memphis Flynns.

[*Margaret moves about the room as she talks, stops before the
mirror, moves on.*]

But I have a piece of Spanish news for Gooper. The Flynns

never had a thing in this world but money and they lost
that, they were nothing at all but fairly successful climbers.
Of course, Mae Flynn came out in Memphis eight years
before I made my début in Nashville, but I had friends at
Ward-Belmont who came from Memphis and they used to
come to see me and I used to go to see them for Christmas
and spring vacations, and so I know who rates an' who
doesn't rate in Memphis society. Why, y'know ole Papa
Flynn, he barely escaped doing time in the Federal pen for
shady manipulations on th' stock market when his chain
stores crashed, and as for Mae having been a cotton carnival
queen, as they remind us so often, lest we forget, well,
that's one honour that I don't envy her for! – Sit on a brass
throne on a tacky float an' ride down Main Street, smilin',
bowin', and blowin' kisses to all the trash on the street –

[*She picks out a pair of jewelled sandals and rushes to the
dressing-table.*]

Why, year before last, when Susan McPheeters was singled
out fo' that honour, y' know what happened to her?
Y'know what happened to poor little Susie McPheeters?

BRICK [*absently*]: No. What happened to little Susie Mc-
Pheeters?

MARGARET: Somebody spit tobacco juice in her face.

BRICK [*dreamily*]: Somebody spit tobacco juice in her face?

MARGARET: That's right, some old drunk leaned out of a
window in the Hotel Gayoso and yelled, 'Hey, Queen,
hey, hey, there, Queenie!' Poor Susie looked up and
flashed him a radiant smile and he shot out a squirt of
tobacco juice right in poor Susie's face.

BRICK: Well, what d'you know about that.

MARGARET [*gaily*]: What do I know about it? I was there, I
saw it!

BRICK [*absently*]: Must have been kind of funny.

MARGARET: Susie didn't think so. Had hysterics. Screamed
like a banshee. They had to stop th' parade an' remove her
from her throne an' go on with –

[*She catches sight of him in the mirror, gasps slightly, wheels
about to face him. Count ten.*]

Why are you looking at me like that?

BRICK [*whistling softly, now*]: Like what, Maggie?

MARGARET [*intensely, fearfully*]: The way y' were lookin' at me just now, befo' I caught your eye in the mirror and you started t' whistle! I don't know how t' describe it but it froze my blood! – I've caught you lookin' at me like that so often lately. What are you thinkin' of when you look at me like that?

BRICK: I wasn't conscious of lookin' at you, Maggie.

MARGARET: Well, I was conscious of it! What were you thinkin'?

BRICK: I don't remember thinking of anything, Maggie.

MARGARET: Don't you think I know that – ? Don't you – ? – Think I know that –?

BRICK [*coolly*]: Know *what*, Maggie?

MARGARET [*struggling for expression*]: That I've gone through this – *hideous!* – *transformation*, become – *hard! Frantic!*

[*Then she adds, almost tenderly:*]

– *cruel!!*

That's what you've been observing in me lately. How could y' help but observe it? That's all right. I'm not – thin-skinned any more, can't afford t' be thin-skinned any more.

[*She is now recovering her power.*]

– But Brick? Brick?

BRICK: Did you say something?

MARGARET: I was *goin'* t' say something: that I get – lonely. Very!

BRICK: Ev'rybody gets that . . .

MARGARET: Living with someone you love can be lonelier – than living entirely *alone*! – if the one that y' love doesn't love you. . . .

[*There is a pause. Brick hobbles downstage and asks, without looking at her:*]

BRICK: Would you like to live alone, Maggie?

[*Another pause: then – after she has caught a quick, hurt breath:*]

MARGARET: *No! – God! – I wouldn't!*

[*Another gasping breath. She forcibly controls what must have been an impulse to cry out. We see her deliberately, very forcibly*] *going all the way back to the world in which you can talk about ordinary matters.*]

Did you have a nice shower?

BRICK: Uh-huh.

MARGARET: Was the water cool?

BRICK: No.

MARGARET: But it made y' feel fresh, huh?

BRICK: Fresher. . . .

MARGARET: I know something would make y' feel *much* fresher!

BRICK: What?

MARGARET: An alcohol rub. Or cologne, a rub with cologne!

BRICK: That's good after a workout but I haven't been workin' out, Maggie.

MARGARET: You've kept in good shape, though.

BRICK [*indifferently*]: You think so, Maggie?

MARGARET: I always thought drinkin' men lost their looks, but I was plainly mistaken.

BRICK [*wryly*]: Why, thanks, Maggie.

MARGARET: You're the only drinkin' man I know that it never seems t' put fat on.

BRICK: I'm gettin' softer, Maggie.

MARGARET: Well, sooner or later it's bound to soften you up. It was just beginning to soften up Skipper when –

[*She stops short.*]

I'm sorry. I never could keep my fingers off a sore – I wish you *would* lose your looks. If you did it would make the martyrdom of Saint Maggie a little more bearable. But no such goddam luck. I actually believe you've gotten better looking since you've gone on the bottle. Yeah, a person who didn't know you would think you'd never had a tense nerve in your body or a strained muscle.

[*There are sounds of croquet on the lawn below: the click of mallets, light voices, near and distant.*]

Of course, you always had that detached quality as if you were playing a game without much concern over whether you won or lost, and now that you've lost the game, not lost but just quit playing, you have that rare sort of charm that usually only happens in very old or hopelessly sick people, the charm of the defeated. – You look so cool, so cool, so enviably cool.

[*Music is heard.*]

They're playing croquet. The moon has appeared and it's white, just beginning to turn a little bit yellow. . . .

You were a wonderful lover. . . .

Such a wonderful person to go to bed with, and I think mostly because you were really indifferent to it. Isn't that right? Never had any anxiety about it, did it naturally, easily, slowly, with absolute confidence and perfect calm, more like opening a door for a lady or seating her at a table than giving expression to any longing for her. Your indifference made you wonderful at lovemaking – *strange?* – but true. . . .

You know, if I thought you would never, never, *never* make love to me again – I would go downstairs to the kitchen and pick out the longest and sharpest knife I could find and stick it straight into my heart, I swear that I would!

But one thing I don't have is the charm of the defeated, my hat is still in the ring, and I am determined to win!

[*There is the sound of croquet mallets hitting croquet balls.*]

– What is the victory of a cat on a hot roof? – I wish I knew. . . .

Just staying on it, I guess, as long as she can. . . .

[*More croquet sounds.*]

Later tonight I'm going to tell you I love you an' maybe by that time you'll be drunk enough to believe me. Yes, they're playing croquet. . . .

Big Daddy is dying of cancer. . . .

What were you thinking of when I caught you looking at me like that? Were you thinking of Skipper?

[*Brick takes up his crutch, rises.*]

Oh, excuse me, forgive me, but laws of silence don't work! No, laws of silence don't work. . . .

[*Brick crosses to the bar, takes a quick drink, and rubs his head with a towel.*]

Laws of silence don't work. . . .

When something is festering in your memory or your imagination, laws of silence don't work, it's just like shutting a door and locking it on a house on fire in hope of forgetting that the house is burning. But not facing a fire doesn't put it out. Silence about a thing just magnifies it. It grows and festers in silence, becomes malignant. . . .

Get dressed, Brick.

[*He drops his crutch.*]

BRICK: I've dropped my crutch.

[*He has stopped rubbing his hair dry but still stands hanging on to the towel rack in a white towel-cloth robe.*]

MARGARET: Lean on me.

BRICK: No, just give me my crutch.

MARGARET: Lean on my shoulder.

BRICK: *I don't want to lean on your shoulder, I want my crutch!*

[*This is spoken like sudden lightning.*]

Are you going to give me my crutch or do I have to get down on my knees on the floor and –

MARGARET: *Here, here, take it, take it!*

[*She has thrust the crutch at him.*]

BRICK [*hobbling out*]: Thanks . . .

MARGARET: We mustn't scream at each other, the walls in this house have ears. . . .

[*He hobbles directly to liquor cabinet to get a new drink.*]

– but that's the first time I've heard you raise your voice in a long time, Brick. A crack in the wall? – Of composure? – I think that's a good sign. . . .

A sign of nerves in a player on the defensive!

[*Brick turns and smiles at her coolly over his fresh drink.*]

BRICK: It just hasn't happened yet, Maggie.

MARGARET: What?

BRICK: The click I get in my head when I've had enough of this stuff to make me peaceful. . . .

Will you do me a favour?

MARGARET: Maybe I will. What favour?

BRICK: Just, just keep your voice down!

MARGARET [*in a hoarse whisper*]: I'll do you that favour, I'll speak in a whisper, if not shut up completely, if *you* will do *me* a favour and make that drink your last one till after the party.

BRICK: What party?

MARGARET: Big Daddy's birthday party.

BRICK: Is this Big Daddy's birthday?

MARGARET: You know this is Big Daddy's birthday!

BRICK: No, I don't, I forgot it.

MARGARET: Well, I remembered it for you. . . .

[*They are both speaking as breathlessly as a pair of kids after a fight, drawing deep exhausted breaths and looking at each other with faraway eyes, shaking and panting together as if they had broken apart from a violent struggle.*]

BRICK: Good for you, Maggie.

MARGARET: You just have to scribble a few lines on this card.

BRICK: You scribble something, Maggie.

MARGARET: It's got to be your handwriting; it's your present, I've given him my present; it's got to be your handwriting!

[*The tension between them is building again, the voices becoming shrill once more.*]

BRICK: I didn't get him a present.

MARGARET: I got one for you.

BRICK: All right. You write the card, then.

MARGARET: And have him know you didn't remember his birthday?

BRICK: I didn't remember his birthday.

MARGARET: You don't have to prove you didn't!

BRICK: I don't want to fool him about it.

MARGARET: Just write 'Love, Brick!' for God's –

BRICK: No.

MARGARET: You've *got* to!

BRICK: I don't have to do anything I don't want to do. You keep forgetting the conditions on which I agreed to stay on living with you.

MARGARET [*out before she knows it*]: I'm not living with you. We occupy the same cage.

BRICK: You've got to remember the conditions agreed on.

MARGARET: They're impossible conditions!

BRICK: Then why don't you –?

MARGARET: HUSH! Who is out there? Is somebody at the door?

[*There are footsteps in hall.*]

MAE [*outside*]: May I enter a moment?

MARGARET: Oh, *you!* Sure. Come in, Mae.

[*Mae enters bearing aloft the bow of a young lady's archery set.*]

MAE: Brick, is this thing yours?

MARGARET: Why, Sister Woman – that's my Diana Trophy. Won it at the intercollegiate archery contest on the Ole Miss campus.

MAE: It's a mighty dangerous thing to leave exposed round a house full of nawmal rid-blooded children attracted t'weapons.

MARGARET: 'Nawmal rid-blooded children attracted t'weapons' ought t'be taught to keep their hands off things that don't belong to them.

MAE: Maggie, honey, if you had children of your own you'd know how funny that is. Will you please lock this up and put the key out of reach?

MARGARET: Sister Woman, nobody is plotting the destruction of your kiddies. – Brick and I still have our special archers' licence. We're goin' deer-huntin' on Moon Lake as soon as the season starts. I love to run with dogs through chilly woods, run, run, leap over obstructions –

[*She goes into the closet carrying the bow.*]

MAE: How's the injured ankle, Brick?

BRICK: Doesn't hurt. Just itches.

MAE: Oh, my! Brick – Brick, you should've been downstairs after supper! Kiddies put on a show. Polly played the piano, Buster an' Sonny drums, an' then they turned out the lights an' Dixie an' Trixie puhfawmed a toe dance in fairy costume with *spahkluhs!* Big Daddy just beamed! He just beamed!

MARGARET [*from the closet with a sharp laugh*]: Oh, I bet. It breaks my heart that we missed it!

[*She re-enters.*]

But Mae? Why did y'give dawgs' names to all your kiddies?

MAE: *Dogs'* names?

[*Margaret has made this observation as she goes to raise the bamboo blinds, since the sunset glare has diminished. In crossing she winks at Brick.*]

MARGARET [*sweetly*]: Dixie, Trixie, Buster, Sonny, Polly! –

Sounds like four dogs and a parrot ... animal act in a circus!

MAE: Maggie?

[*Margaret turns with a smile.*]

Why are you so catty?

MARGARET: 'Cause I'm a cat! But why can't *you* take a joke, Sister Woman?

MAE: Nothin' pleases me more than a joke that's funny. You know the real names of our kiddies. Buster's real name is Robert. Sonny's real name is Saunders. Trixie's real name is Marlene and Dixie's –

[*Someone downstairs calls for her. 'Hey, Mae!' – She rushes to door, saying:*]

Intermission is over!

MARGARET [*as Mae closes door*]: I wonder what Dixie's real name is?

BRICK: Maggie, being catty doesn't help things any ...

MARGARET: I know! *WHY!* – am I so catty? – 'Cause I'm consumed with envy an' eaten up with longing? – Brick, I've laid out your beautiful Shantung silk suit from Rome and one of your monogrammed silk shirts. I'll put your cuff-links in it, those lovely star sapphires I get you to wear so rarely. . . .

BRICK: I can't get trousers on over this plaster cast.

MARGARET: Yes, you can, I'll help you.

BRICK: I'm not going to get dressed, Maggie.

MARGARET: Will you just put on a pair of white silk pyjamas?

BRICK: Yes, I'll do that, Maggie.

MARGARET: *Thank* you, thank you so *much*!

BRICK: Don't mention it.

MARGARET: *Oh, Brick!* How long does it have t' go on? This punishment? Haven't I done time enough, haven't I served my term, can't I apply for a – pardon?

BRICK: Maggie, you're spoiling my liquor. Lately your voice always sounds like you'd been running upstairs to warn somebody that the house was on fire!

MARGARET: Well, no wonder, no wonder. Y'know what I feel like, Brick?

[*Children's and grownups' voices are blended, below, in a loud*

but uncertain rendition of 'My Wild Irish Rose'.]
I feel all the time like a cat on a hot tin roof!

BRICK: Then jump off the roof, jump off it, cats can jump off roofs and land on their four feet uninjured!

MARGARET: Oh, yes!

BRICK: Do it! – fo' God's sake, do it . . .

MARGARET: Do what?

BRICK: Take a lover!

MARGARET: I can't see a man but you! Even with my eyes closed, I just see you! Why don't you get ugly, Brick, why don't you please get fat or ugly or something so I could stand it?

[She rushes to hall door, opens it, listens.]

The concert is still going on! Bravo, no-necks, bravo!

[She slams and locks door fiercely.]

BRICK: What did you lock the door for?

MARGARET: To give us a little privacy for a while.

BRICK: You know better, Maggie.

MARGARET: No, I don't know better. . . .

[She rushes to gallery doors, draws the rose-silk drapes across them.]

BRICK: Don't make a fool of yourself.

MARGARET: I don't mind makin' a fool of myself over you!

BRICK: I mind, Maggie. I feel embarrassed for you.

MARGARET: Feel embarrassed! But don't continue my torture. I can't live on and on under these circumstances.

BRICK: You agreed to –

MARGARET: I know but –

BRICK: – accept that condition!

MARGARET: *I CAN'T! CAN'T! CAN'T!*

[She seizes his shoulder.]

BRICK: Let go!

[He breaks away from her and seizes the small boudoir chair and raises it like a lion-tamer facing a big circus cat.

Count five. She stares at him with her fist pressed to her mouth, then bursts into shrill, almost hysterical laughter. He remains grave for a moment, then grins and puts the chair down.

Big Mama calls through closed door.]

BIG MAMA: Son? Son? Son?

BRICK: What is it, Big Mama?

BIG MAMA [*outside*]: Oh, son! We got the most wonderful news about Big Daddy. I just had t' run up an' tell you right this –

[*She rattles the knob.*]

– What's this door doin', locked, faw? You all think there's robbers in the house?

MARGARET: Big Mama, Brick is dressin', he's not dressed yet.

BIG MAMA: That's all right, it won't be the first time I've seen Brick not dressed. Come on, open this door!

[*Margaret, with a grimace, goes to unlock and open the hall door, as Brick hobbles rapidly to the bathroom and kicks the door shut. Big Mama has disappeared from the hall.*]

MARGARET: Big Mama?

[*Big Mama appears through the opposite gallery doors behind Margaret, huffing and puffing like an old bulldog. She is a short, stout woman; her sixty years and 170 pounds have left her somewhat breathless most of the time; she's always tensed like a boxer, or rather, a Japanese wrestler. Her 'family' was maybe a little superior to Big Daddy's, but not much. She wears a black or silver lace dress and at least half a million in flashy gems. She is very sincere.*]

BIG MAMA [*loudly, startling Margaret*]: Here – I come through Gooper's and Mae's gall'ry door. Where's Brick? *Brick –* Hurry on out of there, son. I just have a second and want to give you the news about Big Daddy. – I hate locked doors in a house. . . .

MARGARET [*with affected lightness*]: I've noticed you do, Big Mama, but people have got to have *some* moments of privacy, don't they?

BIG MAMA: No, ma'am, not in *my* house. [*Without pause.*] Whacha took off you' dress faw? I thought that little lace dress was so sweet on yuh, honey.

MARGARET: I thought it looked sweet on me, too, but one of m' cute little table-partners used it for a napkin so –!

BIG MAMA [*picking up stockings on floor*]: What?

MARGARET: You know, Big Mama, Mae and Gooper's so touchy about those children – thanks, Big Mama . . .

[*Big Mama has thrust the picked-up stockings in Margaret's hand with a grunt.*]

– that you just don't dare to suggest there's any room for improvement in their –

BIG MAMA: Brick, hurry out! – Shoot, Maggie, you just don't like children.

MARGARET: I do SO like children! Adore them! – well brought up!

BIG MAMA [*gentle – loving*]: Well, why don't you have some and bring them up well, then, instead of all the time pickin' on Gooper's an' Mae's?

GOOPER [*shouting up the stairs*]: Hey, hey, Big Mama, Betsy an' Hugh got to go, waitin' t' tell yuh g'by!

BIG MAMA: Tell 'em to hold their hawses, I'll be right down in a jiffy!

[*She turns to the bathroom door and calls out.*]

Son? Can you hear me in there?

[*There is a muffled answer.*]

We just got the full report from the laboratory at the Ochsner Clinic, completely negative, son, ev'rything negative, right on down the line! Nothin' a-tall's wrong with him but some little functional thing called a spastic colon. Can you hear me, son?

MARGARET: He can hear you, Big Mama.

BIG MAMA: Then why don't he say something? God Almighty, a piece of news like that should make him shout. It made *me* shout, I can tell you. I shouted and sobbed and fell right down on my knees! – Look!

[*She pulls up her skirt.*]

See the bruises where I hit my kneecaps? Took both doctors to haul me back on my feet!

[*She laughs – she always laughs like hell at herself.*]

Big Daddy was furious with me! But ain't that wonderful news?

[*Facing bathroom again, she continues:*]

After all the anxiety we been through to git a report like that on Big Daddy's birthday? Big Daddy tried to hide how much of a load that news took off his mind, but didn't fool *me*. He was mighty close to crying about it *himself*!

[*Goodbyes are shouted downstairs, and she rushes to door.*]

Hold those people down there, don't let them go! – Now, git dressed, we're all comin' up to this room fo' Big Daddy's birthday party because of your ankle. – How's his ankle, Maggie?

MARGARET: Well, he broke it, Big Mama.

BIG MAMA: I know he broke it.

[*A phone is ringing in hall. A Negro voice answers: 'Mistuh Polly's res'dence.'*]

I mean does it hurt him much still.

MARGARET: I'm afraid I can't give you that information, Big Mama. You'll have to ask Brick if it hurts much still or not.

SOOKEY [*in the hall*]: It's Memphis, Mizz Polly, it's Miss Sally in Memphis.

BIG MAMA: Awright, Sookey.

[*Big Mama rushes into the hall and is heard shouting on the phone:*]

Hello, Miss Sally. How are you, Miss Sally? – Yes, well, I was just gonna call you about it. *Shoot!* –

[*She raises her voice to a bellow.*]

Miss Sally? Don't ever call me from the Gayoso Lobby, too much talk goes on in that hotel lobby, no wonder you can't hear me! Now listen, Miss Sally. They's nothin' serious wrong with Big Daddy. We got the report just now, they's nothin' wrong but a thing called a – spastic! *SPASTIC!* – colon . . .

[*She appears at the hall door and calls to Margaret.*]

– Maggie, come out here and talk to that fool on the phone. I'm shouted breathless!

MARGARET [*goes out and is heard sweetly at phone*]: Miss Sally? This is Brick's wife, Maggie. So nice to hear your voice. Can you hear *mine*? Well, *good!* – Big Mama just wanted you to know that they've got the report from the Ochsner Clinic and what Big Daddy has is a spastic colon. Yes. Spastic colon, Miss Sally. That's right, spastic colon. *G'bye Miss Sally, hope I'll see you real soon!*

[*Hangs up a little before Miss Sally was probably ready to terminate the talk. She returns through the hall door.*]

She heard me perfectly. I've discovered with deaf people the thing to do is not shout at them but just enunciate clearly. My rich old Aunt Cornelia was deaf as the dead but I could make her hear me just by sayin' each word slowly, distinctly, close to her ear. I read her the *Commercial Appeal* ev'ry night, read her the classified ads in it, even, she never missed a word of it. But was she a mean ole thing! Know what I got when she died? Her unexpired subscriptions to five magazines and the Book-of-the-Month Club and a LIBRARY full of ev'ry dull book ever written! All else went to her hellcat of a sister ... meaner than she was, even!

[*Big Mama has been straightening things up in the room during this speech.*]

BIG MAMA [*closing closet door on discarded clothes*]: Miss Sally *sure is a case!* Big Daddy says she's always got her hand out fo' something. He's not mistaken. That poor ole thing always has her hand out fo' somethin'. I don't think Big Daddy gives her as much as he should.

[*Somebody shouts for her downstairs and she shouts:*]

I'm comin'!

[*She starts out. At the hall door, turns and jerks a forefinger, first towards the bathroom door, then towards the liquor cabinet, meaning: 'Has Brick been drinking?' Margaret pretends not to understand, cocks her head and raises her brows as if the pantomimic performance was completely mystifying to her.*

Big Mama rushes back to Margaret:]

Shoot! Stop playin' so dumb! — I mean has he been drinkin' that stuff much yet?

MARGARET [*with a little laugh*]: Oh! I think he had a highball after supper.

BIG MAMA: Don't laugh about it! — Some single men stop drinkin' when they git married and others start! Brick never touched liquor before he—!

MARGARET [*crying out*]: *THAT'S NOT FAIR!*

BIG MAMA: Fair or not fair I want to ask you a question, one question: D'you make Brick happy in bed?

MARGARET: Why don't you ask if he makes *me* happy in bed?

BIG MAMA: Because I know that —

MARGARET: *It works both ways!*

BIG MAMA: Something's not right! You're childless and my son drinks!

[*Someone has called her downstairs and she has rushed to the door on the line above. She turns at the door and points at the bed.*]

– When a marriage goes on the rocks, the rocks are *there*, right *there*!

MARGARET: *That's –*

[*Big Mama has swept out of the room and slammed the door.*]

– not – fair . . .

[*Margaret is alone, completely alone, and she feels it. She draws in, hunches her shoulders, raises her arms with fists clenched, shuts her eyes tight as a child about to be stabbed with a vaccination needle. When she opens her eyes again, what she sees is the long oval mirror and she rushes straight to it, stares into it with a grimace and says: 'Who are you?' – Then she crouches a little and answers herself in a different voice which is high, thin, mocking: 'I am Maggie the Cat!' – Straightens quickly as bathroom door opens a little and Brick calls out to her.*]

BRICK: Has Big Mama gone?

MARGARET: She's gone.

[*He opens the bathroom door and hobbles out, with his liquor glass now empty, straight to the liquor cabinet. He is whistling softly. Margaret's head pivots on her long, slender throat to watch him.*

She raises a hand uncertainly to the base of her throat, as if it was difficult for her to swallow, before she speaks:]

You know, our sex life didn't just peter out in the usual way, it was cut off short, long before the natural time for it to, and it's going to revive again, just as sudden as that. I'm confident of it. That's what I'm keeping myself attractive for. For the time when you'll see me again like other men see me. Yes, like other men see me. They still see me, Brick, and they like what they see. Uh-huh. Some of them would give their –

Look, Brick!

[*She stands before the long oval mirror, touches her breast and then her hips with her two hands.*]

How high my body stays on me! – Nothing has fallen on
me – not a fraction. . . .

[*Her voice is soft and trembling: a pleading child's. At this
moment as he turns to glance at her – a look which is like a
player passing a ball to another player, third down and goal to
go – she has to capture the audience in a grip so tight that she
can hold it till the first intermission without any lapse of
attention.*]

Other men still want me. My face looks strained, sometimes, but I've kept my figure as well as you've kept yours,
and men admire it. I still turn heads on the street. Why, last
week in Memphis everywhere that I went men's eyes
burned holes in my clothes, at the country club and in
restaurants and department stores, there wasn't a man I met
or walked by that didn't just eat me up with his eyes and
turn around when I passed him and look back at me. Why,
at Alice's party for her New York cousins, the best lookin'
man in the crowd – followed me upstairs and tried to force
his way in the powder room with me, followed me to the
door and tried to force his way in!

BRICK: Why didn't you let him, Maggie?

MARGARET: Because I'm not that common, for one thing.
Not that I wasn't almost tempted to. You like to know who
it was? It was Sonny Boy Maxwell, that's who!

BRICK: Oh, yeah, Sonny Boy Maxwell, he was a good
end-runner but had a little injury to his back and had to
quit.

MARGARET: He has no injury now and has no wife and still
has a lech for me!

BRICK: I see no reason to lock him out of a powder room in
that case.

MARGARET: And have someone catch me at it? I'm not that
stupid. Oh, I might some time cheat on you with someone,
since you're so insultingly eager to have me do it! – But if
I do, you can be damned sure it will be in a place and a
time where no one but me and the man could possibly
know. Because I'm not going to give you any excuse to
divorce me for being unfaithful or anything else. . . .

BRICK: Maggie, I wouldn't divorce you for being unfaithful

or anything else. Don't you know that? Hell. I'd be relieved
to know that you'd found yourself a lover.

MARGARET: Well, I'm taking no chances. No, I'd rather stay
on this hot tin roof.

BRICK: A hot tin roof's 'n uncomfo'table place t' stay on. . . .
[*He starts to whistle softly.*]

MARGARET [*through his whistle*]: Yeah, but I can stay on it
just as long as I have to.

BRICK: You could leave me, Maggie.
[*He resumes whistle. She wheels about to glare at him.*]

MARGARET: *Don't want to and will not!* Besides if I did, you
don't have a cent to pay for it but what you get from Big
Daddy and he's dying of cancer!
[*For the first time a realization of Big Daddy's doom seems to
penetrate to Brick's consciousness, visibly, and he looks at
Margaret.*]

BRICK: Big Mama just said he *wasn't,* that the report was
okay.

MARGARET: That's what she thinks because she got the same
story that they gave Big Daddy. And was just as taken in by
it as he was, poor ole things. . . .
But tonight they're going to tell her the truth about it.
When Big Daddy goes to bed, they're going to tell her
that he is dying of cancer.
[*She slams the dresser drawer.*]
– It's malignant and it's terminal.

BRICK: Does Big Daddy know it?

MARGARET: Hell, do they *ever* know it? Nobody says,
'You're dying.' You have to fool them. They have to fool
themselves.

BRICK: Why?

MARGARET: *Why?* Because human beings dream of life everlasting, that's the reason! But most of them want it on
earth and not in heaven.
[*He gives a short, hard laugh at her touch of humour.*]
Well. . . . [*She touches up her mascara.*] That's how it is,
anyhow. . . . [*She looks about.*] Where did I put down my
cigarette? Don't want to burn up the home-place, at least
not with Mae and Gooper and their five monsters in it!

[*She has found it and sucks at it greedily. Blows out smoke and continues:*]

So this is Big Daddy's last birthday. And Mae and Gooper, they know it, oh, *they* know it, all right. They got the first information from the Ochsner Clinic. That's why they rushed down here with their no-neck monsters. Because. Do you know something? Big Daddy's made no will? Big Daddy's never made out any will in his life, and so this campaign's afoot to impress him, forcibly as possible, with the fact that you drink and I've borne no children!

[*He continues to stare at her a moment, then mutters something sharp but not audible and hobbles rather rapidly out on to the long gallery in the fading, much faded, gold light.*]

MARGARET [*continuing her liturgical chant*]: Y'know, I'm *fond* of Big Daddy, I am genuinely fond of that old man, I really *am*, you know....

BRICK [*faintly, vaguely*]: Yes, I know you are....

MARGARET: I've always sort of admired him in spite of his coarseness, his four-letter words and so forth. Because Big Daddy *is* what he *is,* and he makes no bones about it. He hasn't turned gentleman farmer, he's still a Mississippi red neck, as much of a red neck as he must have been when he was just overseer here on the old Jack Straw and Peter Ochello place. But he got hold of it an' built it into th' biggest an' finest plantation in the Delta. – I've always *liked* Big Daddy....

[*She crosses to the proscenium.*]

Well, this is Big Daddy's last birthday. I'm sorry about it. But I'm facing the facts. It takes money to take care of a drinker and that's the office that I've been elected to lately.

BRICK: You don't have to take care of me.

MARGARET: Yes, I do. Two people in the same boat have got to take care of each other. At least you want money to buy more Echo Spring when this supply is exhausted, or will you be satisfied with a ten-cent beer?

Mae an' Gooper are plannin' to freeze us out of Big Daddy's estate because you drink and I'm childless. But we can defeat that plan. We're *going* to defeat that plan!

Brick, y'know, I've been so God damn disgustingly · poor all my life! – That's the *truth*, Brick!

BRICK: I'm not sayin' it isn't.

MARGARET: Always had to suck up to people I couldn't stand because they had money and I was poor as Job's turkey. You don't know what that's like. Well, I'll tell you, it's like you would feel a thousand miles away from Echo Spring! – And had to get back to it on that broken ankle . . . without a crutch!

That's how it feels to be as poor as Job's turkey and have to suck up to relatives that you hated because they had money and all you had was a bunch of hand-me-down clothes and a few old mouldy three per cent government bonds. My daddy loved his liquor, he fell in love with his liquor the way you've fallen in love with Echo Spring! – And my poor Mama, having to maintain some semblance of social position, to keep appearances up, on an income of one hundred and fifty dollars a month on those old government bonds!

When I came out, the year that I made my début, I had just two evening dresses! One Mother made me from a pattern in *Vogue*, the other a hand-me-down from a snotty rich cousin I hated!

– The dress that I married you in was my grandmother's weddin' gown. . . .

So that's why I'm like a cat on a hot tin roof!

[*Brick is still on the gallery. Someone below calls up to him in a warm Negro voice, 'Hiya, Mistah Brick, how yuh feelin'?' Brick raises his liquor glass as if that answered the question.*]

MARGARET: You can be young without money but you can't be old without it. You've got to be old *with* money because to be old without it is just too awful, you've got to be one or the other, either *young* or *with money,* you can't be old and *without* it. – That's the *truth*, Brick. . . .

[*Brick whistles softly, vaguely.*]

Well, now I'm dressed, I'm all dressed, there's nothing else for me to do.

[*Forlornly, almost fearfully.*]

I'm dressed, all dressed, nothing else for me to do. . . .

[*She moves about restlessly, aimlessly, and speaks, as if to herself.*]

I know when I made my mistake. – What am I –? Oh! – my bracelets. . . .

[*She starts working a collection of bracelets over her hands on to her wrists, about six on each, as she talks.*]

I've thought a whole lot about it and now I know when I made my mistake. Yes, I made my mistake when I told you the truth about that thing with Skipper. Never should have confessed it, a fatal error, tellin' you about that thing with Skipper.

BRICK: Maggie, shut up about Skipper. I mean it, Maggie; you got to shut up about Skipper.

MARGARET: You ought to understand that Skipper and I –

BRICK: You don't think I'm serious, Maggie? You're fooled by the fact that I am saying this quiet? Look, Maggie. What you're doing is a dangerous thing to do. You're – you're – you're – foolin' with something that – nobody ought to fool with.

MARGARET: This time I'm going to finish what I have to say to you. Skipper and I made love, if love you could call it, because it made both of us feel a little bit closer to you. You see, you son of a bitch, you asked too much of people, of me, of him, of all the unlucky poor damned sons of bitches that happen to love you, and there was a whole pack of them, yes, there was a pack of them besides me and Skipper, you asked too goddam much of people that loved you, you – superior creature! – you godlike being! – And so we made love to each other to dream it was you, both of us! Yes, yes, yes! Truth, truth! What's so awful about it? I like it, I think the truth is – yeah! I shouldn't have told you. . . .

BRICK [*holding his head unnaturally still and uptilted a bit*]: It was Skipper that told me about it. Not you, Maggie.

MARGARET: I told you!

BRICK: After he told me!

MARGARET: What does it matter who –?

[*Brick turns suddenly out upon the gallery and calls:*]

BRICK: Little girl! Hey, little girl!

LITTLE GIRL [*at a distance*]: What, Uncle Brick?

BRICK: Tell the folks to come up! – Bring everybody up-stairs!

MARGARET: I can't stop myself! I'd go on telling you this in front of them all, if I had to!

BRICK: Little girl! Go on, go on, will you? Do what I told you, call them!

MARGARET: Because it's got to be told and you, you! – you never let me!

[*She sobs, then controls herself, and continues almost calmly.*]

It was one of those beautiful, ideal things they tell about in the Greek legends, it couldn't be anything else, you being you, and that's what made it so sad, that's what made it so awful, because it was love that never could be carried through to anything satisfying or even talked about plainly. Brick, I tell you, you got to believe me, Brick, I *do* under-stand all about it! I – I think it was – *noble*! Can't you tell I'm sincere when I say I respect it? My only point, the only point that I'm making, is life has got to be allowed to continue even after the *dream* of life is – all – over. . . .

[*Brick is without his crutch. Leaning on furniture, he crosses to pick it up as she continues as if possessed by a will outside herself:*]

Why I remember when we double-dated at college, Gladys Fitzgerald and I and you and Skipper, it was more like a date between you and Skipper. Gladys and I were just sort of tagging along as if it was necessary to chaperone you! – to make a good public impression –

BRICK [*turns to face her, half lifting his crutch*]: Maggie, you want me to hit you with this crutch? Don't you know I could kill you with this crutch?

MARGARET: Good Lord, man, d' you think I'd care if you did?

BRICK: One man has one great good true thing in his life. One great good thing which is true! – I had friendship with Skipper. – You are naming it dirty!

MARGARET: I'm not naming it dirty! I am naming it clean.

BRICK: Not love with you, Maggie, but friendship with Skipper was that one great true thing, and you are naming it dirty!

MARGARET: Then you haven't been listenin', not understood what I'm saying! I'm naming it so damn clean that it killed poor Skipper! – You two had something that had to be kept on ice, yes, incorruptible, yes! – and death was the only icebox where you could keep it. . . .

BRICK: I married you, Maggie. Why would I marry you, Maggie, if I was –?

MARGARET: Brick, don't brain me yet, let me finish! – I know, believe me I know, that it was only Skipper that harboured even any *unconscious* desire for anything not perfectly pure between you two! – Now let me skip a little. You married me early that summer we graduated out of Ole Miss, and we were happy, weren't we, we were blissful, yes, hit heaven together ev'ry time that we loved! But that fall you an' Skipper turned down wonderful offers of jobs in order to keep on bein' football heroes – pro-football heroes. You organized the Dixie Stars that fall, so you could keep on bein' team-mates for ever! But somethin' was not right with it! – *Me included!* – between you. Skipper began hittin' the bottle . . . you got a spinal injury – couldn't play the Thanksgivin' game in Chicago, watched it on TV from a traction bed in Toledo. I joined Skipper. The Dixie Stars lost because poor Skipper was drunk. We drank together that night all night in the bar of the Blackstone and when cold day was comin' up over the Lake an' we were comin' out drunk to take a dizzy look at it, I said, 'SKIPPER! STOP LOVIN' MY HUSBAND OR TELL HIM HE'S GOT TO LET YOU ADMIT IT TO HIM!' – one way or another!

HE SLAPPED ME HARD ON THE MOUTH! – then turned and ran without stopping once, I am sure, all the way back into his room at the Blackstone. . . .

– When I came to his room that night, with a little scratch like a shy little mouse at his door, he made that pitiful, ineffectual little attempt to prove that what I had said wasn't true. . . .

[*Brick strikes at her with crutch, a blow that shatters the gemlike lamp on the table.*]

– In this way, I destroyed him, by telling him truth that

he and his world which he was born and raised in, yours and his world, had told him could not be told?

– From then on Skipper was nothing at all but a receptacle for liquor and drugs. . . .

– *Who shot cock-robin? I with my* –

[*She throws back her head with tight shut eyes.*]

– *merciful arrow!*

[*Brick strikes at her; misses.*]

Missed me! – Sorry, – I'm not tryin' to whitewash my behaviour, Christ, no! Brick, I'm not good. I don't know why people have to pretend to be good, nobody's good. The rich or the well-to-do can afford to respect moral patterns, conventional moral patterns, but I could never afford to, yeah, but – I'm honest! Give me credit for just that, will you *please*? – Born poor, raised poor, expect to die poor unless I manage to get us something out of what Big Daddy leaves when he dies of cancer! But Brick?! – *Skipper is dead! I'm alive!* Maggie the cat is –

[*Brick hops awkwardly forward and strikes at her again with his crutch.*]

– *alive! I am alive! I am* . . .

[*He hurls the crutch at her, across the bed she took refuge behind, and pitches forward on the floor as she completes her speech.*]

– *alive!*

[*A little girl, Dixie, bursts into the room, wearing an Indian war bonnet and firing a cap pistol at Margaret and shouting: 'Bang, bang, bang!'*

Laughter downstairs floats through the open hall door. Margaret had crouched gasping to bed at child's entrance. She now rises and says with cool fury:]

Little girl, your mother or someone should teach you – [*gasping*] – to knock at a door before you come into a room. Otherwise people might think that you – lack – good breeding. . . .

DIXIE: Yanh, yanh, yanh, what is Uncle Brick doin' on th' floor?

BRICK: I tried to kill your Aunt Maggie, but I failed – and I fell. Little girl, give me my crutch so I can get up off th' floor.

MARGARET: Yes, give your uncle his crutch, he's a cripple, honey, he broke his ankle last night jumping hurdles on the high school athletic field!

DIXIE: What were you jumping hurdles for, Uncle Brick?

BRICK: Because I used to jump them, and people like to do what they used to do, even after they've stopped being able to do it. . . .

MARGARET: That's right, that's your answer, now go away, little girl.

[*Dixie fires cap pistol at Margaret three times.*]
Stop, you stop that, monster! You little no-neck monster!
[*She seizes the cap pistol and hurls it through gallery doors.*]

DIXIE [*with a precocious instinct for the cruellest thing*]: You're *jealous!* – You're just jealous because you can't have babies!

[*She sticks out her tongue at Margaret as she sashays past her with her stomach stuck out, to the gallery. Margaret slams the gallery doors and leans panting against them. There is a pause. Brick has replaced his spilt drink and sits, faraway, on the great four-poster bed.*]

MARGARET: You see? – they gloat over us being childless, even in front of their five little no-neck monsters!

[*Pause. Voices approach on the stairs.*]

Brick? – I've been to a doctor in Memphis, a – a gynaecologist. . . .

I've been completely examined, and there is no reason why we can't have a child whenever we want one. And this is my time by the calendar to conceive. Are you listening to me? Are you? Are you LISTENING TO ME!

BRICK: Yes. I hear you, Maggie.

[*His attention returns to her inflamed face.*]

– But how in hell on earth do you imagine – that you're going to have a child by a man that can't stand you?

MARGARET: That's a problem that I will have to work out.

[*She wheels about to face the hall door.*]

Here they come!

[*The lights dim.*]

CURTAIN

ACT TWO

*There is no lapse of time. Margaret and Brick are in the same
positions they held at the end of Act One.*

MARGARET [*at door*]: Here they come!

> [*Big Daddy appears first, a tall man with a fierce, anxious
> look, moving carefully not to betray his weakness even, or
> especially, to himself.*]

BIG DADDY: Well, Brick.

BRICK: Hello, Big Daddy. – Congratulations!

BIG DADDY: – Crap....

> [*Some of the people are approaching through the hall, others
> along the gallery: voices from both directions. Gooper and
> Reverend Tooker become visible outside gallery doors, and
> their voices come in clearly.*
>
> *They pause outside as Gooper lights a cigar.*]

REVEREND TOOKER [*vivaciously*]: Oh, but St Paul's in
Grenada has three memorial windows, and the latest one
is a Tiffany stained-glass window that cost twenty-five hundred dollars, a picture of Christ the Good Shepherd with a
Lamb in His arms.

GOOPER: Who give that window, Preach?

REVEREND TOOKER: Clyde Fletcher's widow. Also presented St Paul's with a baptismal font.

GOOPER: Y'know what somebody ought t' give your church
is a *coolin'* system, Preach.

REVEREND TOOKER: Yes, siree, Bob! And y'know what Gus
Hamma's family gave in his memory to the church at Two
Rivers? A complete new stone parish-house with a basket-
ball court in the basement and a –

BIG DADDY [*uttering a loud barking laugh which is far from truly
mirthful*]: Hey, Preach! What's all this talk about memorials,
Preach? Y'think somebody's about t' kick off around here?
'S that it?

[*Startled by this interjection, Reverend Tooker decides to laugh at the question almost as loud as he can.*

How he would answer the question we'll never know, as he's spared that embarrassment by the voice of Gooper's wife, Mae, rising high and clear as she appears with 'Doc' Baugh, the family doctor, through the hall door.]

MAE [*almost religiously*]: – Let's see now, they've had their *tyyy*-phoid shots, and their tetanus shots, their diphtheria shots and their hepatitis shots and their polio shots, they got *those* shots every month from May through September, and – Gooper? Hey! Gooper! – What all have the kiddies been shot faw?

MARGARET [*overlapping a bit*]: Turn on the Hi-Fi, Brick! Let's have some music t' start off th' party with!

[*The talk becomes so general that the room sounds like a great aviary of chattering birds. Only Brick remains unengaged, leaning upon the liquor cabinet with his faraway smile, an ice cube in a paper napkin with which he now and then rubs his forehead. He doesn't respond to Margaret's command. She bounds forward and stoops over the instrument panel of the console.*]

GOOPER: We gave 'em that thing for a third anniversary present, got three speakers in it.

[*The room is suddenly blasted by the climax of a Wagnerian opera or a Beethoven symphony.*]

BIG DADDY: *Turn that damn thing off!*

[*Almost instant silence, almost instantly broken by the shouting charge of Big Mama, entering through hall door like a charging rhino.*]

BIG MAMA: *Wha's my Brick, wha's mah precious baby!!*

BIG DADDY: *Sorry! Turn it back on!*

[*Everyone laughs very loud. Big Daddy is famous for his jokes at Big Mama's expense, and nobody laughs louder at these jokes than Big Mama herself, though sometimes they're pretty cruel and Big Mama has to pick up or fuss with something to cover the hurt that the loud laugh doesn't quite cover.*

On this occasion, a happy occasion, because the dread in her heart has also been lifted by the false report on Big Daddy's

condition, she giggles, grotesquely, coyly, in Big Daddy's direction
and bears down upon Brick, all very quick and alive.]

BIG MAMA: Here he is, here's my precious baby! What's
that you've got in your hand? You put that liquor down,
son, your hand was made fo' holdin' somethin' better than
that!

GOOPER: Look at Brick put it down!

[Brick has obeyed Big Mama by draining the glass and handing
it to her. Again everyone laughs, some high, some low.]

BIG MAMA: Oh, you bad boy, you, you're my bad little boy.
Give Big Mama a kiss, you bad boy, you! – Look at him
shy away, will you? Brick never liked bein' kissed or made
a fuss over, I guess because he's always had too much of it!
Son, you turn that thing off!

[Brick has switched on the TV set.]

I can't stand TV, radio was bad enough but TV has gone
it one better, I mean – *[Plops wheezing in chair]* – one worse,
ha ha! Now what'm I sittin' down here faw? I want t' sit
next to my sweetheart on the sofa, hold hands with him and
love him up a little!

[Big Mama has on a black and white figured chiffon. The
large irregular patterns, like the markings of some massive
animal, the lustre of her great diamonds and many pearls, the
brilliants set in the silver frames of her glasses, her riotous voice,
booming laugh, have dominated the room since she entered. Big
Daddy has been regarding her with a steady grimace of chronic
annoyance.]

BIG MAMA *[still louder]*: Preacher, Preacher, hey, Preach! Give
me you' hand an' help me up from this chair!

REVEREND TOOKER: None of your tricks, Big Mama!

BIG MAMA: What tricks? You give me you' hand so I can
get up an' –

[Reverend Tooker extends her his hand. She grabs it and pulls
him into her lap with a shrill laugh that spans an octave in two
notes.]

Ever seen a preacher in a fat lady's lap? Hey, hey, folks!
Ever seen a preacher in a fat lady's lap?

[Big Mama is notorious throughout the Delta for this sort of
inelegant horseplay. Margaret looks on with indulgent humour,

*sipping Dubonnet 'on the rocks' and watching Brick, but Mae
and Gooper exchange signs of humourless anxiety over these
antics, the sort of behaviour which Mae thinks may account for
their failure to quite get in with the smartest young married set
in Memphis, despite all. One of the Negroes, Lacy or Sookey,
peeks in, cackling. They are waiting for a sign to bring in the
cake and champagne. But Big Daddy's not amused. He doesn't
understand why, in spite of the infinite mental relief he's received from the doctor's report, he still has these same old fox
teeth in his guts. 'This spastic thing sure is something,' he says
to himself, but aloud he roars at Big Mama:*]

BIG DADDY: *BIG MAMA, WILL YOU QUIT HOR-
SIN'?* – You're too old an' too fat fo' that sort of crazy
kid stuff an' besides a woman with your blood-pressure –
she had two hundred last spring! – is riskin' a stroke when
you mess around like that. . . .

BIG MAMA: *Here comes Big Daddy's birthday!*

[*Negroes in white jackets enter with an enormous birthday
cake ablaze with candles and carrying buckets of champagne
with satin ribbons about the bottle necks.*

*Mae and Gooper strike up song, and everybody, including
the Negroes and Children, joins in. Only Brick remains
aloof.*]

EVERYONE: Happy birthday to you.
            Happy birthday to you.
            Happy birthday, Big Daddy –
[*Some sing: 'Dear, Big Daddy!'*]
            Happy birthday to you.
[*Some sing: 'How old are youu'*]
[*Mae has come down centre and is organizing her children like
a chorus. She gives them a barely audible: 'One, two, three!'
and they are off in the new tune.*]

CHILDREN Skinamarinka – dinka – dink
            Skinamarinka – do
            We love you.
            Skinamarinka – dinka – dink
            Skinamarinka – do.
[*All together, they turn to Big Daddy.*]
            Big Daddy, you!

[*They turn back front, like a musical comedy chorus.*]
> We love you in the morning;
> We love you in the night.
> We love you when we're with you.
> And we love you out of sight.
> Skinamarinka – dinka – dink
> Skinamarinka – do.

[*Mae turns to Big Mama.*]
> Big Mama, too!

[*Big Mama bursts into tears. The Negroes leave.*]

BIG DADDY: Now Ida, what the hell is the matter with you?

MAE: She's just so happy.

BIG MAMA: I'm just so happy, Big Daddy, I have to cry or something.

[*Sudden and loud in the hush:*]

Brick, do you know the wonderful news that Doc Baugh got from the clinic about Big Daddy? Big Daddy's one hundred per cent!

MARGARET: Isn't that wonderful?

BIG MAMA: He's just one hundred per cent. Passed the examination with flying colours. Now that we know there's nothing wrong with Big Daddy but a spastic colon, I can tell you something. I was worried sick, half out of my mind, for fear that Big Daddy might have a thing like –

[*Margaret cuts through this speech, jumping up and exclaiming shrilly:*]

MARGARET: Brick, honey, aren't you going to give Big Daddy his birthday present?

[*Passing by him, she snatches his liquor glass from him.
She picks up a fancily wrapped package.*]

Here it is, Big Daddy, this is from Brick!

BIG MAMA: This is the biggest birthday Big Daddy's ever had, a hundred presents and bushels of telegrams from –

MAE [*at same time*]: What is it, Brick?

GOOPER: I bet 500 to 50 that Brick don't *know* what it is.

BIG MAMA: The fun of presents is not knowing what they are till you open the package. Open your present, Big Daddy.

BIG DADDY: Open it you'self. I want to ask Brick somethin'! Come here, Brick.

MARGARET: Big Daddy's callin' you, Brick.

[*She is opening the package.*]

BRICK: Tell Big Daddy I'm crippled.

BIG DADDY: I see you're crippled. I want to know how you got crippled.

MARGARET [*making diversionary tactics*]: Oh, look, oh, look, why, it's a cashmere robe!

[*She holds the robe up for all to see.*]

MAE: You sound surprised, Maggie.

MARGARET: I never saw one before.

MAE: That's funny. – *Hah!*

MARGARET [*turning on her fiercely, with a brilliant smile*]: Why is it funny? All my family ever had was family – and luxuries such as cashmere robes still surprise me!

BIG DADDY [*ominously*]: Quiet!

MAE [*heedless in her fury*]: I don't see how you could be so surprised when you bought it yourself at Loewenstein's in Memphis last Saturday. You know how I know?

BIG DADDY: I said, Quiet!

MAE: – I know because the salesgirl that sold it to you waited on me and said, Oh, Mrs Pollitt, your sister-in-law just bought a cashmere robe for your husband's father!

MARGARET: Sister Woman! Your talents are wasted as a housewife and mother, you really ought to be with the FBI or –

BIG DADDY: QUIET!

[*Reverend Tooker's reflexes are slower than the others'. He finishes a sentence after the bellow.*]

REVEREND TOOKER [*to Doc Baugh*]: – the Stork and the Reaper are running neck and neck!

[*He starts to laugh gaily when he notices the silence and Big Daddy's glare. His laugh dies falsely.*]

BIG DADDY: Preacher, I hope I'm not butting in on more talk about memorial stained-glass windows, am I, Preacher?

[*Reverend Tooker laughs feebly, then coughs dryly in the embarrassed silence.*]

Preacher?

BIG MAMA: Now, Big Daddy, don't you pick on Preacher!

BIG DADDY [*raising his voice*]: You ever hear that expression all hawk and no spit? You bring that expression to mind with that little dry cough of yours, all hawk an' no spit. . . .

[*The pause is broken only by a short startled laugh from Margaret, the only one there who is conscious of and amused by the grotesque.*]

MAE [*raising her arms and jangling her bracelets*]: I wonder if the mosquitoes are active tonight?

BIG DADDY: What's that, Little Mama? Did you make some remark?

MAE: Yes, I said I wondered if the mosquitoes would eat us alive if we went out on the gallery for a while.

BIG DADDY: Well, if they do, I'll have your bones pulverized for fertilizer!

BIG MAMA [*quickly*]: Last week we had an airplane spraying the place and I think it done some good, at least I haven't had a –

BIG DADDY [*cutting her speech*]: Brick, they tell me, if what they tell me is true, that you done some jumping last night on the high school athletic field?

BIG MAMA: Brick, Big Daddy is talking to you, son.

BRICK [*smiling vaguely over his drink*]: What was that, Big Daddy?

BIG DADDY: They said you done some jumping on the high school track field last night.

BRICK: That's what they told me, too.

BIG DADDY: Was it jumping or humping that you were doing out there? What were you doing out there at three A.M., layin' a woman on that cinder track?

BIG MAMA: Big Daddy, you are off the sick-list, now, and I'm not going to excuse you for talkin' so –

BIG DADDY: Quiet!

BIG MAMA: – *nasty* in front of Preacher and –

BIG DADDY: *QUIET!* – I ast you, Brick, if you was cuttin' you'self a piece o' poon-tang last night on that cinder track? I thought maybe you were chasin' poon-tang on that track an' tripped over something in the heat of the chase – 'sthat it?

[*Gooper laughs, loud and false, others nervously following suit. Big Mama stamps her foot, and purses her lips, crossing*] *to Mae and whispering something to her as Brick meets his father's hard, intent, grinning stare with a slow, vague smile that he offers all situations from behind the screen of his liquor.*]

BRICK: No, sir, I don't think so....

MAE [*at the same time, sweetly*]: Reverend Tooker, let's you and I take a stroll on the widow's walk.

[*She and the preacher go out on the gallery as Big Daddy says:*]

BIG DADDY: Then what the hell were you doing out there at three o'clock in the morning?

BRICK: Jumping the hurdles, Big Daddy, runnin' and jumpin' the hurdles, but those high hurdles have gotten too high for me, now.

BIG DADDY: 'Cause you was drunk?

BRICK [*his vague smile fading a little*]: Sober I wouldn't have tried to jump the *low* ones....

BIG MAMA [*quickly*]: Big Daddy, blow out the candles on your birthday cake!

MARGARET [*at the same time*]: I want to propose a toast to Big Daddy Pollitt on his sixty-fifth birthday, the biggest cotton-planter in –

BIG DADDY [*bellowing with fury and disgust*]: *I told you to stop it, now stop it, quit this –!*

BIG MAMA [*coming in front of Big Daddy with the cake*]: Big Daddy, I will not allow you to talk that way, not even on your birthday, I –

BIG DADDY: I'll talk like I want to on my birthday, Ida, or any other goddam day of the year and anybody here that don't like it knows what they can do!

BIG MAMA: You don't mean that!

BIG DADDY: What makes you think I don't mean it?

[*Meanwhile various discreet signals have been exchanged and Gooper has also gone out on the gallery.*]

BIG MAMA: I just know you don't mean it.

BIG DADDY: You don't know a goddam thing and you never did!

BIG MAMA: Big Daddy, you don't mean that.

BIG DADDY: Oh, yes, I do, oh, yes, I do, I mean it! I put up with a whole lot of crap around here because I thought I was dying. And you thought I was dying and you started taking over, well, you can stop taking over now, Ida, because I'm not gonna die, you can just stop now this business of taking over because you're not taking over because I'm not dying, I went through the laboratory and the goddam exploratory operation and there's nothing wrong with me but a spastic colon. And I'm not dying of cancer which you thought I was dying of. Ain't that so? Didn't you think that I was dying of cancer, Ida?

[*Almost everybody is out on the gallery but the two old people glaring at each other across the blazing cake.*

Big Mama's chest heaves and she presses a fat fist to her mouth.

Big Daddy continues, hoarsely:]

Ain't that so, Ida? Didn't you have an idea I was dying of cancer and now you could take control of this place and everything on it? I got that impression, I seemed to get that impression. Your loud voice everywhere, your fat old body butting in here and there!

BIG MAMA: Hush! The Preacher!

BIG DADDY: Rut the goddam preacher!

[*Big Mama gasps loudly and sits down on the sofa which is almost too small for her.*]

Did you hear what I said? I said rut the goddam preacher!

[*Somebody closes the gallery doors from outside just as there is a burst of fireworks and excited cries from the children.*]

BIG MAMA: I never seen you act like this before and I can't think what's got in you!

BIG DADDY: I went through all that laboratory and operation and all just so I would know if you or me was boss here! Well, now it turns out that I am and you ain't – and that's my birthday present – and my cake and champagne! – because for three years now you been gradually taking over. Bossing. Talking. Sashaying your fat old body around the place I made! I made this place! I was overseer on it! I was the overseer on the old Straw and Ochello plantation. I quit school at ten! I quit school at ten years old and went to work like a nigger in the fields. And I rose to be overseer of the Straw and Ochello plantation. And old Straw died and I was Ochello's partner and the place got bigger and bigger and bigger and bigger and bigger! I did all that myself with no goddam help from you, and now you think you're just about to take over. Well, I am just about to tell you that you are not just about to take over, you are not just about to take over a God damn thing. Is that clear to you, Ida? Is that very plain to you, now? Is that understood completely? I been through the laboratory from A to Z. I've had the goddam exploratory operation, and nothing is wrong with me but a spastic colon — made spastic, I guess, by *disgust*! By all the goddam lies and liars that I have had to put up with, and all the goddam hypocrisy that I lived with all these forty years that we been livin' together!

Hey! Ida! Blow out the candles on the birthday cake! Purse up your lips and draw a deep breath and blow out the goddam candles on the cake!

BIG MAMA: Oh, Big Daddy, oh, oh, oh, Big Daddy!

BIG DADDY: What's the matter with you?

BIG MAMA: *In all these years you never believed that I loved you??*

BIG DADDY: Huh?

BIG MAMA: *And I did, I did so much, I did love you!* — I even loved your hate and your hardness, Big Daddy!

[*She sobs and rushes awkwardly out on to the gallery.*]

BIG DADDY [*to himself*]: *Wouldn't it be funny if that was true. . . .*

[*A pause is followed by a burst of light in the sky from the fireworks.*]

BRICK! HEY, BRICK!

[*He stands over his blazing birthday cake.*

After some moments, Brick hobbles in on his crutch, holding his glass.

Margaret follows him with a bright, anxious smile.]

I didn't call you, Maggie. I called Brick.

MARGARET: I'm just delivering him to you.

[*She kisses Brick on the mouth which he immediately wipes with the back of his hand. She flies girlishly back out. Brick and his father are alone.*]

BIG DADDY: Why did you do that?

BRICK: Do what, Big Daddy?

BIG DADDY: Wipe her kiss off your mouth like she'd spit on you.

BRICK: I don't know. I wasn't conscious of it.

BIG DADDY: That woman of yours has a better shape on her than Gooper's but somehow or other they got the same look about them.

BRICK: What sort of look is that, Big Daddy?

BIG DADDY: I don't know how to describe it but it's the same look.

BRICK: They don't look peaceful, do they?

BIG DADDY: No, they sure in hell don't.

BRICK: They look nervous as cats?

BIG DADDY: That's right, they look nervous as cats.

BRICK: Nervous as a couple of cats on a hot tin roof?

BIG DADDY: That's right, boy, they look like a couple of cats on a hot tin roof. It's funny that you and Gooper being so different would pick out the same type of woman.

BRICK: Both of us married into society, Big Daddy.

BIG DADDY: Crap . . . I wonder what gives them both that look?

BRICK: Well. They're sittin' in the middle of a big piece of land, Big Daddy, twenty-eight thousand acres is a pretty big piece of land and so they're squaring off on it, each determined to knock off a bigger piece of it than the other whenever you let it go.

BIG DADDY: I got a surprise for those women. I'm not gonna let it go for a long time yet if that's what they're waiting for.

BRICK: That's right, Big Daddy. You just sit tight and let them scratch each other's eyes out. . . .

BIG DADDY: You bet your life I'm going to sit tight on it and let those sons of bitches scratch their eyes out, ha ha ha. . . .

But Gooper's wife's a good breeder, you got to admit she's fertile. Hell, at supper tonight she had them all at the table and they had to put a couple of extra leafs in the table to make room for them, she's got five head of them, now, and another one's comin'.

BRICK: Yep, number six is comin'. . . .

BIG DADDY: Brick, you know, I swear to God, I don't know the way it happens?

BRICK: The way what happens, Big Daddy?

BIG DADDY: You git you a piece of land, by hook or crook, an' things start growin' on it, things accumulate on it, and the first thing you know it's completely out of hand, completely out of hand!

BRICK: Well, they say nature hates a vacuum, Big Daddy.

BIG DADDY: That's what they say, but sometimes I think that a vacuum is a hell of a lot better than some of the stuff that nature replaces it with.

Is someone out there by that door?

BRICK: Yep.

BIG DADDY: Who?

[*He has lowered his voice.*]

BRICK: Someone int'rested in what we say to each other.

BIG DADDY: Gooper? – *GOOPER!*

[*After a discreet pause, Mae appears in the gallery door.*]

MAE: Did you call Gooper, Big Daddy?

BIG DADDY: Aw, it was you.

MAE: Do you want Gooper, Big Daddy?

BIG DADDY: No, and I don't want you. I want some privacy here, while I'm having a confidential talk with my son Brick. Now it's too hot in here to close them doors, but if I have to close those rutten doors in order to have a private talk with my son Brick, just let me know and I'll close 'em. Because I hate eavesdroppers, I don't like any kind of sneakin' an' spyin'.

MAE: Why, Big Daddy –

BIG DADDY: You stood on the wrong side of the moon, it threw your shadow!

MAE: I was just –

BIG DADDY: You was just nothing but *spyin'* an' you *know* it!

MAE [*begins to sniff and sob*]: Oh, Big Daddy, you're so unkind for some reason to those that really love you!

BIG DADDY: Shut up, shut up, shut up! I'm going to move you and Gooper out of that room next to this! It's none of your goddam business what goes on in here at night between Brick an' Maggie. You listen at night like a couple of rutten peek-hole spies and go and give a report on what you hear to Big Mama an' she comes to me and says they

say such and such and so and so about what they heard goin'
on between Brick an' Maggie, and Jesus, it makes me sick.
I'm goin' to move you an' Gooper out of that room, I can't
stand sneakin' an' spyin', it makes me sick. . . .

[*Mae throws back her head and rolls her eyes heavenward and
extends her arms as if invoking God's pity for this unjust
martyrdom; then she presses a handkerchief to her nose and
flies from the room with a loud swish of skirts.*]

BRICK [*now at the liquor cabinet*]: They listen, do they?

BIG DADDY: Yeah. They listen and give reports to Big Mama
on what goes on in here between you and Maggie. They
say that –

[*He stops as if embarrassed.*]

– You won't sleep with her, that you sleep on the sofa. Is
that true or not true? If you don't like Maggie, get rid of
Maggie! – What are you doin' there now?

BRICK: Fresh'nin' up my drink.

BIG DADDY: Son, you know you got a real liquor problem?

BRICK: Yes, sir, yes, I know.

BIG DADDY: Is that why you quit sports-announcing, because
of this liquor problem?

BRICK: Yes, sir, yes, sir, I guess so.

[*He smiles vaguely and amiably at his father across his re-
plenished drink.*]

BIG DADDY: Son, don't guess about it, it's too important.

BRICK [*vaguely*]: Yes, sir.

BIG DADDY: And listen to me, don't look at the damn
chandelier. . . .

[*Pause. Big Daddy's voice is husky.*]

– Somethin' else we picked up at th' big fire sale in Europe.

[*Another pause.*]

Life is important. There's nothing else to hold on to. A man
that drinks is throwing his life away. Don't do it, hold on to
your life. There's nothing else to hold on to. . . .

Sit down over here so we don't have to raise our voices,
the walls have ears in this place.

BRICK [*hobbling over to sit on the sofa beside him*]: All right,
Big Daddy.

BIG DADDY: Quit! – how'd that come about? Some disappointment?

BRICK: I don't know. Do you?

BIG DADDY: I'm askin' you, God damn it! How in hell would I know if you don't?

BRICK: I just got out there and found that I had a mouth full of cotton. I was always two or three beats behind what was goin' on on the field and so I –

BIG DADDY: Quit!

BRICK [*amiably*]: Yes, quit.

BIG DADDY: Son?

BRICK: Huh?

BIG DADDY [*inhales loudly and deeply from his cigar; then bends suddenly a little forward, exhaling loudly and raising a hand to his forehead*]: – Whew! – ha ha! – I took in too much smoke, it made me a little light-headed. . . .

[*The mantel clock chimes.*]

Why is it so damn hard for people to talk?

BRICK : Yeah. . . .

[*The clock goes on sweetly chiming till it has completed the stroke of ten.*]

– Nice peaceful-soundin' clock, I like to hear it all night. . . .

[*He slides low and comfortable on the sofa; Big Daddy sits up straight and rigid with some unspoken anxiety. All his gestures are tense and jerky as he talks. He wheezes and pants and sniffs through his nervous speech, glancing quickly, shyly, from time to time, at his son.*]

BIG DADDY: We got that clock the summer we wint to Europe, me an' Big Mama on that damn Cook's Tour, never had such an awful time in my life, I'm tellin' you, son, those gooks over there, they gouge your eyeballs out in their grand hotels. And Big Mama bought more stuff than you could haul in a couple of boxcars, that's no crap. Everywhere she wint on this whirlwind tour, she bought, bought, bought. Why, half that stuff she bought is still crated up in the cellar, under water last spring!

[*He laughs.*]

That Europe is nothin' on earth but a great big auction, that's all it is, that bunch of old worn-out places, it's just a big fire-sale, the whole rutten thing, an' Big Mama wint wild in it, why, you couldn't hold that woman with a mule's harness! Bought, bought, bought! – lucky I'm a rich man, yes siree, Bob, an' half that stuff is mildewin' in th' basement. It's lucky I'm a rich man, it sure is lucky, well, I'm a rich man, Brick, yep, I'm a mighty rich man.

[*His eyes light up for a moment.*]

Y'know how much I'm worth? Guess, Brick! Guess how much I'm worth!

[*Brick smiles vaguely over his drink.*]

Close on ten million in cash an' blue chip stocks, outside, mind you, of twenty-eight thousand acres of the richest land this side of the valley Nile!

[*A puff and crackle and the night sky blooms with an eerie greenish glow. Children shriek on the gallery.*]

But a man can't buy his life with it, he can't buy back his life with it when his life has been spent, that's one thing not offered in the Europe fire-sale or in the American markets or any markets on earth, a man can't buy his life with it, he can't buy back his life when his life is finished. . . .

That's a sobering thought, a very sobering thought, and that's a thought that I was turning over in my head, over and over and over – until today. . . .

I'm wiser and sadder, Brick, for this experience which I just gone through. They's one thing else that I remember in Europe.

BRICK: What is that, Big Daddy?

BIG DADDY: The hills around Barcelona in the country of Spain and the children running over those bare hills in their bare skins beggin' like starvin' dogs with howls and screeches, and how fat the priests are on the streets of Barcelona, so many of them and so fat and so pleasant, ha ha! – Y'know I could feed that country? I got money enough to feed that goddam country, but the human animal is a selfish beast and I don't reckon the money I passed out there to those howling children in the hills around Barcelona would more than upholster one of the chairs in this room, I mean pay to put a new cover on this chair!

Hell, I threw them money like you'd scatter feed corn for chickens, I threw money at them just to get rid of them long enough to climb back into th' car and – drive away. . . .

And then in Morocco, them Arabs, why, prostitution begins at four or five, that's no exaggeration, why, I remember one day in Marrakech that old walled Arab city, I set on a broken-down wall to have a cigar, it was fearful hot there and this Arab woman stood in the road and looked at me till I was embarrassed, she stood stock still in the dusty hot road and looked at me till I was embarrassed. But listen to this. She had a naked child with her, a little naked girl with her, barely able to toddle, and after a while she set this child on the ground and give her a push and whispered something to her.

This child come toward me, barely able t' walk, come toddling up to me and –

Jesus, it makes you sick t' remember a thing like this! It stuck out its hand and tried to unbutton my trousers!

That child was not yet five! Can you believe me? Or do you think that I am making this up? I wint back to the hotel and said to Big Mama, Git packed! We're clearing out of this country. . . .

BRICK: Big Daddy, you're on a talkin' jag tonight.

BIG DADDY [*ignoring this remark*]: Yes, sir, that's how it is, the human animal is a beast that dies but the fact that he's dying don't give him pity for others, no, sir, it –

– Did you say something?

BRICK: Yes.

BIG DADDY: What?

BRICK: Hand me over that crutch so I can get up.

BIG DADDY: Where you goin'?

BRICK: I'm takin' a little short trip to Echo Spring.

BIG DADDY: To where?

BRICK: Liquor cabinet. . . .

BIG DADDY: Yes, sir, boy –

[*He hands Brick the crutch.*]

– The human animal is a beast that dies and if he's got money he buys and buys and buys and I think the reason he buys everything he can buy is that in the back of his mind he has the crazy hope that one of his purchases will be life everlasting! – Which it never can be. . . . The human animal is a beast that –

BRICK [*at the liquor cabinet*]: Big Daddy, you sure are shootin' th' breeze here tonight.

[*There is a pause and voices are heard outside.*]

BIG DADDY: I been quiet here lately, spoke not a word, just sat and stared into space. I had something heavy weighing on my mind but tonight that load was took off me. That's why I'm talking. – The sky looks diff'rent to me. . . .

BRICK: You know what I like to hear most?

BIG DADDY: What?

BRICK: Solid quiet. Perfect unbroken quiet.

BIG DADDY: Why?

BRICK: Because it's more peaceful.

BIG DADDY: Man, you'll hear a lot of that in the grave.

[*He chuckles agreeably.*]

BRICK: Are you through talkin' to me?

BIG DADDY: Why are you so anxious to shut me up?

BRICK: Well, sir, ever so often you say to me, Brick, I want to have a talk with you, but when we talk, it never materializes. Nothing is said. You sit in a chair and gas about this and that and I look like I listen. I try to look like I listen, but I don't listen, not much. Communication is – awful hard between people an' – somehow between you and me, it just don't –

BIG DADDY: Have you ever been scared? I mean have you ever felt downright terror of something?

[*He gets up.*]

Just one moment. I'm going to close these doors. . . .

[*He closes doors on gallery as if he were going to tell an important secret.*]

BRICK: What?

BIG DADDY: Brick?

BRICK: Huh?

BIG DADDY: Son, I thought I had it!

BRICK: Had what? Had what, Big Daddy?

BIG DADDY: Cancer!

BRICK: Oh . . .

BIG DADDY: I thought the old man made out of bones had laid his cold and heavy hand on my shoulder!

BRICK: Well, Big Daddy, you kept a tight mouth about it.

BIG DADDY: A pig squeals. A man keeps a tight mouth about it, in spite of a man not having a pig's advantage.

BRICK: What advantage is that?

BIG DADDY: Ignorance – of mortality – is a comfort. A man don't have that comfort, he's the only living thing that conceives of death, that knows what it is. The others go without knowing, which is the way that anything living should go, go without knowing, without any knowledge of it, and yet a pig squeals, but a man sometimes, he can keep a tight mouth about it. Sometimes he –

[*There is a deep, smouldering ferocity in the old man.*]

– can keep a tight mouth about it. I wonder if –

BRICK: What, Big Daddy?

BIG DADDY: A whisky highball would injure this spastic condition?

BRICK: No, sir, it might do it good.

BIG DADDY [*grins suddenly, wolfishly*]: *Jesus, I can't tell you! The sky is open! Christ, it's open again! It's open, boy, it's open!*

[*Brick looks down at his drink.*]

BRICK: You feel better, Big Daddy?

BIG DADDY: Better? Hell! I can breathe! – All of my life I been like a doubled up fist. . . .

[*He pours a drink.*]

Poundin', smashin', drivin'! – now I'm going to loosen these doubled up hands and touch things *easy* with them. . . .

[*He spreads his hands as if caressing the air.*]

You know what I'm contemplating?

BRICK [*vaguely*]: No, sir. What are you contemplating?

BIG DADDY: Ha ha! – *Pleasure!* – pleasure with *women!*

[*Brick's smile fades a little but lingers.*]

Brick, this stuff burns me! –

– Yes, boy. I'll tell you something that you might not guess. I still have desire for women and this is my sixty-fifth birthday.

BRICK: I think that's mighty remarkable, Big Daddy.

BIG DADDY: Remarkable?

BRICK: *Admirable*, Big Daddy.

BIG DADDY: You're damn right it is, remarkable and admirable both. I realize now that I never had me enough. I let many chances slip by because of scruples about it, scruples, convention – crap.... All that stuff is bull, bull, bull! – It took the shadow of death to make me see it. Now that shadow's lifted, I'm going to cut loose and have, what is it they call it, have me a – ball!

BRICK: A ball, huh?

BIG DADDY: That's right, a ball, a ball! Hell! – I slept with Big Mama till, let's see, five years ago, till I was sixty and she was fifty-eight, and never even liked her, never did!

[*The phone has been ringing down the hall. Big Mama enters, exclaiming:*]

BIG MAMA: Don't you men hear that phone ring? I heard it way out on the gall'ry.

BIG DADDY: There's five rooms off this front gall'ry that you could go through. Why do you go through this one?

[*Big Mama makes a playful face as she bustles out the hall door.*]

Huh! – Why, when Big Mama goes out of a room, I can't remember what that woman looks like, but when Big Mama comes back into the room, boy, then I see what she looks like, and I wish I didn't!

[*Bends over laughing at this joke till it hurts his guts and he straightens with a grimace. The laugh subsides to a chuckle as he puts the liquor glass a little distrustfully down on the table.
Brick has risen and hobbled to the gallery doors.*]

Hey! Where you goin'?

BRICK: Out for a breather.

BIG DADDY: Not yet you ain't. Stay here till this talk is finished, young fellow.

BRICK: I thought it was finished, Big Daddy.

BIG DADDY: It ain't even begun.

BRICK: My mistake. Excuse me. I just wanted to feel that river breeze.

BIG DADDY: Turn on the ceiling fan and set back down in that chair.

[*Big Mama's voice rises, carrying down the hall.*]

BIG MAMA: Miss Sally, you're a case! You're a caution, Miss
Sally. Why didn't you give me a chance to explain it to you?

BIG DADDY: Jesus, she's talking to my old maid sister again.

BIG MAMA: Well, goodbye, now, Miss Sally. You come
down real soon, Big Daddy's dying to see you! Yaisss,
goodbye, Miss Sally. . . .

> [*She hangs up and bellows with mirth. Big Daddy groans and
> covers his ears as she approaches.*
>
> *Bursting in:*]

Big Daddy, that was Miss Sally callin' from Memphis
again! You know what she done, Big Daddy? She called
her doctor in Memphis to git him to tell her what that
spastic thing is! Ha-*HAAAA!* – And called back to tell
me how relieved she was that – Hey! Let me in!

> [*Big Daddy has been holding the door half closed against
> her.*]

BIG DADDY: Naw I ain't. I told you not to come and go
through this room. You just back out and go through those
five other rooms.

BIG MAMA: Big Daddy? Big Daddy? Oh, Big Daddy! – You
didn't meant those things you said to me, did you?

> [*He shuts door firmly against her but she still calls.*]

Sweetheart? Sweetheart? Big Daddy? You didn't mean
those awful things you said to me? – I know you didn't. I
know you didn't mean those things in your heart. . . .

> [*The childlike voice fades with a sob and her heavy footsteps
> retreat down the hall. Brick has risen once more on his crutch
> and starts for the gallery again.*]

BIG DADDY: All I ask of that woman is that she leave me
alone. But she can't admit to herself that she makes me sick.
That comes of having slept with her too many years. Should
of quit much sooner but that old woman she never got
enough of it – and I was good in bed . . . I never should of
wasted so much of it on her. . . . They say you got just so
many and each one is numbered. Well, I got a few left in
me, a few, and I'm going to pick me a good one to spend
'em on! I'm going to pick me a choice one, I don't care
how much she costs, I'll smother her in – minks! Ha ha!
I'll strip her naked and smother her in minks and choke her

with diamonds! Ha ha! I'll strip her naked and choke her
with diamonds and smother her with minks and hump
her from hell to breakfast. *Ha aha ha ha ha!*

MAE [*gaily at door*]: Who's that laughin' in there?

GOOPER: Is Big Daddy laughin' in there?

BIG DADDY: Crap! – them two – *drips.* . . .

> [*He goes over and touches Brick's shoulder.*]

Yes, son. Brick, boy. – I'm – *happy!* I'm happy, son, I'm
happy!

> [*He chokes a little and bites his under lip, pressing his head
> quickly, shyly against his son's head and then, coughing with
> embarrassment, goes uncertainly back to the table where he set
> down the glass. He drinks and makes a grimace as it burns his
> guts. Brick sighs and rises with effort.*]

What makes you so restless? Have you got ants in your
britches?

BRICK: Yes, sir . . .

BIG DADDY: Why?

BRICK: – Something – hasn't – happened. . . .

BIG DADDY: Yeah? What is that!

BRICK [*sadly*]: – the click. . . .

BIG DADDY: Did you say click?

BRICK: Yes, click.

BIG DADDY: What click?

BRICK: A click that I get in my head that makes me peaceful.

BIG DADDY: I sure in hell don't know what you're talking
about, but it disturbs me.

BRICK: It's just a mechanical thing.

BIG DADDY: What is a mechanical thing?

BRICK: This click that I get in my head that makes me peaceful. I got to drink till I get it. It's just a mechanical thing,
something like a – like a – like a –

BIG DADDY: Like a –

BRICK: Switch clicking off in my head, turning the hot light
off and the cool night on and –

> [*He looks up, smiling sadly.*]

– all of a sudden there's – peace!

BIG DADDY [*whistles long and soft with astonishment; he goes
back to Brick and clasps his son's two shoulders*]: Jesus! I didn't

know it had gotten that bad with you. Why, boy, you're –
alcoholic!

BRICK: That's the truth, Big Daddy. I'm alcoholic.

BIG DADDY: This shows how I – let things go!

BRICK: I have to hear that little click in my head that makes
me peaceful. Usually I hear it sooner than this, sometimes
as early as – noon, but –

– Today it's – dilatory. . . .

– I just haven't got the right level of alcohol in my blood-
stream yet!

[*This last statement is made with energy as he freshens his drink.*]

BIG DADDY: Uh – huh. Expecting death made me blind. I
didn't have no idea that a son of mine was turning into a
drunkard under my nose.

BRICK [*gently*]: Well, now you do, Big Daddy, the news has
penetrated.

BIG DADDY: UH-huh, yes, now I do, the news has – penetrated. . . .

BRICK: And so if you'll excuse me –

BIG DADDY: No, I won't excuse you.

BRICK: – I'd better sit by myself till I hear that click in my
head, it's just a mechanical thing but it don't happen except
when I'm alone or talking to no one. . . .

BIG DADDY: You got a long, long time to sit still, boy, and
talk to no one, but now you're talkin' to me. At least I'm
talking to you. And you set there and listen until I tell you
the conversation is over!

BRICK: But this talk is like all the others we've ever had
together in our lives! It's nowhere, nowhere! – it's – it's
painful, Big Daddy. . . .

BIG DADDY: All right, then let it be painful, but don't
you move from that chair! – I'm going to remove that
crutch. . . .

[*He seizes the crutch and tosses it across room.*]

BRICK: I can hop on one foot, and if I fall, I can crawl!

BIG DADDY: If you ain't careful you're gonna crawl off this
plantation and then, by Jesus, you'll have to hustle your
drinks along Skid Row!

BRICK: That'll come, Big Daddy.

BIG DADDY: Naw, it won't. You're my son, and I'm going to straighten you out; now that *I'm* straightened out, I'm going to straighten you out!

BRICK: Yeah?

BIG DADDY: Today the report come in from Ochsner Clinic. Y'know what they told me?

[*His face glows with triumph.*]

The only thing that they could detect with all the instruments of science in that great hospital is a little spastic condition of the colon! And nerves torn to pieces by all that worry about it.

[*A little girl bursts into room with a sparkler clutched in each fist, hops and shrieks like a monkey gone mad and rushes back out again as Big Daddy strikes at her.*

Silence. The two men stare at each other. A woman laughs gaily outside.]

I want you to know I breathed a sigh of relief almost as powerful as the Vicksburg tornado!

BRICK: You weren't ready to go?

BIG DADDY: GO WHERE? – crap. . . .

– When you are gone from here, boy, you are long gone and nowhere! The human machine is not no different from the animal machine or the fish machine or the bird machine or the reptile machine or the insect machine! It's just a whole God damn lot more complicated and consequently more trouble to keep together. Yep. I thought I had it. The earth shook under my foot, the sky come down like the black lid of a kettle and I couldn't breathe! – Today!! – that lid was lifted, I drew my first free breath in – how many years? – *God!* – three. . . .

[*There is laughter outside, running footsteps, the soft, plushy sound and light of exploding rockets.*

Brick stares at him soberly for a long moment; then makes a sort of startled sound in his nostrils and springs up on one foot and hops across the room to grab his crutch, swinging on the furniture for support. He gets the crutch and flees as if in horror for the gallery. His father seizes him by the sleeve of his white silk pyjamas.]

Stay here, you son of a bitch! – till I say go!

BRICK: I can't.

BIG DADDY: You sure in hell will, God damn it.

BRICK: No, I can't. We talk, you talk, in – circles! We get nowhere, nowhere! It's always the same, you say you want to talk to me and don't have a ruttin' thing to say to me!

BIG DADDY: Nothin' to say when I'm tellin' you I'm going to live when I thought I was dying?!

BRICK: Oh – *that!* – Is that what you have to say to me?

BIG DADDY: Why, you son of a bitch! Ain't that, ain't that – *important?!*

BRICK: Well, you said that, that's said, and now I –

BIG DADDY: Now you set back down.

BRICK: You're all balled up, you –

BIG DADDY: I ain't balled up!

BRICK: You are, you're all balled up!

BIG DADDY: Don't tell me what I am, you drunken whelp!

I'm going to tear this coat sleeve off if you don't set down!

BRICK: Big Daddy –

BIG DADDY: Do what I tell you! I'm the boss here, now! I want you to know I'm back in the driver's seat now!

[*Big Mama rushes in, clutching her great heaving bosom.*]

What in hell do you want in here, Big Mama?

BIG MAMA: Oh, Big Daddy! Why are you shouting like that? I just cain't *stainnnnnnd* – it. . . .

BIG DADDY [*raising the back of his hand above his head*]: *GIT!* – outa here.

[*She rushes back out, sobbing.*]

BRICK [*softly, sadly*]: *Christ.* . . .

BIG DADDY [*fiercely*]: Yeah! Christ! – is right. . . .

[*Brick breaks loose and hobbles toward the gallery.*

Big Daddy jerks his crutch from under Brick so he steps with the injured ankle. He utters a hissing cry of anguish, clutches a chair and pulls it over on top of him on the floor.]

Son of a – tub of – hog fat. . . .

BRICK: Big Daddy! Give me my crutch.

[*Big Daddy throws the crutch out of reach.*]

Give me that crutch, Big Daddy.

BIG DADDY: Why do you drink?

BRICK: Don't know, give me my crutch!

BIG DADDY: You better think why you drink or give up drinking!

BRICK: Will you please give me my crutch so I can get up off this floor?

BIG DADDY: First you answer my question. Why do you drink? Why are you throwing your life away, boy, like somethin' disgusting you picked up on the street?

BRICK [getting on to his knees]: Big Daddy, I'm in pain, I stepped on that foot.

BIG DADDY: Good! I'm glad you're not too numb with the liquor in you to feel some pain!

BRICK: You – spilled my – drink. . . .

BIG DADDY: I'll make a bargain with you. You tell me why you drink and I'll hand you one. I'll pour you the liquor myself and hand it to you.

BRICK: Why do I drink?

BIG DADDY: Yeah! Why?

BRICK: Give me a drink and I'll tell you.

BIG DADDY: Tell me first!

BRICK: I'll tell you in one word.

BIG DADDY: What word?

BRICK: DISGUST!

    [*The clock chimes softly, sweetly. Big Daddy gives it a short, outraged glance.*]

    Now how about that drink?

BIG DADDY: What are you disgusted with? You got to tell me that, first. Otherwise being disgusted don't make no sense!

BRICK: Give me my crutch.

BIG DADDY: You heard me, you got to tell me what I asked you first.

BRICK: I told you, I said to kill my disgust!

BIG DADDY: DISGUST WITH WHAT!

BRICK: You strike a hard bargain.

BIG DADDY: What are you disgusted with? – an' I'll pass you the liquor.

BRICK: I can hop on one foot, and if I fall, I can crawl.

BIG DADDY: You want liquor that bad?

BRICK [*dragging himself up, clinging to bedstead*]: Yeah, I want it that bad.

BIG DADDY: If I give you a drink, will you tell me what it is you're disgusted with, Brick?

BRICK: Yes, sir, I will try to.

[*The old man pours him a drink and solemnly passes it to him. There is silence as Brick drinks.*]

Have you ever heard the word 'mendacity'?

BIG DADDY: Sure. Mendacity is one of them five-dollar words that cheap politicians throw back and forth at each other.

BRICK: You know what it means?

BIG DADDY: Don't it mean lying and liars?

BRICK: Yes, sir, lying and liars.

BIG DADDY: Has someone been lying to you?

CHILDREN [*chanting in chorus offstage*]:
We want Big Dad-dee!
We want Big Dad-dee!

[*Gooper appears in the gallery door.*]

GOOPER: Big Daddy, the kiddies are shouting for you out there.

BIG DADDY [*fiercely*]: Keep out, Gooper!

GOOPER: 'Scuse *me!*

[*Big Daddy slams the doors after Gooper.*]

BIG DADDY: Who's been lying to you, has Margaret been lying to you, has your wife been lying to you about something, Brick?

BRICK: Not her. That wouldn't matter.

BIG DADDY: Then who's been lying to you, and what about?

BRICK: No one single person and no one lie. . . .

BIG DADDY: Then what, what then, for Christ's sake?

BRICK: – The whole, the whole – thing. . . .

BIG DADDY: Why are you rubbing your head? You got a headache?

BRICK: No, I'm tryin' to –

BIG DADDY: – Concentrate, but you can't because your brain's all soaked with liquor, is that the trouble? Wet brain!

[*He snatches the glass from Brick's hand.*]

What do you know about this mendacity thing? Hell! I
could write a book on it! Don't you know that? I could
write a book on it and still not cover the subject? Well, I
could, I could write a goddam book on it and still not
cover the subject anywhere near enough!! – Think of all
the lies I got to put up with! – Pretences! Ain't that mendacity? Having to pretend stuff you don't think or feel or
have any idea of? Having for instance to act like I care for
Big Mama! – I haven't been able to stand the sight, sound,
or smell of that woman for forty years now! – even when
I *laid* her! – regular as a piston. . . .

   Pretend to love that son of a bitch of a Gooper and his
wife Mae and those five same screechers out there like
parrots in a jungle? Jesus! Can't stand to look at 'em!

   Church! – it bores the Bejesus out of me but I go! – I go
an' sit there and listen to the fool preacher!

   Clubs! – Elks! Masons! Rotary! – *crap!*

   [*A spasm of pain makes him clutch his belly. He sinks into
   a chair and his voice is softer and hoarser.*]

   You I *do* like for some reason, did always have some kind
of real feeling for – affection – respect – yes, always. . . .

   You and being a success as a planter is all I ever had any
devotion to in my whole life! – and that's the truth. . . .

   I don't know why, but it is!

   I've lived with mendacity! – Why can't *you* live with it?
Hell, you *got* to live with it, there's nothing *else* to *live* with
except mendacity, is there?
BRICK: Yes, sir. Yes, sir, there is something else that you can
   live with!
BIG DADDY: What?
BRICK [*lifting his glass*]: This! – Liquor. . . .
BIG DADDY: That's not living, that's dodging away from life.
BRICK: I want to dodge away from it.
BIG DADDY: Then why don't you kill yourself, man?
BRICK: I like to drink. . . .
BIG DADDY: Oh, God, I can't talk to you. . . .
BRICK: I'm sorry, Big Daddy.
BIG DADDY: Not as sorry as I am. I'll tell you something. A
   little while back when I thought my number was up –

[*This speech should have torrential pace and fury.*]

– before I found out it was just this – spastic – colon. I thought about you. Should I or should I not, if the jig was up, give you this place when I go – since I hate Gooper an' Mae an' know that they hate me, and since all five same monkeys are little Maes an' Goopers. – And I thought, No! – Then I thought, Yes! – I couldn't make up my mind. I hate Gooper and his five same monkeys and that bitch Mae! Why should I turn over twenty-eight thousand acres of the richest land this side of the valley Nile to not my kind? – But why in hell, on the other hand, Brick – should I subsidize a goddam fool on the bottle? – Liked or not liked, well, maybe even – *loved!* – Why should I do that? – Subsidize worthless behaviour? Rot? Corruption?

BRICK [*smiling*]: I understand.

BIG DADDY: Well, if you do, you're smarter than I am, God damn it, because I don't understand. And this I will tell you frankly. I didn't make up my mind at all on that question and still to this day I ain't made out no will! – Well, now I don't *have* to. The pressure is gone. I can just wait and see if you pull yourself together or if you don't.

BRICK: That's right, Big Daddy.

BIG DADDY: You sound like you thought I was kidding.

BRICK [*rising*]: No, sir, I know you're not kidding.

BIG DADDY: But you don't care –?

BRICK [*hobbling toward the gallery door*]: No, sir, I don't care. . . . Now how about taking a look at your birthday fireworks and getting some of that cool breeze off the river?

[*He stands in the gallery doorway as the night sky turns pink and green and gold with successive flashes of light.*]

BIG DADDY: *WAIT!* – Brick. . . .

[*His voice drops. Suddenly there is something shy, almost tender, in his restraining gesture.*]

Don't let's – leave it like this, like them other talks we've had, we've always – talked around things, we've – just talked around things for some rutten reason, I don't know what, it's always like something was left not spoken, something avoided because neither of us was honest enough with the – other. . . .

BRICK: I never lied to you, Big Daddy.

BIG DADDY: Did I ever to *you*?

BRICK: No, sir. . . .

BIG DADDY: Then there is at least two people that never lied to each other.

BRICK: But we've never *talked* to each other.

BIG DADDY: We can *now*.

BRICK: Big Daddy, there don't seem to be anything much to say.

BIG DADDY: You say that you drink to kill your disgust with lying.

BRICK: You said to give you a reason.

BIG DADDY: Is liquor the only thing that'll kill this disgust?

BRICK: Now. Yes.

BIG DADDY: But not once, huh?

BRICK: Not when I was still young an' believing. A drinking man's someone who wants to forget he isn't still young an' believing.

BIG DADDY: Believing what?

BRICK: Believing. . . .

BIG DADDY: Believing *what*?

BRICK [*stubbornly evasive*]: Believing. . . .

BIG DADDY: I don't know what the hell you mean by believing and I don't think you know what you mean by believing, but if you still got sports in your blood, go back to sports announcing and –

BRICK: Sit in a glass box watching games I can't play? Describing what I can't do while players do it? Sweating out their disgust and confusion in contests I'm not fit for? Drinkin' a coke, half bourbon, so I can stand it? That's no goddam good any more, no help – time just outran me, Big Daddy – got there first . . .

BIG DADDY: I think you're passing the buck.

BRICK: You know many drinkin' men?

BIG DADDY [*with a slight, charming smile*]: I have known a fair number of that species.

BRICK: Could any of them tell you why he drank?

BIG DADDY: Yep, you're passin' the buck to things like time and disgust with 'mendacity' and – crap! – if you got to use that kind of language about a thing, it's ninety-proof bull, and I'm not buying any.

BRICK: I had to give you a reason to get a drink!

BIG DADDY: You started drinkin' when your friend Skipper died.

[*Silence for five beats. Then Brick makes a startled movement, reaching for his crutch.*]

BRICK: What are you suggesting?

BIG DADDY: I'm suggesting nothing.

[*The shuffle and clop of Brick's rapid hobble away from his father's steady, grave attention.*]

– But Gooper an' Mae suggested that there was something not right exactly in your –

BRICK [*stopping short downstage as if backed to a wall*]: 'Not right'?

BIG DADDY: Not, well, exactly *normal* in your friendship with –

BRICK: They suggested that, too? I thought that was Maggie's suggestion.

[*Brick's detachment is at last broken through. His heart is accelerated; his forehead sweat-beaded; his breath becomes more rapid and his voice hoarse. The thing they're discussing, timidly and painfully on the side of Big Daddy, fiercely, violently on Brick's side, is the inadmissible thing that Skipper died to disavow between them. The fact that if it existed it had to be disavowed to 'keep face' in the world they lived in, may be at the heart of the 'mendacity' that Brick drinks to kill his disgust with. It may be the root of his collapse. Or maybe it is only a single manifestation of it, not even the most important. The bird that I hope to catch in the net of this play is not the solution of one man's psychological problem. I'm trying to catch the true quality of experience in a group of people, that cloudy, flickering, evanescent – fiercely charged! – interplay of live human beings in the thundercloud of a common crisis. Some mystery should be left in the revelation of character in a play, just as a great deal of mystery is always left in the revelation of character in life, even in one's own character to himself. This does not absolve the playwright of his duty to observe and probe as clearly and deeply as he legitimately* can: *but it should steer him away from*] *'pat' conclusions, facile definitions which make a play just a play, not a snare for the truth of human experience.*

The following scene should be played with great concentration, with most of the power leashed but palpable in what is left unspoken.]

Who else's suggestion is it, is it *yours?* How many others thought that Skipper and I were –

BIG DADDY [*gently*]: Now, hold on, hold on a minute, son. – I knocked around in my time.

BRICK: What's that got to do with –

BIG DADDY: I said 'Hold on!' – I bummed, I bummed this country till I was –

BRICK: Whose suggestion, who else's suggestion is it?

BIG DADDY: Slept in hobo jungles and railroad Y's and flop-houses in all cities before I –

BRICK: Oh, *you* think so, too, you call me your son and a queer. Oh! Maybe that's why you put Maggie and me in this room that was Jack Straw's and Peter Ochello's, in which that pair of old sisters slept in a double bed where both of 'em died!

BIG DADDY: *Now just don't go throwing rocks at* –

[*Suddenly Reverend Tooker appears in the gallery doors, his head slightly, playfully, fatuously cocked, with a practised clergyman's smile, sincere as a bird-call blown on a hunter's whistle, the living embodiment of the pious, conventional lie.*

Big Daddy gasps a little at this perfectly timed, but incongruous, apparition.]

– What're you looking for, Preacher?

REVEREND TOOKER: The gentlemen's lavatory, ha ha! – heh, heh . . .

BIG DADDY [*with strained courtesy*]: – Go back out and walk down to the other end of the gallery, Reverend Tooker, and use the bathroom connected with my bedroom, and if you can't find it, ask them where it is!

REVEREND TOOKER: Ah, thanks.

[*He goes out with a deprecatory chuckle.*]

BIG DADDY: It's hard to talk in this place . . .

BRICK: Son of a –!

BIG DADDY [*leaving a lot unspoken*]: – I seen all things and

understood a lot of them, till 1910. Christ, the year that –
I had worn my shoes through, hocked my – I hopped off
a yellow dog freight car half a mile down the road, slept in
a wagon of cotton outside the gin – Jack Straw an' Peter
Ochello took me in. Hired me to manage this place which
grew into this one. – When Jack Straw died – why, old
Peter Ochello quit eatin' like a dog does when its master's
dead, and died, too!

BRICK: Christ!

BIG DADDY: I'm just saying I understand such –

BRICK [*violently*]: Skipper is dead. I have not quit eating!

BIG DADDY: No, but you started drinking.

[*Brick wheels on his crutch and hurls his glass across the room
shouting.*]

BRICK: YOU THINK SO, TOO?

BIG DADDY: *Shhh!*

[*Footsteps run on the gallery. There are women's calls.
Big Daddy goes toward the door.*]

Go 'way! – Just broke a glass. . . .

[*Brick is transformed, as if a quiet mountain blew suddenly
up in volcanic flame.*]

BRICK: You think so, too? You think so, too? You think me
an' Skipper did, did, did! – *sodomy!* – together?

BIG DADDY: Hold –!

BRICK: That what you –

BIG DADDY: – *ON* – a minute!

BRICK: You think we did dirty things between us, Skipper
an' –

BIG DADDY: Why are you shouting like that? Why are you –

BRICK: – Me, is that what you think of Skipper, is that –

BIG DADDY: – so excited? I don't think nothing. I don't
know nothing. I'm simply telling you what –

BRICK: You think that Skipper and me were a pair of dirty
old men?

BIG DADDY: Now that's –

BRICK: Straw? Ochello? A couple of –

BIG DADDY: Now just –

BRICK: – ducking sissies? Queers? Is that what you –

BIG DADDY: Shhh.

BRICK: – think?

[*He loses his balance and pitches to his knees without noticing the pain. He grabs the bed and drags himself up.*]

BIG DADDY: Jesus! – Whew.... Grab my hand!

BRICK: Naw, I don't want your hand....

BIG DADDY: Well, I want yours. Git up!

[*He draws him up, keeps an arm about him with concern and affection.*]

You broken out in a sweat! You're panting like you'd run a race with –

BRICK [*freeing himself from his father's hold*]: Big Daddy, you shock me, Big Daddy, you, you – *shock* me! Talkin' so –

[*He turns away from his father.*]

– casually! – about a – thing like that . . .

– Don't you know how people *feel* about things like that? How, how *disgusted* they are by things like that? Why, at Ole Miss when it was discovered a pledge to our fraternity, Skipper's and mine, did a, *attempted* to do a, unnatural thing with –

We not only dropped him like a hot rock! – We told him to git off the campus, and he did, he got! – All the way to –

[*He halts, breathless.*]

BIG DADDY: – Where?

BRICK: North Africa, last I heard!

BIG DADDY: Well, I have come back from further away than that, I have just now returned from the other side of the moon, death's country, son, and I'm not easy to shock by anything here.

[*He comes downstage and faces out.*]

Always, anyhow, lived with too much space around me to be infected by ideas of other people. One thing you can grow on a big place more important than cotton! – is *tolerance!* – I grown it.

[*He returns toward Brick.*]

BRICK: Why can't exceptional friendship, *real, real, deep, deep friendship!* between two men be respected as something clean and decent without being thought of as –

BIG DADDY: It can, it is, for God's sake.

BRICK: – *Fairies.* . . .

[*In his utterance of this word, we gauge the wide and profound reach of the conventional mores he got from the world that crowned him with early laurel.*]

BIG DADDY: I told Mae an' Gooper –

BRICK: Frig Mae and Gooper, frig all dirty lies and liars! – Skipper and me had a clean, true thing between us! – had a clean friendship, practically all our lives, till Maggie got the idea you're talking about. Normal? No! – It was too rare to be normal, any true thing between two people is too rare to be normal. Oh, once in a while he put his hand on my shoulder or I'd put mine on his, oh, maybe even, when we were touring the country in pro-football an' shared hotel-rooms we'd reach across the space between the two beds and shake hands to say goodnight, yeah, one or two times we –

BIG DADDY: Brick, nobody thinks that that's not normal!

BRICK: Well, they're mistaken, it was! It was a pure an' true thing an' that's not normal.

[*They both stare straight at each other for a long moment. The tension breaks and both turn away as if tired.*]

BIG DADDY: Yeah, it's – hard t' – talk. . . .

BRICK: All right, then, let's – let it go. . . .

BIG DADDY: Why did Skipper crack up? Why have you?

[*Brick looks back at his father again. He has already decided, without knowing that he has made this decision, that he is going to tell his father that he is dying of cancer. Only this could even the score between them: one inadmissible thing in return for another.*]

BRICK [*ominously*]: All right. You're asking for it, Big Daddy. We're finally going to have that real true talk you wanted. It's too late to stop it, now, we got to carry it through and cover every subject.

[*He hobbles back to the liquor cabinet.*]

Uh-huh.

[*He opens the ice bucket and picks up the silver tongs with slow admiration of their frosty brightness.*]

Maggie declares that Skipper and I went into pro-football

after we left 'Ole Miss' because we were scared to grow up . . .

[*He moves downstage with the shuffle and clop of a cripple on a crutch. As Margaret did when her speech became 'recitative', he looks out into the house, commanding its attention by his direct, concentrated gaze – a broken, 'tragically elegant' figure telling simply as much as he knows of ' the Truth':*]

– Wanted to – keep on tossing – those long, long! – high, high! – passes that – couldn't be intercepted except by time, the aerial attack that made us famous! And so we did, we did, we kept it up for one season, that aerial attack, we held it high! – Yeah, but –

– that summer, Maggie, she laid the law down to me, said, Now or never, and so I married Maggie. . . .

BIG DADDY: How was Maggie in bed?

BRICK [*wryly*]: Great! the greatest!

[*Big Daddy nods as if he thought so.*]

She went on the road that fall with the Dixie Stars. Oh, she made a great show of being the world's best sport. She wore a – wore a – tall bearskin cap! A shako, they call it, a dyed moleskin coat, a moleskin coat dyed red! – Cut up crazy! Rented hotel ballrooms for victory celebrations, wouldn't cancel them when it – turned out – defeat. . . .

MAGGIE THE CAT! Ha ha!

[*Big Daddy nods.*]

– But Skipper, he had some fever which came back on him which doctors couldn't explain and I got that injury – turned out to be just a shadow on the X-ray plate – and a touch of bursitis. . . .

I lay in a hospital bed, watched our games on TV, saw Maggie on the bench next to Skipper when he was hauled out of a game for stumbles, fumbles! – Burned me up the way she hung on his arm! – Y'know, I think that Maggie had always felt sort of left out because she and me never got any closer together than two people just get in bed, which is not much closer than two cats on a – fence humping. . . .

So! She took this time to work on poor dumb Skipper. He was a less than average student at Ole Miss, you know that, don't you?! – Poured in his mind the dirty, false idea that what we were, him and me, was a frustrated case of that ole pair of sisters that lived in this room, Jack Straw and Peter Ochello! – He, poor Skipper, went to bed with Maggie to prove it wasn't true, and when it didn't work out, he thought it *was* true! – Skipper broke in two like a rotten stick – nobody ever turned so fast to a lush – or died of it so quick. . . .

– Now are you satisfied?

[*Big Daddy has listened to this story, dividing the grain from the chaff. Now he looks at his son.*]

BIG DADDY: Are *you* satisfied?

BRICK: With what?

BIG DADDY: That half-ass story!

BRICK: What's half-ass about it?

BIG DADDY: Something's left out of that story. What did you leave out?

[*The phone has started ringing in the hall. As if it reminded him of something, Brick glances suddenly toward the sound and says:*]

BRICK: Yes! – I left out a long-distance call which I had from Skipper, in which he made a drunken confession to me and on which I hung up! – last time we spoke to each other in our lives. . . .

[*Muted ring stops as someone answers phone in a soft, indistinct voice in hall.*]

BIG DADDY: You hung up?

BRICK: Hung up. Jesus! Well –

BIG DADDY: Anyhow now! – we have tracked down the lie with which you're disgusted and which you are drinking to kill your disgust with, Brick. You been passing the buck. This disgust with mendacity is disgust with yourself.

You! – dug the grave of your friend and kicked him in it! – before you'd face truth with him!

BRICK: *His* truth, not *mine!*

BIG DADDY: His truth, okay! But you wouldn't face it with him!

BRICK: Who *can* face truth? Can *you?*

BIG DADDY: Now don't start passin' the rotten buck again, boy!

BRICK: *How about these birthday congratulations, these many, many happy returns of the day, when ev'rybody but you knows there won't be any!*

[*Whoever has answered the hall phone lets out a high, shrill laugh; the voice becomes audible saying: 'no, no, you got it all wrong! Upside down! Are you crazy?'*

Brick suddenly catches his breath as he realizes that he has made a shocking disclosure. He hobbles a few paces, then freezes, and without looking at his father's shocked face, says:]

Let's, let's – go out, now, and –

[*Big Daddy moves suddenly forward and grabs hold of the boy's crutch like it was a weapon for which they were fighting for possession.*]

BIG DADDY: Oh, no, no! No one's going out! What did you start to say?

BRICK: I don't remember.

BIG DADDY: 'Many happy returns when they know there won't be any'?

BRICK: Aw, hell, Big Daddy, forget it. Come on out on the gallery and look at the fireworks they're shooting off for your birthday. . . .

BIG DADDY: First you finish that remark you were makin' before you cut off. 'Many happy returns when they know there won't be any'? – Ain't that what you just said?

BRICK: Look, now. I can get around without that crutch if I have to but it would be a lot easier on the furniture an' glassware if I didn' have to go swinging along like Tarzan of th' –

BIG DADDY: FINISH WHAT YOU WAS SAYIN'!

[*An eerie green glow shows in sky behind him.*]

BRICK [*sucking the ice in his glass, speech becoming thick*]: Leave th' place to Gooper and Mae an' their five little same little monkeys. All I want is –

BIG DADDY: 'LEAVE TH' PLACE,' did you say?

BRICK [*vaguely*]: All twenty-eight thousand acres of the richest land this side of the valley Nile.

BIG DADDY: Who said I was 'leaving the place' to Gooper or anybody? This is my sixty-fifth birthday! I got fifteen

years or twenty years left in me! I'll outlive *you!* I'll bury
you an' have to pay for your coffin!

BRICK: Sure. Many happy returns. Now let's go watch the
fireworks, come on, let's –

BIG DADDY: Lying, have they been lying? About the report
from th' – clinic? Did they, did they – find something? –
Cancer. Maybe?

BRICK: Mendacity is a system that we live in. Liquor is one
way out an' death's the other. . . .

[*He takes the crutch from Big Daddy's loose grip and swings
out on the gallery leaving the doors open.*

A song, 'Pick a Bale of Cotton', is heard.]

MAE [*appearing in door*]: Oh, Big Daddy, the field-hands are singin'
fo' you!

BIG DADDY [*shouting hoarsely*]: BRICK! BRICK!

MAE: He's outside drinkin', Big Daddy.

BIG DADDY: *BRICK!*

[*Mae retreats, awed by the passion of his voice. Children call
Brick in tones mocking Big Daddy. His face crumbles like
broken yellow plaster about to fall into dust.*

*There is a glow in the sky. Brick swings back through the
doors, slowly, gravely, quite soberly.*]

BRICK: I'm sorry, Big Daddy. My head don't work any more
and it's hard for me to understand how anybody could care
if he lived or died or was dying or cared about anything but
whether or not there was liquor left in the bottle and so I
said what I said without thinking. In some ways I'm no
better than the others, in some ways worse because I'm
less alive. Maybe it's being alive that makes them lie, and
being almost *not* alive makes me sort of accidentally truthful – I don't know but – anyway – we've been friends . . .
– And being friends is telling each other the truth. . . .

[*There is a pause.*]

You told *me!* I told *you!*

[*A child rushes into the room and grabs a fistful of fire-cracker,
and runs out again.*]

CHILD [*screaming*]: Bang, bang, bang, bang, bang, bang,
bang, bang, bang!

BIG DADDY [*slowly and passionately*]: CHRIST – DAMN –

ALL – LYING SONS OF – LYING BITCHES!

[*He straightens at last and crosses to the inside door. At the
door he turns and looks back as if he had some desperate question
he couldn't put into words. Then he nods reflectively and says in
a hoarse voice:*]

Yes, all liars, all liars, all lying dying liars!

[*This is said slowly, slowly, with a fierce revulsion. He goes
on out.*]

– Lying! Dying! Liars!

[*His voice dies out. There is the sound of a child being slapped.
It rushes, hideously bawling, through room and out the hall door.*

*Brick remains motionless as the lights dim out and the curtain
falls.*]

CURTAIN

ACT THREE

There is no lapse of time.
Mae enters with Reverend Tooker.

MAE: Where is Big Daddy! Big Daddy?

BIG MAMA [*entering*]: Too much smell of burnt fireworks makes me feel a little bit sick at my stomach. – Where is Big Daddy?

MAE: That's what I want to know, where has Big Daddy gone?

BIG MAMA: He must have turned in, I reckon he went to baid....
　　[*Gooper enters.*]

GOOPER: Where is Big Daddy?

MAE: We don't know where he is!

BIG MAMA: I reckon he's gone to baid.

GOOPER: Well, then, now we can talk.

BIG MAMA: What *is* this talk, *what* talk?
　　[*Margaret appears on gallery, talking to Dr Baugh.*]

MARGARET [*musically*]: My family freed their slaves ten years before abolition, my great-great-grandfather gave his slaves their freedom five years before the war between the States started!

MAE: Oh, for God's sake! Maggie's climbed back up in her family tree!

MARGARET [*sweetly*]: What, Mae? – Oh, where's Big Daddy?!
　　[*The pace must be very quick. Great Southern animation.*]

BIG MAMA [*addressing them all*]: I think Big Daddy was just worn out. He loves his family, he loves to have them around him, but it's a strain on his nerves. He wasn't himself tonight, Big Daddy wasn't himself, I could tell he was all worked up.

REVEREND TOOKER: I think he's remarkable.

BIG MAMA: Yaisss! Just remarkable. Did you all notice the

food he ate at that table? Did you all notice the supper he put away? Why, he ate like a hawss!

GOOPER: I hope he doesn't regret it.

BIG MAMA: Why, that man – ate a huge piece of cawn-bread with molasses on it! Helped himself twice to hoppin' john.

MARGARET: Big Daddy loves hoppin' john. – We had a real country dinner.

BIG MAMA [*overlapping Margaret*]: Yais, he simply adores it! An' candied yams? That man put away enough food at that table to stuff a nigger *field*-hand!

GOOPER [*with grim relish*]: I hope he don't have to pay for it later on. . . .

BIG MAMA [*fiercely*]: What's *that,* Gooper?

MAE: Gooper says he hopes Big Daddy doesn't suffer tonight.

BIG MAMA: Oh, shoot, Gooper says, Gooper says! Why should Big Daddy suffer for satisfying a normal appetite? There's nothin' wrong with that man but nerves, he's sound as a dollar! And now he knows he is an' that's why he ate such a supper. He had a big load off his mind, knowin' he wasn't doomed t' – what he thought he was doomed to. . . .

MARGARET [*sadly and sweetly*]: Bless his old sweet soul. . . .

BIG MAMA [*vaguely*]: Yais, bless his heart, wher's Brick?

MAE: Outside.

GOOPER: – Drinkin' . . .

BIG MAMA: I know he's drinkin'. You all don't have to keep tellin' *me* Brick is drinkin'. Cain't I see he's drinkin' without you continually tellin' me that boy's drinkin'?

MARGARET: Good for you, Big Mama!

[*She applauds.*]

BIG MAMA: Other people *drink* and *have* drunk an' will *drink,* as long as they make that stuff an' put it in bottles.

MARGARET: That's the truth. I never trusted a man that didn't drink.

MAE: Gooper never drinks. Don't you trust Gooper?

MARGARET: Why, Gooper, don't you drink? If I'd known you didn't drink, I wouldn't of made that remark –

BIG MAMA: *Brick?*

MARGARET: – at least, not in your presence.

[*She laughs sweetly.*]

BIG MAMA: *Brick!*

MARGARET: He's still on the gall'ry. I'll go bring him in so we can talk.

BIG MAMA [*worriedly*]: I don't know what this mysterious family conference is about.

> [*Awkward silence. Big Mama looks from face to face, then belches slightly and mutters, 'Excuse me. . . .' She opens an ornamental fan suspended about her throat, a black lace fan to go with her black lace gown and fans her wilting corsage, sniffing nervously and looking from face to face in the uncomfortable silence as Margaret calls 'Brick?' and Brick sings to the moon on the gallery.*]

I don't know what's wrong here, you all have such long faces! Open that door on the hall and let some air circulate through here, will you please, Gooper?

MAE: I think we'd better leave that door closed, Big Mama, till after the talk.

BIG MAMA: Reveren' Tooker, will *you* please open that door?!

REVEREND TOOKER: I sure will, Big Mama.

MAE: I just didn't think we ought t' take any chance of Big Daddy hearin' a word of this discussion.

BIG MAMA: *I swan!* Nothing's going to be said in Big Daddy's house that he cain't hear if he wants to!

GOOPER: Well, Big Mama, it's –

> [*Mae gives him a quick, hard poke to shut him up. He glares at her fiercely as she circles before him like a burlesque ballerina, raising her skinny bare arms over her head, jangling her bracelets, exclaiming:*]

MAE: *A breeze! A breeze!*

REVEREND TOOKER: I think this house is the coolest house in the Delta. – Did you all know that Halsey Banks' widow put air-conditioning units in the church and rectory at Friar's Point in memory of Halsey?

> [*General conversation has resumed; everybody is chatting so that the stage sounds like a big bird-cage.*]

GOOPER: Too bad nobody cools your church off for you. I bet you sweat in that pulpit these hot Sundays, Reverend Tooker.

REVEREND TOOKER: Yes, my vestments are drenched.

MAE [*at the same time to Dr Baugh*]: You think those vitamin B$_{12}$ injections are what they're cracked up t' be, Doc Baugh?

DOCTOR BAUGH: Well, if you want to be stuck with something I guess they're as good to be stuck with as anything else.

BIG MAMA [*at gallery door*]: *Maggie, Maggie, aren't you comin' with Brick?*

MAE [*suddenly and loudly, creating a silence*]: *I have a strange feeling, I have a peculiar feeling!*

BIG MAMA [*turning from gallery*]: What feeling?

MAE: That Brick said somethin' he shouldn't of said t' Big Daddy.

BIG MAMA: Now what on earth could Brick of said t' Big Daddy that he shouldn't say?

GOOPER: Big Mama, there's somethin' –

MAE: NOW, WAIT!

[*She rushes up to Big Mama and gives her a quick hug and kiss. Big Mama pushes her impatiently off as the Reverend Tooker's voice rises serenely in a little pocket of silence:*]

REVEREND TOOKER: Yes, last Sunday the gold in my chasuble faded into th' purple. . . .

GOOPER: Reveren', you must of been preachin' hell's fire last Sunday!

[*He guffaws at this witticism but the Reverend is not sincerely amused. At the same time Big Mama has crossed over to Dr Baugh and is saying to him:*]

BIG MAMA [*her breathless voice rising high-pitched above the others*]:

In my day they had what they call the Keeley cure for heavy drinkers. But now I understand they just take some kind of tablets, they call them 'Annie Bust' tablets. But *Brick* don't need to take *nothin'*.

[*Brick appears in gallery doors with Margaret behind him.*]

BIG MAMA [*unaware of his presence behind her*]: That boy is just broken up over Skipper's death. You know how poor Skipper died. They gave him a big, big dose of that sodium amytal stuff at his home and then they called the ambulance and give him another big, big dose of it at the hospital and that and all of the alcohol in his system fo' months an'

months an' months just proved too much for his heart. . . .
I'm scared of needles! I'm more scared of a needle than the
knife. . . . I think more people have been needled out of this
world than –

[*She stops short and wheels about.*]

OH! – here's Brick! My precious baby –

[*She turns upon Brick with short, fat arms extended, at the same
time uttering a loud, short sob, which is both comic and touching.*

*Brick smiles and bows slightly, making a burlesque gesture of
gallantry for Maggie to pass before him into the room. Then he
hobbles on his crutch directly to the liquor cabinet and there is
absolute silence, with everybody looking at Brick as everybody has
always looked at Brick when he spoke or moved or appeared.
One by one he drops ice cubes in his glass, then suddenly, but
not quickly, looks back over his shoulder with a wry, charming
smile, and says:*]

BRICK: I'm sorry! Anyone else?

BIG MAMA [*sadly*]: No, son. I *wish* you wouldn't!

BRICK: I wish I didn't have to, Big Mama, but I'm still waiting for that click in my head which makes it all smooth out!

BIG MAMA: Aw, Brick, you – BREAK MY HEART!

MARGARET [*at the same time*]: Brick, go sit with Big Mama!

BIG MAMA: I just cain't staiiiiiiii-nnnnd – it. . . .

[*She sobs.*]

MAE: Now that we're all assembled –

GOOPER: We kin talk. . . .

BIG MAMA: Breaks my heart. . . .

MARGARET: Sit with Big Mama, Brick, and hold her hand.

[*Big Mama sniffs very loudly three times, almost like three drum
beats in the pocket of silence.*]

BRICK: You do that, Maggie. I'm a restless cripple. I got to
stay on my crutch.

[*Brick hobbles to the gallery door; leans there as if waiting.*

*Mae sits beside Big Mama, while Gooper moves in front and
sits on the end of the couch, facing her. Reverend Tooker moves
nervously into the space between them; on the other side, Dr
Baugh stands looking at nothing in particular and lights a cigar.
Margaret turns away.*]

BIG MAMA: Why're you all *surroundin'* me – like this? Why're you all starin' at me like this an' makin' signs at each other?

[*Reverend Tooker steps back startled.*]

MAE: Calm yourself, Big Mama.

BIG MAMA: Calm you'self, *you'self*, Sister Woman. How could I calm myself with everyone starin' at me as if big drops of blood had broken out on m'face? What's this all about, Annh! What?

[*Gooper coughs and takes a centre position.*]

GOOPER: Now, Doc Baugh.

MAE: Doc Baugh?

BRICK [*suddenly*]: SHHH – !

[*Then he grins and chuckles and shakes his head regretfully.*]

– Naw! – that wasn't th' click.

GOOPER: Brick, shut up or stay out there on the gallery with your liquor! We got to talk about a serious matter. Big Mama wants to know the complete truth about the report we got today from the Ochsner Clinic.

MAE [*eagerly*]: – on Big Daddy's condition!

GOOPER: Yais, on Big Daddy's condition, we got to face it.

DOCTOR BAUGH: Well. . . .

BIG MAMA [*terrified, rising*]: Is there? Something? Something that I? Don't – Know?

[*In these few words, this startled, very soft, question, Big Mama reviews the history of her forty-five years with Big Daddy, her great, almost embarrassingly true-hearted and simple-minded devotion to Big Daddy, who must have had something Brick has, who made himself loved so much by the 'simple expedient' of not loving enough to disturb his charming detachment, also once coupled, like Brick's, with virile beauty.*

Big Mama has a dignity at this moment: she almost stops being fat.]

DOCTOR BAUGH [*after a pause, uncomfortably*]: Yes? – Well –

BIG MAMA: I!!! – want to – knowwwwwww. . . .

[*Immediately she thrusts her fist to her mouth as if to deny that statement.*

Then, for some curious reason, she snatches the withered corsage from her breast and hurls it on the floor and steps on it with her short, fat feet.]

– Somebody must be lyin'! – I want to know!

MAE: Sit down, Big Mama, sit down on this sofa.

MARGARET [*quickly*]: Brick, go sit with Big Mama.

BIG MAMA: *What is it, what is it?*

DOCTOR BAUGH: I never have seen a more thorough examination than Big Daddy Pollitt was given in all my experience with the Ochsner Clinic.

GOOPER: It's one of the best in the country.

MAE: It's *THE* best in the country – bar *none!*

[*For some reason she gives Gooper a violent poke as she goes past him. He slaps at her hand without removing his eyes from his mother's face.*]

DOCTOR BAUGH: Of course they were ninety-nine and nine-tenths per cent sure before they even started.

BIG MAMA: Sure of what, sure of what, sure of – *what? – what!*

[*She catches her breath in a startled sob. Mae kisses her quickly. She thrusts Mae fiercely away from her, staring at the doctor.*]

MAE: Mommy, be a brave girl!

BRICK [*in the doorway, softly*]:
  '*By the light, by the light,
  Of the sil-ve-ry mo-ooo-n*

GOOPER: Shut up! – Brick.

BRICK: – Sorry....

[*He wanders out on the gallery.*]

DOCTOR BAUGH: But now, you see, Big Mama, they cut a piece off this growth, a specimen of the tissue and –

BIG MAMA: Growth? You told Big Daddy –

DOCTOR BAUGH: Now wait.

BIG MAMA [*fiercely*]: You told me and Big Daddy there wasn't a thing wrong with him but –

MAE: Big Mama, they always –

GOOPER: Let Doc Baugh talk, will yuh?

BIG MAMA: – little spastic condition of –

[*Her breath gives out in a sob.*]

DOCTOR BAUGH: Yes, that's what we told Big Daddy. But we had this bit of tissue run through the laboratory and I'm sorry to say the test was positive on it. It's – well – malignant....

[*Pause.*]

BIG MAMA: – Cancer?! Cancer?!
> [*Dr Baugh nods gravely.*
> *Big Mama gives long gasping cry.*]

MAE and GOOPER: Now, now, now, Big Mama, you had to know. . . .

BIG MAMA: *WHY DIDN'T THEY CUT IT OUT OF HIM? HANH? HANH?*

DOCTOR BAUGH: Involved too much, Big Mama, too many organs affected.

MAE: Big Mama, the liver's affected and so's the kidneys, both! It's gone way past what they call a –

GOOPER: A surgical risk.

MAE: – Uh-huh. . . .
> [*Big Mama draws a breath like a dying gasp.*]

REVEREND TOOKER: Tch, tch, tch, tch, tch!

DOCTOR BAUGH: Yes, it's gone past the knife.

MAE: *That's why he's turned yellow, Mommy!*

BIG MAMA: *Git away from me, git away from me, Mae!*
> [*She rises abruptly.*]
> *I want Brick! Where's Brick? Where is my only son?*

MAE: Mama! Did she say '*only* son'?

GOOPER: What does that make *me*?

MAE: A sober responsible man with five precious children! – *Six!*

BIG MAMA: I want Brick to tell me! Brick! Brick!

MARGARET [*rising from her reflections in a corner*]: Brick was so upset he went back out.

BIG MAMA: *Brick!*

MARGARET: Mama, let *me* tell you!

BIG MAMA: No, no, leave me alone, you're not my blood!

GOOPER: *Mama, I'm your son! Listen to me!*

MAE: Gooper's your son, Mama, he's your first-born!

BIG MAMA: Gooper never liked Daddy.

MAE [*as if terribly shocked*]: *That's not TRUE!*
> [*There is a pause. The minister coughs and rises.*]

REVEREND TOOKER [*to Mae*]: I think I'd better slip away at this point.

MAE [*sweetly and sadly*]: Yes, Doctor Tooker, you go.

REVEREND TOOKER [*discreetly*]: Good night, good night, everybody, and God bless you all . . . on this place. . . .

[*He slips out.*]

DOCTOR BAUGH: That man is a good man but lacking in tact. Talking about people giving memorial windows – if he mentioned one memorial window, he must have spoke of a dozen, and saying how awful it was when somebody died intestate, the legal wrangles, and so forth.

[*Mae coughs, and points at Big Mama.*]

DOCTOR BAUGH: Well, Big Mama. . . .

[*He sighs.*]

BIG MAMA: It's all a mistake. I know it's just a bad dream.

DOCTOR BAUGH: We're gonna keep Big Daddy as comfortable as we can.

BIG MAMA: Yes, it's just a bad dream, that's all it is, it's just an awful dream.

GOOPER: In my opinion Big Daddy is having some pain but won't admit that he has it.

BIG MAMA: Just a dream, a bad dream.

DOCTOR BAUGH: That's what lots of them do, they think if they don't admit they're having the pain they can sort of escape the fact of it.

GOOPER [*with relish*]: Yes, they get sly about it, they get real sly about it.

MAE: Gooper and I think –

GOOPER: Shut up, Mae! – Big Daddy ought to be started on morphine.

BIG MAMA: Nobody's going to give Big Daddy morphine.

DOCTOR BAUGH: Now, Big Mama, when that pain strikes it's going to strike mighty hard and Big Daddy's going to need the needle to bear it.

BIG MAMA: I tell you, nobody's going to give him morphine.

MAE: Big Mama, you don't want to see Big Daddy suffer, you know you –

[*Gooper standing beside her gives her a savage poke.*]

DOCTOR BAUGH [*placing a package on the table*]: I'm leaving this stuff here, so if there's a sudden attack you all won't have to send out for it.

MAE: I know how to give a hypo.

GOOPER: Mae took a course in nursing during the war.

MARGARET: Somehow I don't think Big Daddy would want Mae to give him a hypo.

MAE: You think he'd want *you* to do it?

[*Dr Baugh rises.*]

GOOPER: Doctor Baugh is goin'.

DOCTOR BAUGH: Yes, I got to be goin'. Well, keep your chin up, Big Mama.

GOOPER [*with jocularity*]: She's gonna keep *both* chins up, aren't you, Big Mama?

[*Big Mama sobs.*]

Now stop that, Big Mama.

MAE: Sit down with me, Big Mama.

GOOPER [*at door with Dr Baugh*]: Well, Doc, we sure do appreciate all you done. I'm telling you, we're surely obligated to you for –

[*Dr Baugh has gone out without a glance at him.*]

GOOPER: – I guess that doctor has got a lot on his mind but it wouldn't hurt him to act a little more human. . . .

[*Big Mama sobs.*]

Now be a brave girl, Mommy.

BIG MAMA: It's not true, I know that it's just not true!

GOOPER: Mama, those tests are infallible!

BIG MAMA: Why are you so determined to see your father daid?

MAE: Big Mama!

MARGARET [*gently*]: I know what Big Mama means.

MAE [*fiercely*]: Oh, do you?

MARGARET [*quietly and very sadly*]: Yes, I think I do.

MAE: For a newcomer in the family you sure do show a lot of understanding.

MARGARET: Understanding is needed on this place.

MAE: I guess you must have needed a lot of it in your family Maggie, with your father's liquor problem and now you've got Brick with his!

MARGARET: Brick does not have a liquor problem at all. Brick is devoted to Big Daddy. This thing is a terrible strain on him.

BIG MAMA: Brick is Big Daddy's boy, but he drinks too much and it worries me and Big Daddy, and, Margaret, you've got to cooperate with us, you've got to cooperate with Big Daddy and me in getting Brick straightened out. Because it will break Big Daddy's heart if Brick don't pull himself together and take hold of things.

MAE: Take hold of *what* things, Big Mama?

BIG MAMA: The place.

[*There is a quick violent look between Mae and Gooper.*]

GOOPER: Big Mama, you've had a shock.

MAE: Yais, we've all had a shock, but . . .

GOOPER: Let's be realistic –

MAE: – Big Daddy would never, would *never*, be foolish enough to –

GOOPER: – put this place in irresponsible hands!

BIG MAMA: Big Daddy ain't going to leave the place in anybody's hands; Big Daddy is *not* going to die. I want you to get that in your heads, all of you!

MAE: Mommy, Mommy, Big Mama, we're just as hopeful an' optimistic as you are about Big Daddy's prospects, we have faith in *prayer* – but nevertheless there are certain matters that have to be discussed an' dealt with, because otherwise –

GOOPER: Eventualities have to be considered and now's the time. . . . Mae, will you please get my briefcase out of our room?

MAE: Yes, honey.

[*She rises and goes out through the hall door.*]

GOOPER [*standing over Big Mama*]: Now, Big Mom. What you said just now was not at all true and you know it. I've always loved Big Daddy in my own quiet way. I never made a show of it, and I know that Big Daddy has always been fond of me in a quiet way, too, and he never made a show of it neither.

[*Mae returns with Gooper's briefcase.*]

MAE: Here's your briefcase, Gooper, honey.

GOOPER [*handing the briefcase back to her*]: Thank you. . . . Of ca'use, my relationship with Big Daddy is different from Brick's.

MAE: You're eight years older'n Brick an' always had t' carry a bigger load of th' responsibilities than Brick ever had t' carry. He never carried a thing in his life but a football or a highball.

GOOPER: Mae, will y' let me talk, please?

MAE: Yes, honey.

GOOPER: Now, a twenty-eight thousand acre plantation's a mighty big thing t'run.

MAE: Almost singlehanded.

[*Margaret has gone out on to the gallery, and can be heard calling softly to Brick.*]

BIG MAMA: You never had to run this place! What are you talking about? As if Big Daddy was dead and in his grave, you had to run it? Why, you just helped him out with a few business details and had your law practice at the same time in Memphis!

MAE: Oh, Mommy, Mommy, Big Mommy! Let's be fair! Why, Gooper has given himself body and soul to keeping this place up for the past five years since Big Daddy's health started failing. Gooper won't say it, Gooper never thought of it as a duty, he just did it. And what did Brick do? Brick kept living in his past glory at college! Still a football player at twenty-seven!

MARGARET [*returning alone*]: Who are you talking about, now? Brick? A football player? He isn't a football player and you know it. Brick is a sports announcer on TV and one of the best-known ones in the country!

MAE: I'm talking about what he was.

MARGARET: Well, I wish you would just stop talking about my husband.

GOOPER: I've got a right to discuss my brother with other members of MY OWN family which don't include *you*. Why don't you go out there and drink with Brick?

MARGARET: I've never seen such malice toward a brother.

GOOPER: How about his for me? Why, he can't stand to be in the same room with me!

MARGARET: This is a deliberate campaign of vilification for the most disgusting and sordid reason on earth, and I know what it is! It's *avarice, avarice, greed, greed!*

BIG MAMA: *Oh, I'll scream! I will scream in a moment unless this stops!*

[*Gooper has stalked up to Margaret with clenched fists at his sides as if he would strike her. Mae distorts her face again into a hideous grimace behind Margaret's back.*]

MARGARET: We only remain on the place because of Big Mom and Big Daddy. If it is true what they say about Big Daddy we are going to leave here just as soon as it's over. Not a moment later.

BIG MAMA [*sobs*]: Margaret. Child. Come here. Sit next to Big Mama.

MARGARET: Precious Mommy. I'm sorry, I'm so sorry, I –!

[*She bends her long graceful neck to press her forehead to Big Mama's bulging shoulder under its black chiffon.*]

GOOPER: How beautiful, how touching, this display of devotion!

MAE: Do you know why she's childless? She's childless because that big beautiful athlete husband of hers won't go to bed with her!

GOOPER: You jest won't let me do this in a nice way, will yah? Aw right – Mae and I have five kids with another one coming! I don't give a goddam if Big Daddy likes me or don't like me or did or never did or will or will never! I'm just appealing to a sense of common decency and fair play. I'll tell you the truth. I've resented Big Daddy's partiality to Brick ever since Brick was born, and the way I've been treated like I was just barely good enough to spit on and sometimes not even good enough for that. Big Daddy is dying of cancer, and it's spread all through him and it's attacking all his vital organs including the kidneys and right now he is sinking into uraemia, and you all know what uraemia is, it's poisoning of the whole system due to the failure of the body to eliminate its poisons.

MARGARET [*to herself, downstage, hissingly*]: *Poisons, poisons! Venomous thoughts and words! In hearts and minds! – That's poisons!*

GOOPER [*overlapping her*]: I am asking for a square deal, and I expect to get one. But if I don't get one, if there's any peculiar shenanigans going on around here behind my back,

or before me, well, I'm not a corporation lawyer for nothing,
I know how to protect my own interests. – *OH! A late
arrival!*

> [*Brick enters from the gallery with a tranquil, blurred smile,
> carrying an empty glass with him.*]

MAE: Behold the conquering hero comes!

GOOPER: The fabulous Brick Pollitt! Remember him? –
Who could forget him!

MAE: He looks like he's been injured in a game!

GOOPER: Yep, I'm afraid you'll have to warm the bench at the
Sugar Bowl this year, Brick!

> [*Mae laughs shrilly.*]

Or was it the Rose Bowl that he made that famous run in?

MAE: The punch bowl, honey. It was in the punch bowl, the
cut-glass punch bowl!

GOOPER: Oh, that's right, I'm getting the bowls mixed up!

MARGARET: Why don't you stop venting your malice and
envy on a sick boy?

BIG MAMA: *Now you two hush, I mean it, hush, all of you, hush!*

GOOPER: All right, Big Mama. A family crisis brings out the
best and the worst in every member of it.

MAE: *That's the truth.*

MARGARET: *Amen!*

BIG MAMA: *I said, hush!* I won't tolerate any more catty talk
in my house.

> [*Mae gives Gooper a sign indicating briefcase.*
> *Brick's smile has grown both brighter and vaguer. As he*
> *prepares a drink, he sings softly:*]

BRICK: *Show me the way to go home,*
> *I'm tired and I wanta go to bed,*
> *I had a little drink about an hour ago –*

GOOPER [*at the same time*]: Big Mama, you know it's necessary
for me t'go back to Memphis in th' mornin' t'represent the
Parker estate in a lawsuit.

> [*Mae sits on the bed and arranges papers she has taken from the
> briefcase.*]

BRICK [*continuing the song*]:
> *Wherever I may roam,*
> *On land or sea or foam.*

BIG MAMA: Is it, Gooper?

MAE: Yaiss.

GOOPER: That's why I'm forced to – to bring up a problem that –

MAE: Somethin' that's too important t' be put off!

GOOPER: If Brick was sober, he ought to be in on this.

MARGARET: Brick is present; we're here.

GOOPER: Well, good. I will now give you this outline my partner, Tom Bullitt, an' me have drawn up – a sort of dummy – trusteeship.

MARGARET: Oh, that's it! You'll be in charge an' dole out remittances, will you?

GOOPER: This we did as soon as we got the report on Big Daddy from th' Ochsner Laboratories. We did this thing, I mean we drew up this dummy outline with the advice and assistance of the Chairman of the Boa'd of Directors of th' Southern Plantahs Bank and Trust Company in Memphis, C. C. Bellowes, a man who handles estates for all th' prominent fam'lies in West Tennessee and th' Delta.

BIG MAMA: Gooper?

GOOPER [crouching in front of Big Mama]: Now this is not – not final, or anything like it. This is just a preliminary outline. But it does provide a basis – a design – a – possible, feasible – plan!

MARGARET: Yes, I'll bet.

MAE: It's a plan to protect the biggest estate in the Delta from irresponsibility an' –

BIG MAMA: Now you listen to me, all of you, you listen here! They's not goin' to be any more catty talk in my house! And Gooper, you put that away before I grab it out of your hand and tear it right up! I don't know what the hell's in it, and I don't want to know what the hell's in it. I'm talkin' in Big Daddy's language now; I'm his *wife*, not his *widow*, I'm still his *wife*! And I'm talkin' to you in his language an' –

GOOPER: Big Mama, what I have here is –

MAE: Gooper explained that it's just a plan. . . .

BIG MAMA: I don't care what you got there. Just put it back where it came from, an' don't let me see it again, not even the outside of the envelope of it! Is that understood? Basis!

Plan! Preliminary! Design! I say – what is it Big Daddy always says when he's disgusted?

BRICK [*from the bar*]: Big Daddy says 'crap' when he's disgusted.

BIG MAMA [*rising*]: That's right – *CRAP!* I say *CRAP* too, like Big Daddy!

MAE: Coarse language doesn't seem called for in this –

GOOPER: Somethin' in me is *deeply outraged* by hearin' you talk like this.

BIG MAMA: *Nobody's goin' to take nothin'!* – till Big Daddy lets go of it, and maybe, just possibly, not – not even then! No, not even then!

BRICK: *You can always hear me singin' this song,*
        Show me the way to go home.

BIG MAMA: Tonight Brick looks like he used to look when he was a little boy, just like he did when he played wild games and used to come home all sweaty and pink-cheeked and sleepy, with his – red curls shining. . . .

[*She comes over to him and runs her fat shaky hand through his hair. He draws aside as he does from all physical contact and continues the song in a whisper, opening the ice bucket and dropping in the ice cubes one by one as if he were mixing some important chemical formula.*]

BIG MAMA [*continuing*]: Time goes by so fast. Nothin' can outrun it. Death commences too early – almost before you're half-acquainted with life – you meet with the other. . . .

Oh, you know we just got to love each other an' stay together, all of us, just as close as we can, especially now that such a *black* thing has come and moved into this place without invitation.

[*Awkwardly embracing Brick, she presses her head to his shoulder.*

Gooper has been returning papers to Mae who has restored them to briefcase with an air of severely tried patience.]

GOOPER: Big Mama? Big Mama?

[*He stands behind her, tènse with sibling envy.*]

BIG MAMA [*oblivious of Gooper*]: Brick, you hear me, don't you?

MARGARET: Brick hears you, Big Mama, he understands what you're saying.

BIG MAMA: Oh, Brick, son of Big Daddy! Big Daddy does so love you! Y'know what would be his fondest dream come true? If before he passed on, if Big Daddy has to pass on, you gave him a child of yours, a grandson as much like his son as his son is like Big Daddy!

MAE [*zipping briefcase shut: an incongruous sound*]: *Such a pity that Maggie an' Brick can't oblige!*

MARGARET [*suddenly and quietly but forcefully*]: Everybody listen.

[*She crosses to the centre of the room, holding her hands rigidly together.*]

MAE: Listen to what, Maggie?

MARGARET: I have an announcement to make.

GOOPER: A sports announcement, Maggie?

MARGARET: Brick and I are going to – *have a child!*

[*Big Mama catches her breath in a loud gasp.*]
Pause. Big Mama rises.]

BIG MAMA: Maggie! Brick! This is too good to believe!

MAE: That's right, too good to believe.

BIG MAMA: Oh, my, my! This is Big Daddy's dream, his dream come true! I'm going to tell him right now before he –

MARGARET: We'll tell him in the morning. Don't disturb him now.

BIG MAMA: I want to tell him before he goes to sleep, I'm going to tell him his dream's come true this minute! And Brick! A child will make you pull yourself together and quit this drinking!

[*She seizes the glass from his hand.*]
The responsibilities of a father will –

[*Her face contorts and she makes an excited gesture; bursting into sobs, she rushes out, crying.*]
I'm going to tell Big Daddy right this minute!

[*Her voice fades out down the hall.*
Brick shrugs slightly and drops an ice cube into another glass. Margaret crosses quickly to his side, saying something under her breath, and she pours the liquor for him, staring up almost fiercely into his face.]

BRICK [*coolly*]: Thank you, Maggie, that's a nice big shot.

[*Mae has joined Gooper and she gives him a fierce poke, making a low hissing sound and a grimace of fury.*]

GOOPER [*pushing her aside*]: Brick, could you possibly spare me one small shot of that liquor?

BRICK: Why, help yourself, Gooper boy.

GOOPER: I will.

MAE [*shrilly*]: Of course we know that this is –

GOOPER: *Be still, Mae!*

MAE: I won't be still! I know she's made this up!

GOOPER: God damn it, I said to shut up!

MARGARET: Gracious! I didn't know that my little announcement was going to provoke such a storm!

MAE: *That* woman isn't *pregnant!*

GOOPER: Who said she was?

MAE: *She* did.

GOOPER: The doctor didn't. Doc Baugh didn't.

MARGARET: I haven't gone to Doc Baugh.

GOOPER: Then who'd you go to, Maggie?

MARGARET: One of the best gynaecologists in the South.

GOOPER: Uh huh, uh huh! – I see. . . .

   [*He takes out pencil and notebook.*]

– May we have his name, please?

MARGARET: No, you may not, Mister Prosecuting Attorney!

MAE: He doesn't have any name, he doesn't exist!

MARGARET: Oh, he exists all right, and so does my child, Brick's baby!

MAE: You can't conceive a child by a man that won't sleep with you unless you think you're –

   [*Brick has turned on the phonograph. A scat song cuts Mae's speech.*]

GOOPER: *Turn that off!*

MAE: We know it's a lie because we hear you in here; he won't sleep with you, we hear you! So don't imagine you're going to put a trick over on us, to fool a dying man with a–

   [*A long drawn cry of agony and rage fills the house. Margaret turns phonograph down to a whisper.*
       The cry is repeated.]

MAE [*awed*]: Did you hear that, Gooper, did you hear that?

GOOPER: Sounds like the pain has struck.

MAE: Go see, Gooper!

GOOPER: Come along and leave these love birds together in their nest!

[*He goes out first, Mae follows but turns at the door, contorting her face and hissing at Margaret.*]

MAE: *Liar!*

[*She slams the door.*

Margaret exhales with relief and moves a little unsteadily to catch hold of Brick's arm.]

MARGARET: Thank you for – keeping still . . .

BRICK: OK, Maggie.

MARGARET: It was gallant of you to save my face!

BRICK: – It hasn't happened yet.

MARGARET: What?

BRICK: The click. . . .

MARGARET: – the click in your head that makes you peaceful, honey?

BRICK: Uh-huh. It hasn't happened. . . . I've got to make it happen before I can sleep. . . .

MARGARET: – I – know what you – mean. . . .

BRICK: Give me that pillow in the big chair, Maggie.

MARGARET: I'll put it on the bed for you.

BRICK: No, put it on the sofa, where I sleep.

MARGARET: Not tonight, Brick.

BRICK: I want it on the sofa. That's where I sleep.

[*He has hobbled to the liquor cabinet. He now pours down three shots in quick succession and stands waiting, silent. All at once he turns with a smile and says:*]

There!

MARGARET: What?

BRICK: The *click.* . . .

[*His gratitude seems almost infinite as he hobbles out on the gallery with a drink. We hear his crutch as he swings out of sight. Then, at some distance, he begins singing to himself a peaceful song.*

Margaret holds the big pillow forlornly as if it were her only companion, for a few moments, then throws it on the bed. She rushes to the liquor cabinet, gathers all the bottles in her arms,] *turns about undecidedly, then runs out of the room with them, leaving the door ajar on the dim yellow hall. Brick is heard hobbling back along the gallery, singing his peaceful song. He comes back in, sees the pillow on the bed, laughs lightly, sadly, picks it up. He has it under his arm as Margaret returns to the room. Margaret softly shuts the door and leans against it, smiling softly at Brick.*]

MARGARET: Brick, I used to think that you were stronger than me and I didn't want to be overpowered by you. But now, since you've taken to liquor – you know what? – I guess it's bad, but now I'm stronger than you and I can love you more truly!

Don't move that pillow. I'll move it right back if you do! – Brick?

[*She turns out all the lamps but a single rose-silk-shaded one by the bed.*]

I really have been to a doctor and I know what to do and – Brick? – this is my time by the calendar to conceive!

BRICK: Yes, I understand, Maggie. But how are you going to conceive a child by a man in love with his liquor?

MARGARET: By locking his liquor up and making him satisfy my desire before I unlock it!

BRICK: Is that what you've done, Maggie?

MARGARET: Look and see. That cabinet's mighty empty compared to before!

BRICK: Well, I'll be a son of a –

[*He reaches for his crutch but she beats him to it and rushes out on the gallery, hurls the crutch over the rail and comes back in, panting.*

There are running footsteps. Big Mama bursts into the room, her face all awry, gasping, stammering.]

BIG MAMA: Oh, my God, oh, my God, oh, my God, where is it?

MARGARET: Is this what you want, Big Mama?

[*Margaret hands her the package left by the doctor.*]

BIG MAMA: I can't bear it, oh! God! Oh, Brick! Brick, baby!

[*She rushes at him. He averts his face from her sobbing kisses. Margaret watches with a tight smile.*]

My son, Big Daddy's boy! Little Father!

[*The groaning cry is heard again. She runs out, sobbing.*]

MARGARET: And so tonight we're going to make the lie true, and when that's done, I'll bring the liquor back here and we'll get drunk together, here, tonight, in this place that death has come into. . . .

– What do you say?

BRICK: I don't say anything. I guess there's nothing to say.

MARGARET: Oh, you weak people, you weak, beautiful people! – who give up. – What you want is someone to –

[*She turns out the rose-silk lamp.*]

– take hold of you. – Gently, gently, with love! And –

[*The curtain begins to fall slowly.*]

I *do* love you, Brick, I *do*!

BRICK [*smiling with charming sadness*]: Wouldn't it be funny if that was true?

THE CURTAIN COMES DOWN

THE END

NOTE OF EXPLANATION

SOME day when time permits I would like to write a piece
about the influence, its dangers and its values, of a powerful
and highly imaginative director upon the development of a
play, before and during production. It does have dangers, but
it has them only if the playwright is excessively malleable or
submissive, or the director is excessively insistent on ideas or
interpretations of his own. Elia Kazan and I have enjoyed the
advantages and avoided the dangers of this highly explosive
relationship because of the deepest mutual respect for each
other's creative function: we have worked together three
times with a phenomenal absence of friction between us and
each occasion has increased the trust.

If you don't want a director's influence on your play, there
are two ways to avoid it, and neither is good. One way is to
arrive at an absolutely final draft of your play before you let
your director see it, then hand it to him saying, Here it is,
take it or leave it! The other way is to select a director who is
content to put your play on the stage precisely as you con-
ceived it with no ideas of his own. I said neither is a good way,
and I meant it. No living playwright, that I can think of,
hasn't something valuable to learn about his own work from a
director so keenly perceptive as Elia Kazan. It so happened
that in the case of *Streetcar*, Kazan was given a script that was
completely finished. In the case of *Cat*, he was shown the first
typed version of the play, and he was excited by it, but he had
definite reservations about it which were concentrated in the
third act. The gist of his reservations can be listed as three
points: one, he felt that Big Daddy was too vivid and important a character to disappear from the play except as an
offstage cry after the second act curtain; two, he felt that the
character of Brick should undergo some apparent mutation
as a result of the virtual vivisection that he undergoes in his
interview with his father in Act Two. Three, he felt that the
character of Margaret, while he understood that I sympathized

with her and liked her myself, should be, if possible, more clearly sympathetic to an audience.

It was only the third of these suggestions that I embraced wholeheartedly from the outset, because it so happened that Maggie the Cat had become steadily more charming to me as I worked on her characterization. I didn't want Big Daddy to reappear in Act Three and I felt that the moral paralysis of Brick was a root thing in his tragedy, and to show a dramatic progression would obscure the meaning of that tragedy in him and because I don't believe that a conversation, however revelatory, ever effects so immediate a change in the heart or even conduct of a person in Brick's state of spiritual disrepair.

However, I wanted Kazan to direct the play, and though these suggestions were not made in the form of an ultimatum, I was fearful that I would lose his interest if I didn't re-examine the script from his point of view. I did. And you will find included in this published script the new third act that resulted from his creative influence on the play. The reception of the playing-script has more than justified, in my opinion, the adjustments made to that influence. A failure reaches fewer people, and touches fewer, than does a play that succeeds.

It may be that *Cat* number one would have done just as well, or nearly, as *Cat* number two; it's an interesting question. At any rate, with the publication of both third acts in this volume, the reader can, if he wishes, make up his own mind about it.

TENNESSEE WILLIAMS

ACT THREE

Big Daddy is seen leaving as at the end of Act Two.

BIG DADDY [*shouts, as he goes out D R on gallery*]: ALL – LYIN' – DYIN' – LIARS! LIARS! LIARS!

[*After Big Daddy has gone, Margaret enters from D R on gallery, into room through D S door. She X to Brick at L C.*]

MARGARET: Brick, what in the name of God was goin' on in this room?

[*Dixie and Trixie rush through the room from the hall, L to gallery R, brandishing cap pistols, which they fire repeatedly, as they shout: 'Bang! Bang! Bang!'*

Mae appears from D R gallery entrance, and turns the children back U L, along gallery. At the same moment, Gooper, Reverend Tooker and Dr Baugh enter from L in the hall.]

MAE: Dixie! You quit that! Gooper, will y'please git these kiddies t'baid? Right now?

[*Gooper and Reverend Tooker X along upper gallery, Dr Baugh holds, U C, near hall door. Reverend Tooker X to Mae near section of gallery just outside doors, R.*]

GOOPER [*urging the children along*]: Mae – you seen Big Mama?

MAE: Not yet.

[*Dixie and Trixie vanish through hall, L.*]

REVEREND TOOKER [*to Mae*]: Those kiddies are so full of vitality. I think I'll have to be startin' back to town.

[*Margaret turns to watch and listen.*]

MAE: Not yet, Preacher. You know we regard you as a member of this fam'ly, one of our closest an' dearest, so you just got t'be with us when Doc Baugh gives Big Mama th' actual truth about th' report from th' clinic.

[*Calls through door:*]

Has Big Daddy gone to bed, Brick?

[*Gooper has gone out DR at the beginning of the exchange between Mae and Reverend Tooker.*]

MARGARET [*replying to Mae*]: Yes, he's gone to bed.

[*To Brick:*]
Why'd Big Daddy shout 'liars'?

GOOPER [*off DR*]: Mae!

[*Mae exits DR. Reverend Tooker drifts along upper gallery.*]

BRICK: I didn't lie to Big Daddy. I've lied to nobody, nobody but myself, just lied to myself. The time has come to put me in Rainbow Hill, put me in Rainbow Hill, Maggie, I ought to go there.

MARGARET: Over my dead body!

[*Brick starts R. She holds him.*]
Where do you think you're goin'?

[*Mae enters from DR on gallery, X to Reverend Tooker, who comes to meet her.*]

BRICK [*X below to C*]: Out for some air, I want air –

GOOPER [*entering from DR to Mae, on gallery*]: Now, where is that old lady?

MAE: Cantcha find her, Gooper?

[*Reverend Tooker goes out DR.*]

GOOPER [*X to Doc above hall door*]: She's avoidin' this talk.

MAE: I think she senses somethin'.

GOOPER [*calls off L*]: Sookey! Go find Big Mama an' tell her Doc Baugh an' the Preacher've got to go soon.

MAE: Don't let Big Daddy hear yuh!

[*Brings Dr Baugh to R on gallery.*]

REVEREND TOOKER [*off DR, calls*]: Big Mama.

SOOKEY and DAISY [*running from L to R in lawn, calling*]: Miss Ida! Miss Ida!

[*They go out UR.*]

GOOPER [*calling off upper gallery*]: Lacey, you look downstairs for Big Mama!

MARGARET: Brick, they're going to tell Big Mama the truth now, an' she needs you!

[*Reverend Tooker appears in lawn area, UR, X C.*]

DOCTOR BAUGH [*to Mae, on R gallery*]: This is going to be painful.

MAE: Painful things can't always be avoided.

DOCTOR BAUGH: That's what I've noticed about 'em, Sister Woman.

REVEREND TOOKER [*on lawn, points off* R]: I see Big Mama!

[*Hurries off* L *and reappears shortly in hall.*]

GOOPER [*hurrying into hall*]: She's gone round the gall'ry to Big Daddy's room. Hey, Mama!

[*Off:*]

Hey, Big Mama! Come here!

MAE [*calls*]: Hush, Gooper! Don't holler, go to her!

[*Gooper and Reverend Tooker now appear together in halls. Big Mama runs in from* D R, *carrying a glass of milk. She X past Dr Baugh to Mae, on* R *gallery. Dr Baugh turns away.*]

BIG MAMA: Here I am! What d'you all want with me?

GOOPER [*steps toward Big Mama*]: Big Mama, I told you we got to have this talk.

BIG MAMA: What talk you talkin' about? I saw the light go on in Big Daddy's bedroom an' took him his glass of milk, an' he just shut the shutters right in my face.

[*Steps into room through* R *door.*]

When old couples have been together as long as me an' Big Daddy, they, they get irritable with each other just from too much – devotion! Isn't that so?

[*X below wicker seat to* R C *area.*]

MARGARET [*X to Big Mama, embracing her*]: Yes, of course it's so.

[*Brick starts out* U C *through hall, but sees Gooper and Reverend Tooker entering, so he hobbles through* C *out* D S *door and on to gallery.*]

BIG MAMA: I think Big Daddy was just worn out. He loves his fam'ly. He loves to have 'em around him, but it's a strain on his nerves. He wasn't himself tonight, Brick–

[*X C toward Brick, Brick passes her on his way out,* D S.]

Big Daddy wasn't himself, I could tell he was all worked up.

REVEREND TOOKER [*U S C*]: I think he's remarkable.

BIG MAMA: Yaiss! Just remarkable.

[*Faces* U S, *turns, X to bar, puts down glass of milk.*]

Did you notice all the food he ate at that table?

[*X* R *a bit.*]

Why he ate like a hawss!

GOOPER [*USC*]: I hope he don't regret it.

BIG MAMA [*turns US toward Gooper*]: What! Why that man ate a huge piece of cawn bread with molasses on it! Helped himself twice to hoppin' john!

MARGARET [*X to Big Mama*]: Big Daddy loves hoppin' john. We had a real country dinner.

BIG MAMA: Yais, he simply adores it! An' candied yams. Son –

[*X to DS door, looking out at Brick. Margaret X above Big Mama to her L.*]

That man put away enough food at that table to stuff a field-hand.

GOOPER: I hope he don't have to pay for it later on.

BIG MAMA [*turns US*]: What's that, Gooper?

MAE: Gooper says he hopes Big Daddy doesn't suffer tonight.

BIG MAMA [*turns to Margaret, DC*]: Oh, shoot, Gooper says, Gooper says! Why should Big Daddy suffer for satisfyin' a nawmal appetite? There's nothin' wrong with that man but nerves; he's sound as a dollar! An' now he knows he is, an' that's why he ate such a supper. He had a big load off his mind, knowin' he wasn't doomed to – what – he thought he was – doomed t' –

[*She wavers.*
Margaret puts her arms around Big Mama.]

GOOPER [*urging Mae forward*]: MAE!

[*Mae runs forward below wicker seat. She stands below Big Mama, Margaret above Big Mama. They help her to the wicker seat. Big Mama sits. Margaret sits above her. Mae stands behind her.*]

MARGARET: Bless his ole sweet soul.

BIG MAMA: Yes – bless his heart.

BRICK [*DS on gallery, looking out front*]: Hello, moon, I envy you, you cool son of a bitch.

BIG MAMA: I want Brick!

MARGARET: He just stepped out for some fresh air.

BIG MAMA: Honey! I want Brick!

MAE: Bring li'l Brother in here so we cin talk.

[*Margaret rises, X through DS door to Brick on gallery.*]

BRICK [*to the moon*]: I envy you – you cool son of a bitch.

MARGARET: Brick what're you doin' out here on the gall'ry, baby?

BRICK: Admirin' an' complimentin' th' man in the moon.

[*Mae X to Dr Baugh on R gallery. Reverend Tooker and Gooper move R U C, looking at Big Mama.*]

MARGARET [*to Brick*]: Come in, baby. They're gettin' ready to tell Big Mama the truth.

BRICK: I can't witness that thing in there.

MAE: Doc Baugh, d'you think those vitamin B$_{12}$ injections are all they're cracked up t'be?

[*Enters room to upper side, behind wicker seat.*]

DOCTOR BAUGH [*X to below wicker seat*]: Well, I guess they're as good t'be stuck with as anything else.

[*Looks at watch; X through to L C.*]

MARGARET [*to Brick*]: Big Mama needs you!

BRICK: I can't witness that thing in there!

BIG MAMA: What's wrong here? You all have such long faces, you sit here waitin' for somethin' like a bomb – to go off.

GOOPER: We're waitin' for Brick an' Maggie to come in for this talk.

MARGARET [*X above Brick, to his R*]: Brother Man an' Mae have got a trick up their sleeves, an' if you don't go in there t'help Big Mama, y'know what I'm goin' to do –?

BIG MAMA: Talk. Whispers! Whispers!

[*Looks out D R.*]

Brick! . . .

MARGARET [*answering Big Mama's call*]: Comin', Big Mama!
[*To Brick.*]

I'm goin' to take every dam' bottle on this place an' pitch it off th' levee into th' river!

BIG MAMA: Never had this sort of atmosphere here before.

MAE [*sits above Big Mama on wicker seat*]: Before what, Big Mama?

BIG MAMA: This occasion. What's Brick an' Maggie doin' out there now?

GOOPER [*X D C, looks out*]: They seem to be havin' some little altercation.

[*Brick X toward D S step. Maggie moves R above him to portal D R. Reverend Tooker joins Dr Baugh, L C.*]

BIG MAMA [*taking a pill from pill box on chain at her wrist*]: Give me a little somethin' to wash this tablet down with. Smell of burnt fireworks always makes me sick.

[*Mae X to bar to pour glass of water. Dr Baugh joins her. Gooper X to Reverend Tooker, L C.*]

BRICK [*to Maggie*]: You're a live cat, aren't you?

MARGARET: You're dam' right I am!

BIG MAMA: Gooper, will y'please open that hall door – an' let some air circulate in this stiflin' room?

[*Gooper starts U S, but is restrained by Mae who X through C with glass of water. Gooper turns to men D L C.*]

MAE [*X to Big Mama with water, sits above her*]: Big Mama, I think we ought to keep that door closed till after we talk.

BIG MAMA: I swan!

[*Drinks water. Washes down pill.*]

MAE: I just don't think we ought to take any chance of Big Daddy hearin' a word of this discussion.

BIG MAMA [*hands glass to Mae*]: What discussion of what? Maggie! Brick! Nothin' is goin' to be said in th' house of Big Daddy Pollitt that he can't hear if he wants to!

[*Mae rises, X to bar, puts down glass, joins Gooper and the two men, L C.*]

BRICK: How long are you goin' to stand behind me, Maggie?

MARGARET: Forever, if necessary.

[*Brick X U S to R gallery door.*]

BIG MAMA: Brick!

[*Mae rises, looks out D S, sits.*]

GOOPER: That boy's gone t'pieces – he's just gone t'pieces.

DOCTOR BAUGH: Y'know, in my day they used to have somethin' they called the Keeley cure for drinkers.

BIG MAMA: Shoot!

DOCTOR BAUGH: But nowadays, I understand they take some kind of tablets that kill their taste for the stuff.

GOOPER [*turns to Dr Baugh*]: Call 'em anti-bust tablets.

BIG MAMA: Brick don't need to take nothin'. That boy is just broken up over Skipper's death. You know how poor

Skipper died. They gave him a big, big dose of that sodium amytal stuff at his home an' then they called the ambulance an' give him another big, big dose of it at th' hospital an' that an' all the alcohol in his system fo' months an' months just proved too much for his heart an' his heart quit beatin'. I'm scared of needles! I'm more scared of a needle than th' knife –

[*Brick has entered the room to behind the wicker seat. He rests his hand on Big Mama's head. Gooper has moved a bit U R C, facing Big Mama.*]

BIG MAMA: Oh! Here's Brick! My precious baby!

[*Dr Baugh X to bar, puts down drink. Brick X below Big Mama through C to bar.*]

BRICK: Take it, Gooper!

MAE [*rising*]: What?

BRICK: Gooper knows what. Take it, Gooper!

[*Mae turns to Gooper U R C. Dr Baugh X to Reverend Tooker. Margaret, who has followed Brick U S on R gallery before he entered the room, now enters room, to behind wicker seat.*]

BIG MAMA [*to Brick*]: You just break my heart.

BRICK [*at bar*]: Sorry – anyone else?

MARGARET: Brick, sit with Big Mama an' hold her hand while we talk.

BRICK: You do that, Maggie. I'm a restless cripple. I got to stay on my crutch.

[*Mae sits above Big Mama, Gooper moves in front, below, and sits on couch, facing Big Mama. Reverend Tooker closes in to R C. Dr Baugh X D C, faces upstage, smoking cigar. Margaret turns away to R doors.*]

BIG MAMA: Why're you all *surroundin'* me? – like this? Why're you all starin' at me like this an' makin' signs at each other?

[*Brick hobbles out hall door and X along R gallery.*]

I don't need nobody to hold my hand. Are you all crazy? Since when did Big Daddy or me need anybody –?

[*Reverend Tooker moves behind wicker seat.*]

MAE: Calm yourself, Big Mama.

BIG MAMA: Calm *you'self you'self*, Sister Woman! How could I calm myself with everyone starin' at me as if big drops of blood had broken out on m'face? What's this all about Annh! What?

GOOPER: Doc Baugh —

[*Mae rises.*]

Sit down, Mae —

[*Mae sits.*]

— Big Mama wants to know the complete truth about th' report we got today from the Ochsner Clinic!

[*Dr Baugh buttons his coat, faces group at R C.*]

BIG MAMA: Is there somethin' — somethin' that I don't know?

DOCTOR BAUGH: Yes — well . . .

BIG MAMA [*rises*]: I — want to — *knowwwww!*

[*X to Dr Baugh.*]

Somebody must be lyin'! *I want to know!*

[*Mae, Gooper, Reverend Tooker surround Big Mama.*]

MAE: Sit down, Big Mama, sit down on this sofa!

[*Brick has passed Margaret Xing D R on gallery.*]

MARGARET: Brick! Brick!

BIG MAMA: *What is it, what is it?*

[*Big Mama drives Dr Baugh a bit D L C. Others follow, surrounding Big Mama.*]

DOCTOR BAUGH: I never have seen a more thorough examination than Big Daddy Pollitt was given in all my experience at the Ochsner Clinic.

GOOPER: It's one of th' best in th' country.

MAE: It's *THE* best in th' country — bar none!

DOCTOR BAUGH: Of course they were ninety-nine and nine-tenths per cent certain before they even started.

BIG MAMA: Sure of what, sure of what, sure of what — *what!?*

MAE: Now, Mommy, be a brave girl!

BRICK [*on D R gallery, covers his ears, sings*]: 'By the light, by the light, of the silvery moon!'

GOOPER [*breaks D R. Calls out to Brick*]: Shut up, Brick!

[*Returns to group L C.*]

BRICK: Sorry . . .

[*Continues singing.*]

DOCTOR BAUGH: But now, you see, Big Mama, they cut a piece off this growth, a specimen of the tissue, an' —

BIG MAMA: Growth? You told Big Daddy —

DOCTOR BAUGH: Now, wait –

BIG MAMA: You told me an' Big Daddy there wasn't a thing wrong with him but –

MAE: Big Mama, they always –

GOOPER: Let Doc Baugh talk, will yuh?

BIG MAMA: – little spastic condition of –

REVEREND TOOKER [*throughout all this*]: Shh! Shh! Shh!

[*Big Mama breaks U C, they all follow.*]

DOCTOR BAUGH: Yes, that's what we told Big Daddy. But we had this bit of tissue run through the laboratory, an' I'm sorry t'say the test was positive on it. It's malignant.

[*Pause.*]

BIG MAMA: *Cancer! Cancer!*

MAE: Now now, Mommy –

GOOPER [*at the same time*]: You had to know, Big Mama.

BIG MAMA: *Why didn't they cut it out of him? Hanh? Hannh?*

DOCTOR BAUGH: Involved too much, Big Mama, too many organs affected.

MAE: Big Mama, the liver's affected, an' so's the kidneys, both. It's gone way past what they call a –

GOOPER: – a surgical risk.

[*Big Mama gasps.*]

REVEREND TOOKER: Tch, tch, tch.

DOCTOR BAUGH: Yes, it's gone past the knife.

MAE: That's why he's turned yellow!

[*Brick stops singing, turns away U R on gallery.*]

BIG MAMA [*pushes Mae D S*]: Git away from me, git away from me, Mae!

[*X D S R.*]

I want Brick! Where's Brick! *Where's my only son?*

MAE [*a step after Big Mama*]: Mama! Did she say 'only' son?

GOOPER [*following Big Mama*]: What does that make me?

MAE [*above Gooper*]: A sober responsible man with five precious children – *six!*

BIG MAMA: I want Brick! Brick! Brick!

MARGARET [*a step to Big Mama above couch*]: Mama, let *me* tell you.

BIG MAMA [*pushing her aside*]: No, no, leave me alone, you're not my blood!

[*She rushes on to the D S gallery.*]

GOOPER [*X to Big Mama on gallery*]: Mama! I'm your son! Listen to me!

MAE: Gooper's your son, Mama, he's your first-born!

BIG MAMA: Gooper never liked Daddy!

MAE: That's not true!

REVEREND TOOKER [*U C*]: I think I'd better slip away at this point. Good night, good night everybody, and God bless you all – on this place.

[*Goes out through hall.*]

DOCTOR BAUGH [*X D R to above D S door*]: Well, Big Mama –

BIG MAMA [*leaning against Gooper, on lower gallery*]: It's all a mistake, I know it's just a bad dream.

DOCTOR BAUGH: We're gonna keep Big Daddy as comfortable as we can.

BIG MAMA: Yes, it's just a bad dream, that's all it is, it's just an awful dream.

GOOPER: In my opinion Big Daddy is havin' some pain but won't admit that he has it.

BIG MAMA: Just a dream, a bad dream.

DOCTOR BAUGH: That's what lots of 'em do, they think if they don't admit they're havin' the pain they can sort of escape th' fact of it.

[*Brick X US on R gallery. Margaret watches him from R doors.*]

GOOPER: Yes, they get sly about it, get real sly about it.

MAE [*X to R of Dr Baugh*]: Gooper an' I think –

GOOPER: Shut up, Mae! – Big Mama, I really do think Big Daddy should be started on morphine.

BIG MAMA [*pulling away from Gooper*]: Nobody's goin' to give Big Daddy morphine!

DOCTOR BAUGH: Now, Big Mama, when that pain strikes it's goin' to strike mighty hard an' Big Daddy's goin' t'need the needle to bear it.

BIG MAMA [*X to Dr Baugh*]: I tell you, nobody's goin' to give him morphine!

MAE: Big Mama, you don't want to see Big Daddy suffer, y'know y' –

DOCTOR BAUGH [*X to bar*]: Well, I'm leavin' this stuff here.
    [*Puts packet of morphine, etc., on bar.*]
so if there's a sudden attack you won't have to send out for
it.
    [*Big Mama hurries to L side bar.*]

MAE [*X C, below Dr Baugh*]: I know how to give a hypo.

BIG MAMA: Nobody's goin' to give Big Daddy morphine!

GOOPER [*X C*]: Mae took a course in nursin' durin' th' war.

MARGARET: Somehow I don't think Big Daddy would want
Mae t'give him a hypo.

MAE [*to Margaret*]: You think he'd want *you* to do it?

DOCTOR BAUGH: Well –

GOOPER: Well, Doc Baugh is goin' –

DOCTOR BAUGH: Yes, I got to be goin'. Well, keep your
chin up, Big Mama.
    [*X to hall.*]

GOOPER [*as he and Mae follow Dr Baugh into the hall*]: She's
goin' to keep her ole chin up, aren't you, Big Mama?
    [*They go out L.*]
Well, Doc, we sure do appreciate all you've done. I'm
telling you, we're obligated –

BIG MAMA: Margaret!
    [*X R C.*]

MARGARET [*meeting Big Mama in front of wicker seat*]: I'm
right here, Big Mama.

BIG MAMA: Margaret, you've got to cooperate with me an'
Big Daddy to straighten Brick out now –

GOOPER [*off L, returning with Mae*]: I guess that Doctor has
got a lot on his mind, but it wouldn't hurt him to act a
little more human –

BIG MAMA: – because it'll break Big Daddy's heart if Brick
don't pull himself together an' take hold of things here.
    [*Brick X D S R on gallery.*]

MAE [*U C, overhearing*]: Take hold of what things, Big Mama?

BIG MAMA [*sits in wicker chair, Margaret standing behind chair*]:
The place.

GOOPER [*U C*]: Big Mama, you've had a shock.

MAE [*X with Gooper to Big Mama*]: Yais, we've all had a shock,
but –

GOOPER: Let's be realistic –

MAE: Big Daddy would not, would *never*, be foolish enough to –

GOOPER: – put this place in irresponsible hands!

BIG MAMA: Big Daddy ain't goin' t'put th' place in anybody's hands, Big Daddy is *not* goin' t'die! I want you to git that into your haids, all of you!

> [*Mae sits above Big Mama, Margaret turns R to door, Gooper X L C a bit.*]

MAE: Mommy, Mommy, Big Mama, we're just as hopeful an' optimistic as you are about Big Daddy's prospects, we have faith in prayer – but nevertheless there are certain matters that have to be discussed an' dealt with, because otherwise –

GOOPER: Mae, will y'please get my briefcase out of our room?

MAE: Yes, honey.

> [*Rises, goes out through hall L.*]

MARGARET [*X to Brick on D S gallery*]: Hear them in there?

> [*X back to R gallery door.*]

GOOPER [*stands above Big Mama. Leaning over her*]: Big Mama, what you said just now was not at all true, an' you know it. I've always loved Big Daddy in my own quiet way. I never made a show of it. I know that Big Daddy has always been fond of me in a quiet way, too.

> [*Margaret drifts U R on gallery. Mae returns, X to Gooper's L with briefcase.*]

MAE: Here's your briefcase, Gooper, honey.

> [*Hands it to him.*]

GOOPER [*hands briefcase back to Mae*]: Thank you. Of ca'use, my relationship with Big Daddy is different from Brick's.

MAE: You're eight years older'n Brick an' always had t' carry a bigger load of th' responsibilities than Brick ever had t'carry; he never carried a thing in his life but a football or a highball.

GOOPER: Mae, will y'let me talk, please?

MAE: Yes, honey.

GOOPER: Now, a twenty-eight thousand acre plantation's a mighty big thing t'run.

MAE: Almost single-handed!

BIG MAMA: You never had t'run this place, Brother Man,

what're you talkin' about, as if Big Daddy was dead an' in his grave, you had to run it? Why, you just had t'help him out with a few business details an' had your law practice at the same time in Memphis.

MAE: Oh, Mommy, Mommy, Mommy! Let's be fair! Why, Gooper has given himself body an' soul t'keepin' this place up fo' the past five years since Big Daddy's health started fallin'. Gooper won't say it, Gooper never thought of it as a duty, he just did it. An' what did Brick do? Brick kep' livin' in his past glory at college!

[*Gooper places a restraining hand on Mae's leg; Margaret drifts DS in gallery.*]

GOOPER: Still a football player at twenty-seven!

MARGARET [*bursts into UR door*]: Who are you talkin' about now? Brick? A football player? He isn't a football player an' you know it! Brick is a sports announcer on TV an' one of the best-known ones in the country!

MAE [*breaks UC*]: I'm talkin' about what he was!

MARGARET [*X to above lower gallery door*]: Well, I wish you would just stop talkin' about my husband!

GOOPER [*X to above Margaret*]: Listen, Margaret, I've got a right to discuss my own brother with other members of my own fam'ly, which don't include *you*!

[*Pokes finger at her; she slaps his finger away.*]

Now, why don't you go on out there an' drink with Brick?

MARGARET: I've never seen such malice toward a brother.

GOOPER: How about his for me? Why he can't stand to be in the same room with me!

BRICK [*on lower gallery*]: That's the truth!

MARGARET: This is a deliberate campaign of vilification for the most disgusting and sordid reason on earth, and I know what it is! *It's avarice, avarice, greed, greed!*

BIG MAMA: Oh, I'll scream, I will scream in a moment unless this stops! Margaret, child, come here, sit next to Big Mama.

MARGARET [*X to Big Mama, sits above her*]: Precious Mommy.

[*Gooper X to bar.*]

MAE: How beautiful, how touchin' this display of devotion! Do you know why she's childless? She's childless because that big, beautiful athlete husband of hers won't go to bed with her, that's why!

[*X to L of bed, looks at Gooper.*]

GOOPER: You jest won't let me do this the nice way, will yuh? Aw right –

[*X to above wicker seat.*]

I don't give a goddam if Big Daddy likes me or don't like me or did or never did or will or will never! I'm just appealin' to a sense of common decency an' fair play! I'm tellin' you th' truth –

[*X D S through lower door to Brick on D R gallery.*]

I've resented Big Daddy's partiality to Brick ever since th' goddam day you were born, son, an' th' way I've been treated, like I was just barely good enough to spit on, an' sometimes not even good enough for that.

[*X back through room to above wicker seat.*]

Big Daddy is dyin' of cancer an' it's spread all through him an' it's attacked all his vital organs includin' the kidneys an' right now he is sinkin' into uraemia, an' you all know what uraemia is, it's poisonin' of the whole system due to th' failure of th' body to eliminate its poisons.

MARGARET: Poisons, poisons, venomous thoughts and words! In hearts and minds! That's poisons!

GOOPER: I'm askin' for a square deal an' by God I expect to get one. But if I don't get one, if there's any peculiar shenanigans goin' on around here behind my back, well I'm not a corporation lawyer for nothin'!

[*X D S toward lower gallery door, on apex.*]

I know how to protect my own interests.

[*Rumble of distant thunder.*]

BRICK [*entering the room through D S door*]: Storm comin' up.

GOOPER: Oh, a late arrival!

MAE [*X through C to below bar, L C O*]: Behold, the conquerin' hero comes!

GOOPER [*X through C to bar, following Brick, imitating his limp*]: The fabulous Brick Pollitt! Remember him? Who could forget him?

MAE: He looks like he's been injured in a game!

GOOPER: Yep, I'm afraid you'll have to warm th' bench at

the Sugar Bowl this year, Brick! Or was it the Rose Bowl that he made his famous run in.

[*Another rumble of thunder, sound of wind rising.*]

MAE [*X to L of Brick, who has reached the bar*]: The punch bowl, honey, it was the punch bowl, the cut-glass punch bowl!

GOOPER: That's right! I'm always gettin' the boy's *bowls* mixed up!

[*Pats Brick on the butt.*]

MARGARET [*rushes at Gooper, striking him*]: Stop that! You stop that!

[*Thunder.*

Mae X toward Margaret from L of Gooper, flails at Margaret; Gooper keeps the women apart. Lacey runs through the US lawn area in a raincoat.]

DAISY and SOOKEY [*off UL*]: Storm! Storm comin'! Storm! Storm!

LACEY [*running out UR*]: Brightie, close them shutters!

GOOPER [*X on to R gallery, calls after Lacey*]: Lacey, put the top up on my Cadillac, will yuh?

LACEY [*off R*]: Yes, sur, Mistah Pollitt!

GOOPER [*X to above Big Mama*]: Big Mama, you know it's goin' to be necessary for me t'go back to Memphis in th' mornin' t'represent the Parker estate in a lawsuit.

[*Mae sits on L side bed, arranges papers she removes from briefcase.*]

BIG MAMA: Is it, Gooper?

MAE: Yaiss.

GOOPER: That's why I'm forced to – to bring up a problem that –

MAE: Somethin' that's too important t' be put off!

GOOPER: If Brick was sober, he ought to be in on this. I think he ought to be present when I present this plan.

MARGARET [*UC*]: Brick is present, we're present!

GOOPER: Well, good. I will now give you this outline my partner, Tom Bullitt, an' me have drawn up – a sort of dummy – trusteeship!

MARGARET: Oh, that's it! You'll be in charge an' dole out remittances, will you?

GOOPER: This we did as soon as we got the report on Big Daddy from th' Ochsner Laboratories. We did this thing, I mean we drew up this dummy outline with the advice and assistance of the Chairman of the Boa'd of Directors of th' Southern Plantuhs Bank and Trust Company in Memphis, C. C. Bellowes, a man who handles estates for all th' prominent fam'lies in West Tennessee and th' Delta!

BIG MAMA: Gooper?

GOOPER [*X behind seat to below Big Mama*]: Now this is not – not final, or anything like it, this is just a preliminary outline. But it does provide a – basis – a design – a – possible, feasible – *plan*!

[*He waves papers Mae has thrust into his hand, US.*]

MARGARET [*X DL*]: Yes, I'll bet it's a plan!

[*Thunder rolls. Interior lighting dims.*]

MAE: It's a plan to protect the biggest estate in the Delta from irresponsibility an' –

BIG MAMA: Now you listen to me, all of you, you listen here! They's not goin' to be no more catty talk in my house! And Gooper, you put that away before I grab it out of your hand and tear it right up! I don't know what the hell's in it, and I don't want to know what the hell's in it. I'm talkin' in Big Daddy's language now, I'm his *wife*, not his *widow*, I'm still his *wife*! And I'm talkin' to you in his language an' –

GOOPER: Big Mama, what I have here is –

MAE: Gooper explained that it's just a plan. . . .

BIG MAMA: I don't care what you got there, just put it back where it come from an' don't let me see it again, not even the outside of the envelope of it! Is that understood? Basis! Plan! Preliminary! Design! – I say – what is it that Big Daddy always says when he's disgusted?

[*Storm clouds race across sky.*]

BRICK [*from bar*]: Big Daddy says 'crap' when he is disgusted.

BIG MAMA [*rising*]: That's right – *CRAPPPP!* I say *CRAP* too, like Big Daddy!

[*Thunder rolls.*]

MAE: Coarse language don't seem called for in this –

GOOPER: Somethin' in me is *deeply outraged* by this.

BIG MAMA: *Nobody's goin' to do nothin'!* till Big Daddy lets go

of it, and maybe just possibly not – not even then! No, not
even then!

[*Thunder clap. Glass crash, off L.*

*Off U R, children commence crying. Many storm sounds,
L and R: barnyard animals in terror, papers crackling, shutters
rattling. Sookey and Daisy hurry from L to R in lawn area.
Inexplicably, Daisy hits together two leather pillows. They
cry, 'Storm! Storm!' Sookey waves a piece of wrapping paper
to cover lawn furniture. Mae exits to hall and upper gallery.
Strange man runs across lawn, R to L.*

Thunder rolls repeatedly.]

MAE: Sookey, hurry up an' git that po'ch fu'niture covahed;
want th' paint to come off?

[*Starts D R on gallery.*

Gooper runs through hall to R gallery.]

GOOPER [*yells to Lacey, who appears from R*]: Lacey, put mah
car away!

LACEY: Cain't, Mistah Pollitt, you got the keys!

[*Exit U S.*]

GOOPER: Naw, you got 'em, man.

[*Exit D R. Reappears U R, calls to Mae:*]

Where th' keys to th' car, honey?

[*Runs C.*]

MAE [*D R on gallery*]: You got 'em in your pocket!

[*Exit D R.*

*Gooper exits U R. Dog howls. Daisy and Sookey sing off
U R to comfort children. Mae is heard placating the children.*

Storm fades away.

*During the storm, Margaret X and sits on couch, D R. Big
Mama X D C.*]

BIG MAMA: BRICK! Come here, Brick, I need you.

[*Thunder distantly.*

*Children whimper, off L. Mae consoles them. Brick X to
R of Big Mama.*]

BIG MAMA: Tonight Brick looks like he used to look when
he was a little boy just like he did when he played wild
games in the orchard back of the house and used to come
home when I hollered myself hoarse for him! all – sweaty –
and pink-cheeked – an' sleepy with his curls shinin' –

[*Thunder distantly.*

Children whimper off L. Mae consoles them. Dog howls, off.]

Time goes by so fast. Nothin' can outrun it. Death commences too early – almost before you're half-acquainted with life – you meet with the other. Oh, you know we just got to love each other, an' stay together all of us just as close as we can, specially now that such a *black* thing has come and moved into this place without invitation.

[*Dog howls, off.*]

Oh, Brick, son of Big Daddy, Big Daddy does so love you. Y'know what would be his fondest dream come true? If before he passed on, if Big Daddy has to pass on . . .

[*Dog howls, off.*]

You give him a child of yours, a grandson as much like his son as his son is like Big Daddy. . . .

MARGARET: I know that's Big Daddy's dream.

BIG MAMA: That's his dream.

BIG DADDY [*off D R on gallery*]: Looks like the wind was takin' liberties with this place.

[*Lacey appears U L, X to U C in lawn area; Brightie and Small appear U R on lawn. Big Daddy X on to the U R gallery.*]

LACEY: Evenin', Mr Pollitt.

BRIGHTIE and SMALL: Evenin', Cap'n. Hello, Cap'n.

MARGARET [*X to R door*]: Big Daddy's on the gall'ry.

BIG DADDY: Stawm crossed th' river, Lacey?

LACEY: Gone to Arkansas, Cap'n.

[*Big Mama has turned toward the hall door at the sound of Big Daddy's voice on the gallery. Now she X's D S R an out the D S door on to the gallery.*]

BIG MAMA: I can't stay here. He'll see somethin' in my eyes.

BIG DADDY [*on upper gallery, to the boys*]: Stawm done any damage around here?

BRIGHTIE: Took the po'ch off ole Aunt Crawley's house.

BIG DADDY: Ole Aunt Crawley should of been settin' on it. It's time fo' th' wind to blow that ole girl away!

[*Field-hands laugh, exit, U R. Big Daddy enters room, U C, hall door.*]

Can I come in?

[*Puts his cigar in ash tray on bar.*
   Mae and Gooper hurry along the upper gallery and stand behind Big Daddy in hall door.]

MARGARET: Did the storm wake you up, Big Daddy?

BIG DADDY: Which stawm are you talkin' about – th' one outside or th' hullaballoo in here?

   [*Gooper squeezes past Big Daddy.*]

GOOPER [*X toward bed, where legal papers are strewn*]: 'Scuse me, sir . . .

   [*Mae tries to squeeze past Big Daddy to join Gooper, but Big Daddy puts his arm firmly around her.*]

BIG DADDY: I heard some mighty loud talk. Sounded like somethin' important was bein' discussed. What was the powwow about?

MAE [*flustered*]: Why – nothin', Big Daddy . . .

BIG DADDY [*X DLC, taking Mae with him*]: What is that pregnant-lookin' envelope you're puttin' back in your briefcase, Gooper?

GOOPER [*at foot of bed, caught, as he stuffs papers into envelope*]: That? Nothin', suh – nothin' much of anythin' at all . . .

BIG DADDY: Nothin'? It looks like a whole lot of nothing!

   [*Turns US to group:*]

You all know th' story about th' young married couple –

GOOPER: Yes, sir!

BIG DADDY: Hello, Brick –

BRICK: Hello, Big Daddy.

   [*The group is arranged in a semi-circle above Big Daddy, Margaret at the extreme R, then Mae and Gooper, then Big Mama, with Brick at L.*]

BIG DADDY: Young married couple took Junior out to th' zoo one Sunday, inspected all of God's creatures in their cages, with satisfaction.

GOOPER: Satisfaction.

BIG DADDY [*X USC, face front*]: This afternoon was a warm afternoon in spring an' that ole elephant had somethin' else on his mind which was bigger'n peanuts. You know this story, Brick?

   [*Gooper nods.*]

BRICK: No, sir, I don't know it.

BIG DADDY: Y'see, in th' cage adjoinin' they was a young female elephant in heat!

BIG MAMA [*at Big Daddy's shoulder*]: Oh, Big Daddy!

BIG DADDY: What's the matter, preacher's gone, ain't he? All right. That female elephant in the next cage was permeatin' the atmosphere about her with a powerful and excitin' odour of female fertility! Huh! Ain't that a nice way to put it, Brick?

BRICK: Yes, sir, nothin' wrong with it.

BIG DADDY: Brick says the's nothin' wrong with it!

BIG MAMA: Oh, Big Daddy!

BIG DADDY [*X DSC*]: So this ole bull elephant still had a couple of fornications left in him. He reared back his trunk an' got a whiff of that elephant lady next door! – began to paw at the dirt in his cage an' butt his head against the separatin' partition and, first thing y'know, there was a conspicuous change in his *profile* – very *conspicuous*! Ain't I tellin' this story in decent language, Brick?

BRICK: Yes, sir, too ruttin' decent!

BIG DADDY: So, the little boy pointed at it and said, 'What's that?' His Mam said, 'Oh, that's nothin'!' – His Papa said, 'She's spoiled!'

[*Field-hands sing off R, featuring Sookey: 'I Just Can't Stay Here by Myself,' through following scene.*
Big Daddy X to Brick at L.]

BIG DADDY: You didn't laugh at that story, Brick.

[*Big Mama X DRC crying. Margaret goes to her. Mae and Gooper hold URC.*]

BRICK: No, sir, I didn't laugh at that story.

[*On the lower gallery, Big Mama sobs. Big Daddy looks toward her.*]

BIG DADDY: What's wrong with that long, thin woman over there, loaded with diamonds? Hey, what's-your-name, what's the matter with you?

MARGARET [*X toward Big Daddy*]: She had a slight dizzy spell, Big Daddy.

BIG DADDY [*ULC*]: You better watch that, Big Mama. A stroke is a bad way to go.

MARGARET [*X to Big Daddy at C*]: Oh, Brick, Big Daddy

has on your birthday present to him, Brick, he has on your cashmere robe, the softest material I have ever felt.

BIG DADDY: Yeah, this is my soft birthday, Maggie. . . .

Not my gold or my silver birthday, but my soft birthday, everything's got to be soft for Big Daddy on this soft birthday.

[*Maggie kneels before Big Daddy C. As Gooper and Mae speak, Big Mama X USRC in front of them, hushing them with a gesture.*]

GOOPER: Maggie, I hate to make such a crude observation, but there is somethin' a little indecent about your –

MAE: Like a slow-motion football tackle –

MARGARET: Big Daddy's got on his Chinese slippers that I gave him, Brick. Big Daddy, I haven't given you my big present yet, but now I will, now's the time for me to present it to you! I have an announcement to make!

MAE: What? What kind of announcement?

GOOPER: A sports announcement, Maggie?

MARGARET: Announcement of life beginning! A child is coming, sired by Brick, and out of Maggie the Cat! I have Brick's child in my body, an' that's my birthday present to Big Daddy on this birthday!

[*Big Daddy looks at Brick who X behind Big Daddy to DS portal, L.*]

BIG DADDY: Get up, girl, get up off your knees, girl.

[*Big Daddy helps Margaret rise. He X above her, to her R, bites off the end of a fresh cigar, taken from his bathrobe pocket, as he studies Margaret.*]

Uh-huh, this girl has life in her body, that's no lie!

BIG MAMA: BIG DADDY'S DREAM COME TRUE

BRICK: *JESUS!*

BIG DADDY [*X R below wicker seat*]: Gooper, I want my lawyer in the mornin'.

BRICK: Where are you goin', Big Daddy?

BIG DADDY: Son, I'm goin' up on the roof to the belvedere on th' roof to look over my kingdom before I give up my kingdom – twenty-eight thousand acres of th' richest land this side of the Valley Nile!

[*Exit through R doors, and D R on gallery.*]

BIG MAMA [*following*]: Sweetheart, sweetheart, sweetheart –
can I come with you?
  [*Exits D R.*
    Margaret is D S C in mirror area.]

GOOPER [*X to bar*]: Brick, could you possibly spare me one
small shot of that liquor?

BRICK [*D L C*]: Why, help yourself, Gooper boy.

GOOPER: I will.

MAE [*X forward*]: Of course we know that this is a lie!

GOOPER [*drinks*]: Be still, Mae!

MAE [*X to Gooper at bar*]: I won't be still! I know she's made
this up!

GOOPER: God damn it, I said to shut up!

MAE: That woman isn't pregnant!

GOOPER: Who said she was?

MAE: She did!

GOOPER: The doctor didn't. Doc Baugh didn't.

MARGARET [*X R to above couch*]: I haven't gone to Doc Baugh.

GOOPER [*X through to L of Margaret*]: Then who'd you go to,
Maggie?
  [*Offstage song finishes.*]

MARGARET: One of the best gynaecologists in the South.

GOOPER: Uh-huh, I see –
  [*Foot on end of couch, trapping Margaret:*]
May we have his name please?

MARGARET: No, you may not, Mister – Prosecutin' Attorney!

MAE [*X to R of Margaret, above*]: He doesn't have any name,
he doesn't exist!

MARGARET: He does so exist, and so does my baby, Brick's
baby!

MAE: You can't conceive a child by a man that won't sleep
with you unless you think you're –
  [*Forces Margaret on to couch, turns away C.*
    Brick starts C for Mae.]
He drinks all the time to be able to tolerate you! Sleeps on
the sofa to keep out of contact with you!

GOOPER [*X above Margaret, who lies face down on couch*]: Don't
try to kid us, Margaret –

MAE [*X to bed, L side, rumpling pillows*]: How can you conceive
a child by a man that won't sleep with you? How can you
conceive? How can you? How can you!

GOOPER [*sharply*]: *MAE!*

BRICK [*X below Mae to her R, takes hold of her*]: Mae, Sister Woman, how d'you know that I don't sleep with
Maggie?

MAE: We occupy the next room an' th' wall between isn't
soundproof.

BRICK: Oh . . .

MAE: We hear the nightly pleadin' and the nightly refusal.
So don't imagine you're goin' t'put a trick over on us, to
fool a dyin' man with – a –

BRICK: Mae, Sister Woman, not everybody makes much
noise about love. Oh, I know some people are huffers an'
puffers, but others are silent lovers.

GOOPER [*behind seat, R*]: This talk is pointless, completely.

BRICK: How d'y'know that we're not silent lovers?
    Even if y'got a peep-hole drilled in the wall, how can
y'tell if sometime when Gooper's got business in Memphis
an' you're playin' scrabble at the country club with other
ex-queens of cotton, Maggie and I don't come to some
temporary agreement? How do you know that –?
    [*He X above wicker seat to above R end couch.*]

MAE: Brick, I never thought that you would stoop to her
level, I just never dreamed that you would stoop to her
level.

GOOPER: I don't think Brick will stoop to her level.

BRICK [*sits R of Margaret on couch*]: What is your level? Tell
me your level so I can sink or rise to it.
    [*Rises.*]
    You heard what Big Daddy said. This girl has life in her
body.

MAE: That is a lie!

BRICK: No, truth is something desperate, an' she's got it.
Believe me, it's somethin' desperate, an' she's got it.
    [*X below seat to below bar.*]
    An' now if you will stop actin' as if Brick Pollitt was dead
an' buried, invisible, not heard, an' go on back to your

peep-hole in the wall – I'm drunk, and sleepy – not as alive as Maggie, but still alive. ...

[*Pours drink, drinks.*]

GOOPER [*picks up briefcase from R foot of bed*]: Come on, Mae. We'll leave these love birds together in their nest.

MAE: Yeah, nest of lice! Liars!

GOOPER: Mae – Mae, you jes' go on back to our room –

MAE: Liars!

[*Exits through hall.*]

GOOPER [*D R above Margaret*]: We're jest goin' to wait an' see. Time will tell.

[*X to R of bar.*]

Yes, sir, little brother, we're just goin' to wait an' see!

[*Exit, hall.*

The clock strikes twelve.

Maggie and Brick exchange a look. He drinks deeply, puts his glass on the bar. Gradually, his expression changes. He utters a sharp exhalation.

The exhalation is echoed by the singers, off U R, who commence vocalizing with 'Gimme a Cool Drink of Water Fo' I Die', and continue till end of act.]

MARGARET [*as she hears Brick's exhalation*]: The click?

[*Brick looks toward the singers, happily, almost gratefully. He X R to bed, picks up his pillow, and starts toward head of couch, D R, Xing above wicker seat. Margaret seizes the pillow from his grasp, rises, stands facing C, holding the pillow close. Brick watches her with growing admiration. She moves quickly U S C, throwing pillow on to bed. She X to bar. Brick counters below wicker seat, watching her. Margaret grabs all the bottles from the bar. She goes into hall, pitches the bottles, one after the other, off the platform into the U L lawn area. Bottles break, off L. Margaret re-enters the room, stands U C, facing Brick.*]

Echo Spring has gone dry, and no one but me could drive you to town for more.

BRICK: Lacey will get me –

MARGARET: Lacey's been told not to!

BRICK: I could drive –

MARGARET: And you lost your driver's licence! I'd phone ahead and have you stopped on the highway before you got halfway to Ruby Lightfoot's gin mill. I told a lie to Big Daddy, but we can make that lie come true. And then I'll bring you liquor, and we'll get drunk together, here, tonight, in this place that death has come into! What do you say? What do you say, baby?

BRICK [*X to L side bed*]: I admire you, Maggie.

[*Brick sits on edge of bed. He looks up at the overhead light, then at Margaret. She reaches for the light, turns it out; then she kneels quickly beside Brick at foot of bed.*]

MARGARET: Oh, you weak, beautiful people who give up with such grace. What you need is someone to take hold of you – gently, with love, and hand your life back to you, like something gold you let go of – and I can! I'm determined to do it – and nothing's more determined than a cat on a tin roof – is there? Is there, baby?

[*She touches his cheek gently.*]

CURTAIN

The Milk Train Doesn't Stop
Here Anymore

AUTHOR'S NOTES

SOMETIMES theatrical effects and devices such as those I have adopted in the third (and I hope final) version of this play are ascribed to affectation or 'artiness', so it may be helpful for me to explain a bit of my intention in the use of these effects and devices, and let the play's production justify or condemn them.

I have added to the cast a pair of stage assistants that function in a way that's between the Kabuki Theatre of Japan and the chorus of Greek theatre. My excuse, or reason, is that I think the play will come off better the further it is removed from conventional theatre since it's been rightly described as an allegory and as a 'sophisticated fairy-tale'.

Stage assistants in Japanese Kabuki are a theatrical expedient. They work on-stage during the performance, shifting set-pieces, placing and removing properties and furniture. Now and then in this play they have lines to speak, very short ones that serve as cues to the principal performers. . . . They should be regarded, therefore, as members of the cast. They sometimes take a balletic part in the action of the play. They should be dressed in black, very simply, to represent invisibility to the other players. The other players should never appear to see them, even when they speak or take part in the action, except when they appear 'in costume'.

The setting represents the library and bedroom of the white villa, downstage, and the bedrooms of the pink and blue villinos: most importantly, the terrace of the white villa, which I think should extend the whole width of the proscenium with a small apron for a white iron bench, a step down from the terrace.

Separations between interior and exterior should not be clearly defined except by lighting. When a single interior is being used, the other interior areas should be masked by light, folding screens, painted to blend with the cyclorama, that is, in sea-and-sky colours: they should be set in place and removed by the stage assistants. The cyclorama and these folding screens represent, preferably in a semi-abstract style, the mountain-sea-sky of Italy's 'Divina Costiera' in summer.

Since the villas are, naturally, much further apart than they can appear on the stage, the director could adopt a convention of having actors, going from one villa to another, make their exits into the wings: wait till the stage assistants have removed the screens that mask the next interior to be used: then come back out and enter that area.

August 1963

PROLOGUE

At rise: the STAGE ASSISTANTS *are onstage: All the interior areas are masked by their individual screens: the light on the cyclorama suggests early dawn.*

ONE: Daybreak: flag-raising ceremony on Mrs Goforth's mountain.

TWO: Above the oldest sea in the Western world.

ONE: Banner.

> [TWO *hands it to him.* TWO *places the staff in a socket near the right wings and attaches the flag to it. A fan in the wings whips it out as it is being raised so that the audience can see the device on it clearly.*]

ONE: The device on the banner is a golden griffin.

TWO: A mythological monster, half lion and half eagle.

ONE: And completely human.

TWO: Yes, wholly and completely human, that's true.

ONE: We are also a device.

TWO: A theatrical device of ancient and oriental origin.

ONE: With occidental variations, however.

TOGETHER: We are Stage Assistants. We move the screens that mask the interior playing areas of the stage presentation.

ONE: We fetch and carry.

TWO: Furniture and props.

ONE: To make the presentation – the play or masque or pageant – move more gracefully quickly through the course of the two final days of Mrs Goforth's existence.

MRS GOFORTH'S VOICE [*off, half-sleeping*]: AHHHHHHHH, MEEEEEEEEE ...

> [*The harmonium player produces a sound of distant church bells.*]

ONE: The actors will not seem to hear us except when we're in costume.

TWO: They will never see us, except when we're in costume.

ONE: Sometimes we will give them cues for speech and participate in the action.

MRS GOFORTH'S VOICE [*off*]: AHHHHHH, AHHHHHH,
  AHHHHHH ...

  [THEY *show no reaction to this human cry.*]

MRS GOFORTH'S VOICE [*off, more wakefully*]: ANOTHER DAY,
  OH, CHRIST, OH, MOTHER OF CHRIST!

  [*There is silence, a pause, as the cyclorama's lighting indicates the
  progress of the day toward the meridian.*]

TOGETHER: Our hearts are invisible, too.

  [*The fan that whipped out the flag bearing the personal emblem,
  the griffin, of* MRS GOFORTH, *dies down and the flag subsides
  with it and will not whip out again till the flag-lowering ceremony
  which will take place near the end of the play.*

  *Now it is Noon. Electric buzzers sound from various points on
  the stage. The* STAGE ASSISTANTS *cross rapidly up centre and
  remove a screen, the middle panel of which is topped by* MRS
  GOFORTH'S *heraldic device, the gold griffin. The library of
  the white villa is unmasked and the play begins.*]

SCENE ONE

MRS GOFORTH *and her secretary*, BLACKIE.

MRS GOFORTH: I made my greatest mistake when I put a fast car in his hands, that red demon sports car, his fighting cock, I called it, which he drove insanely, recklessly, between my estate and the Casino at Monte Carlo, so recklessly that the police commissioner of Monaco came personally to ask me. Correction, *beg* me. Correction, *implore* me! – To insist that he go with me in the Rolls with a chauffeur at the wheel, as a protection of his life and of the lives of others. – M. Le Commissionaire, I said, for me there are no others. – I know, Madame, he said, but for the others there are others. – Then I confessed to the Commissioner of Police that over this young poet with Romanov blood in his veins, I had no more control than my hands had over the sea-wind or the storms of the sea. At night he had flying dreams, he would thrash his arms like wings, and once his hand on which he wore a signet ring with the heavy Romanov crest struck me in the mouth and drew blood. After *that, necessarily – twin beds.* . . .

BLACKIE: Mrs Goforth, excuse me, but the last thing I have typed up is – oh, here it is. – 'My first two husbands were ugly as apes and my third one resembled an ostrich.' – Now if this passage you're dictating to me comes in direct sequence it will sound as if you had put the fast car in the hands of the ostrich.

[*A long, tempestuous pause.*]

MRS GOFORTH: Aren't you the sly one, oh, you're sly as ten flies when you want to give me the needle, aren't you, Miss Blackie? My first three marriages were into Dun and Bradstreet's, and the Social Register, both! – My first husband, Harlon Goforth, whose name I still carry after three later marriages – that dignified financier, TYCOON! – was a man that Presidents put next to their wives at banquets in the White House, and you sit there smoking in my face, when you know I've been told to quit smoking, and you make a joke of my work with a dead-pan expression on your Vassar-girl face, in your Vassar-girl voice, and *I WILL NOT TOLERATE IT!* – You know goddam well. I'm talking about my *fourth* husband, the *last* one, the one I married for love, who plunged off the Grande Corniche between Monte Carlo and – died that night in my arms in a clinic at Nice: and my heart died with him! Forever.

[*Her voice breaks.*]

BLACKIE: I'm sorry, Mrs Goforth. [*Puts out cigarette.*] – I'm no writer but I do think in writing there has to be some kind of logical – sequence, continuity – between one bit and the next bit, and the last thing you dictated to me –

MRS GOFORTH: Was it something I put on the tape-recorder in my bedroom after I'd been given one of those injections that upset my balance at night?

BLACKIE: I took it off your bedroom tape this morning.

MRS GOFORTH: Always check those night recordings with me before we begin to work the following morning. We're working against time, Blackie. Remember, try to remember, I've got two dead-lines to meet, my New York publishers and my London publishers, both, have my memoirs on their Fall List. I said Fall. It's already late in August. Now do you see why there's no time for goofing or must I draw you a picture of autumn leaves falling?

BLACKIE: Mrs Goforth, I think those publishers' dead-lines are unrealistic, not to say cruel, and as for me, I not only have to function as a secretary but as an *editor,* I have to *collate* the material you dictate to me and I'm not being sly or cruel, I'm just being *honest* with you when I tell you –

MRS GOFORTH [*cutting in*]: All cruel people describe themselves as paragons of frankness!

BLACKIE: I think we'd better stop now.

MRS GOFORTH: I think we'd better go *on*, now!

BLACKIE: Mrs Goforth, the Police Commissioner of Monaco was right when he told you that there were 'others'. I am one of those 'others'. I've had no sleep, scarcely any at all and –

MRS GOFORTH: *You've* had no sleep? What about me, how much sleep do *I* get?

BLACKIE: You sleep till noon or after!

MRS GOFORTH: Under sedation, with nightmares!

BLACKIE: – Your broker is on the phone. . . .

[THE STAGE ASSISTANTS *have entered with phone.*]

MRS GOFORTH [*immediately brightening*]: Chuck, baby, how're we doing? Ah-huh, glamour stocks still slipping? Don't hold on to 'em, dump them before they drop under what I bought 'em at, baby. We'll start buying back when they hit the basement level. – Don't give me an argument, SELL! SELL! HELL! – It's building into a crash! So, baby, I'm hitting the silk! High, low, Jack and the game! Ho ho!

[*She bangs down the phone, exhilarated, and it is removed by one of the* STAGE ASSISTANTS. *The other* ASSISTANT *has rushed to the stage right wings and he now appears in a white doctor's jacket. This is one of the costumes that make the assistants seen and heard by the other actors.*]

ASSISTANT (*as* DR LULLO): *Buon' giorno!*

MRS GOFORTH: *What's he wheeling in here that looks like a baby-buggy for a baby from Mars?*

[*He is pushing a 'mock-up' of a portable X-ray machine.*]

BLACKIE: It's something your doctor in Rome, Dr. – what? Rengucci? – had sent up here to spare you the trouble of interrupting your work to take a new set of pictures to show what progress there is in the healing of the lesion, the lung-abscess, that –

MRS GOFORTH: Oh, so you're having private consultations with that quack in Rome?

BLACKIE: Just routine calls that he told me to make sure to spare you the trouble of –

MRS GOFORTH: Spare me no trouble, just spare me your goddam PRESUMPTION!

DR LULLO: *Forse più tarde, fors' un po più tarde?*

MRS GOFORTH: *Will you get your sneaky grin out of here? VA. VA. PRESTO!*

[*He retires quickly from the lighted area.* MRS GOFORTH *advances both fearfully and threateningly upon the medical apparatus.*]

My outside is *public,* but my insides are *private,* and the Rome quack was hired by my bitch daughter that wants to hang black crepe on me. Wants to know if I'm going and when I'll go. Doesn't know that if and when I do go, she gets one dollar, the rest goes to a – a *cultural Foundation!* – named for *me*? Blackie, wheel this thing off the terrace, to the cliff-side of the mountain and shove it over!

BLACKIE: Mrs Goforth, you mustn't ask me to do ridiculous things.

MRS GOFORTH: I don't do ridiculous things and don't ask anyone else to do 'em for me. But if you think it's ridiculous of me to show my opinion of Rengucci's presumption and – *Look, watch this! Here we go, perambulator from Mars. Out, down, go!*

[*She thrusts it violently on to the forestage, where it is seized by the* STAGE ASSISTANTS *and rushed into the wings: she crosses on to the forestage, leaning forward to watch its fall off the cliff. After a couple of moments, we hear a muted crash that signifies its destruction on the rocky beach under the mountain. Then she straightens, dizzily, with a fierce laugh, and staggers back toward the library area, where* BLACKIE, *meanwhile, has closed her notebook and rushed off stage.*

Heart-beat sounds as MRS GOFORTH *moves distractedly about the library area, calling out breathlessly for* BLACKIE. *She presses several buttons on the inter-com. box on the desk: electric buzzers sound from here and there on the stage but no one responds: She washes down a pill with a swig of brandy: the heartbeat sounds subside as her agitation passes. She sinks into the desk-chair.*]

MRS GOFORTH: – Ahhh. . . .

[*Then she activates her tape-recorder and speaks into it with a voice that is plaintively childlike.*]

– Blackie, the boss is sorry she took her nerves out on you. It's those night-injections I take nights for my – neuralgia – neuritis – bursitis. The pick-up pills and the quiet-down pills: nerves shot. . . .

[*A wave booms under the mountain.*]

– Oh, God, Blackie, I'm *scared!* You know what I'm scared of? Possibly, maybe, the Boss is – *dying* this summer! On the Divina Costiera, under that, that – angry old lion, the sun, and the – insincere sympathy of the – [*Her mood suddenly reverses again.*] No, no, no, I don't want her goddam sympathy, I'll take that slobbery stuff off the tape and – BEGIN! CONTINUE! DICTATION!

[*She rises, paces the forestage with a portable 'mike'.*

HARMONIUM: *a phrase of lyrical music: she stops short, lifting a jewelled hand as if to say 'Listen' – Then suddenly the hard accretion of years is broken through. The stage dims out except for her follow-spot on the forestage.*]

'Cloudy symbols of a – high romance. . . .' – Who said that, where is that from? Check tomorrow, Blackie, in Book of Familiar Quotations. . . .

Begin, continue dictation. [*Pause: paces*] – The love of true understanding isn't something a man brings up the road to you every day or once in a blue moon, even. But it was brought to me once, almost too late but not quite. . . .

The hard shell of my heart, the calcium deposits grown around it, could still be cracked, broken through, and my last husband broke through it, and I was brought back to life and almost back to – what? – Youth. . . .

– The nights, the nights, especially the first one I spent with Alex! – The way that a lover undresses, removes his clothes the first night you pass together, is a clue, a definite clue, to your whole future relationship with him, you know. – Alex unclothed himself *unconsciously gracefully,* as if before no one in a – room made of windows, and then, unclothed – *correction:* clothed in a god's perfection, his naked body! – He went from window to window, all the way round the bedroom, drawing the curtains together so that daybreak beginning wouldn't wake us early from the sleep after love, which is a heavenly sleep that shouldn't be broken early. Then came to rest in a god's perfection beside me: reached up to turn off the light: I reached up and turned it *back on!*

[*At this point,* MRS GOFORTH'S *watchdogs (Lupos) set up a great clamour on the inland side of the mountain. A* MAN *shouts.* WOMEN SERVANTS *scream in Italian. Somebody calls, 'Rudy, Rudy!'*

MRS GOFORTH *is very annoyed by this disruption of her tender recollections: she presses various buttons on the inter-com. box on her desk.*]

MRS GOFORTH [*shouting over the dogs*]: CHE SUCCEDE! CHE FA, CRETINI! STRONZE!! (etc.).

[*The savage barking continues but diminishes a little in volume as a* YOUNG MAN, *who has been just assaulted by dogs, limps and stumbles on to the terrace: He bears a heavy white sack over his shoulder: looks back as if to make sure he's no longer pursued.* BLACKIE *appears behind him, panting, looking as if she'd also been roughed-up by the dogs.*]

BLACKIE [*To the young man*]: Places go mad, it's catching, people catch it! [*Draws a breath.*] There's a doctor up here, I'll get him for you.

CHRIS: Can I see Mrs Goforth?

BLACKIE: Sit down somewhere. I'll see if she can see you, and I'll –

[*The young man,* CHRIS, *limps out upon the forestage: sinks on to a white iron bench: a wave crashes below the mountain. He looks blankly out at the audience for a moment: then shakes his head and utters a desperate-sounding laugh.* BLACKIE *rushes into the library area.*]

– Mrs Goforth, I can't stand this sort of thing!

MRS GOFORTH: *What?*

BLACKIE: Those dogs of Rudy's, those wolves, attacked a young man just now.

MRS GOFORTH: What young man, doing what?

BLACKIE: He was climbing the mountain to see you!

MRS GOFORTH: Who is he, what does he want?

BLACKIE: I didn't stop to ask that. I had to drive the dogs off to keep him from being torn to pieces before I – asked him questions: Look! [*She shows* MRS GOFORTH *a laceration on her thigh, just over the knee*] – The others just watched and screamed like children at a circus!

MRS GOFORTH: Sit down, have a brandy. A place like this is always protected by dogs.

[*Sound of another wave crashing.*]

CHRIS: BOOM.

> [*He discovers that his leather pants,* lederhosen, *have been split down his thigh.*]

BLACKIE: That gangster's bodyguard, Rudy, just stood there and watched!

MRS GOFORTH: Blackie, this estate contains things appraised by Lloyd's at over two million pounds sterling, besides my jewels and summer furs, and that's why it has to be guarded against trespassers, uninvited intruders. Have you had your anti-tetanus shot, or – whatever they call it?

BLACKIE: Yes, I'm all right but he isn't. [*She presses a button on the inter-com. box.*]

MRS GOFORTH: Who're you calling?

BLACKIE: I'm calling Dr Lullo.

MRS GOFORTH: Stop that, leave that to me! Do you think I want to be sued by this trespasser? Get away from my desk. I'm going to buzz Rudy. [*Presses another button.*] Rudy, dov'è Rudy? Io lo voglio in liberia, subito, presto! Capito?

> [*The young man staggers to his feet and calls:* 'MRS GOFORTH!'
> MRS GOFORTH *picks up a pair of binoculars and gazes out at the terrace.*
>
> BLACKIE *stares at her with consternation.*]

CHRIS: MRS GOFORTH?

> [RUDY, *the watchman, in semi-military costume, appears on the terrace.*]

RUDY: Shut up, stop that shouting. [*Enters the library area.*]

MRS GOFORTH: Aw. Rudy. What happened, what's the report?

RUDY: I caught this man out there climbing up here from the highway.

BLACKIE: He set the dogs on him.

MRS GOFORTH: That's what the dogs are here for. Rudy, what's the sign say on the gate on the highway?

RUDY: Private property.

MRS GOFORTH: Just 'Private Property', not 'Beware of Dogs'?

RUDY: There's nothing about dogs down there.

MRS GOFORTH: Well, for Chrissake, put up 'Beware of dogs',

too. Put it up right away. If this man sues me, I've got to prove THERE WAS A BEWARE OF DOGS sign.

BLACKIE: How can you prove what's not true?

MRS GOFORTH [*to* RUDY]: Go on, hurry it up!

[RUDY *exits.* MRS GOFORTH *to* BLACKIE.]

Now pull yourself together: what a day! It's too much for me, I'll have to go back to bed. . . .

[GIULIO, *the gardener's son, a boy of seventeen, appears on the terrace.*]

GIULIO [*to the young man, who is applying an antiseptic to his lacerations*]: *Come va? Meglior?*

CHRIS: Sì, meglior, grazie. Do you understand English?

GIULIO: Yes, English.

CHRIS: Good. Would you please tell Mrs Goforth that Mr Christopher Flanders is here to see her, and – Oh, give her this book, there's a letter in it, and – ask her if I may see her, don't – don't mention the dogs, just say I – I want very much to see her, if she's willing to see me. . . .

[*During this exchange on the forestage,* MRS GOFORTH *has picked up the pair of binoculars.*

GIULIO *knocks at the screen that represents the door between the terrace and the library.*]

MRS GOFORTH: Come in, come in, avante!

[*The boy enters, excitedly.*]

GIULIO: Man bring this up road.

MRS GOFORTH [*Gingerly accepting the book in her hand*]: Young man that dogs bite bring this – [*Squints at book.*] – POEMS! – to me?

GIULIO: This, this, brings! Up mountains!

[*She turns the book and squints at a photograph of the author.*]

MRS GOFORTH: – Man resemble this photo?

[BLACKIE *is still quietly weeping at the desk.*]

GIULIO: Non capito.

MRS GOFORTH: Man! – Uomo! – resemble, look like – this photo!

GIULIO: Yes, this man. This man that dogs bite on mountain. [*Points out excitedly toward the young man on the bench.*]

MRS GOFORTH: Well, go back out – va fuori e dica – Blackie! Tell him to go back out there and say that I am very upset over the accident with the dogs but that I would like to know why he came here without invitation and that I am not responsible for anybody that comes here without invitation!

BLACKIE [*strongly, rising*]: No, I will not. I will not give a man nearly killed by dogs such an inhuman message.

MRS GOFORTH: He hasn't been seriously hurt, he's standing up now. Listen, he's shouting my name.

[*The young man has called* 'MRS GOFORTH?' *in a hoarse, panting voice. His shirt and one leg of his* lederhosen *have been nearly stripped off him.*

He has the opposite appearance to that which is ordinarily encountered in poets as they are popularly imagined. His appearance is rough and weathered: his eyes wild, haggard: He has the look of a powerful, battered but still undefeated, fighter.]

CHRIS: *MRS GOFORTH!* [*The call is almost imperious.*]

[*A wave crashes under the mountain:* CHRIS *closes his eyes: opens them: crosses to the lounge chair on the terrace and throws himself down in it, dropping a large canvas sack on the terrace tiles.*

The excited, distant barking of the dogs has now died out.

Female voices are still heard exclaiming at a distance, in Italian.]

MRS GOFORTH [*looking again through her binoculars*]: Pull yourself together. The continent has been over-run by beatniks lately. I've been besieged by them, Blackie. Writers that don't write, painters that don't paint. A bunch of freeloaders, Blackie. They come over here on a Yugoslavian freighter with about a hundred dollars in travellers' cheques and the summer addresses of everybody they think they can free-load on. That's why I'm not so sympathetic about them. Look, I made it, I got it because I made it, but they'll never work for a living as long as there is a name on their sucker-list, Blackie. Now cut the hysterics out, now, and go out there and –

BLACKIE: – *What?*

MRS GOFORTH: Interrogate him for me!

BLACKIE: Interrogate? A badly injured young man?

MRS GOFORTH: *Trespasser!* Get that straight in case he tries to sue me. [*She continues inspecting him through the binoculars.*] Hmm, he's not bad looking in a wild sort of way, but I'm afraid he's a beatnik, he has a beard and looks like he hadn't seen water for bathing purposes in a couple of weeks.

BLACKIE: You would, too, if a pack of wild dogs had attacked you.

MRS GOFORTH: *Watch-dogs*, *lupos*, defending private property: get that straight. He has on *lederhosen*. Hmm. – The first time I saw Alex, in the Bavarian Alps, he had on *lederhosen* and the right legs for 'em, too. And it's odd, it's a coincidence that I was dictating some recollections of Alex, who was a poet, when this young – *trespasser* – got here. Now if the sweat and – the filthy appearance just come from the dogs' attack on him, I mean from *meeting* the dogs, you can tell by the smell of him while you're talking to him.

BLACKIE: You want me to go out and smell him? I'm not a dog, Mrs Goforth.

MRS GOFORTH: You don't have to be a dog to smell a beatnik. Sometimes they smell to high heaven because not washing is almost a religion with 'em, why, last summer one of those ones you see in *Life* and *Look*, came up here. I had to talk to him with a handkerchief held to my nose: it was a short conversation and the last one between us.

[CHRIS *staggers up from the lounge-chair and shouts* 'MRS GOFORTH'.]

MRS GOFORTH: – What impudence, going on shouting at me like that!

BLACKIE: I think the least you could do is go out there yourself and show some decent concern over the dogs' attack on him.

MRS GOFORTH: I'm not going to see him till I've checked with my lawyers about my liability, if any. So be a good scout, a nice Brownie den-mother, and go out there and –

BLACKIE: *Interrogate* him?

MRS GOFORTH: Ask him politely what he wants here, why he came to see me without invitation, and if you get the right answers, put him in the pink villino. And I'll see him later, after my siesta. He might be OK for a while, and I could use some male companionship up here since all I've got is you and Generalissimo Rudy for company this summer. I do need male company, Blackie, that's what I need to be me, the old Sissy Goforth, high, low, jack and the game!

BLACKIE: I'll go see if he's seriously hurt. [*She crosses out, to the terrace, and approaches* CHRIS *limping about the forestage. To* CHRIS.] How are you, are you all right, now?

CHRIS: Not all right: but better. Could I see Mrs Goforth?

BLACKIE: Not yet, not right now, but she told me to put you in the little pink guest house, if you can – walk a little. It's a little way down the mountain.

CHRIS: – Well, thank God, and – [*Tries to lift his sack and stumbles under its weight.*] – Mrs Goforth, of course . . .

BLACKIE [*calling*]: GIULIO! VIENE QUI!

[GIULIO *comes on to the terrace.*]

BLACKIE: – Porta questo sacco al villino rosa.

GIULIO [*lifting sack*]: Pesante! – Dio . . .

BLACKIE: *Tu sei pesante, nella testa!* [*Then to* CHRIS.] – You can bathe and rest till Mrs Goforth feels better and is ready to see you.

CHRIS: Oh. – Thanks. . . .

[*He follows her off the terrace. The* STAGE ASSISTANTS *fold and remove the screen masking a bed upstage. The bed is small but rococo, and all pink.*

The STAGE ASSISTANTS *return downstage with the screen and wait near* MRS GOFORTH, *who is still watching the terrace scene through her binoculars.*]

MRS GOFORTH [*to herself*]: Ah, God . . . [*Raises a hand unconsciously to a pain in her chest.*]

[*The* STAGE ASSISTANTS *unfold the screen before her, as the library area is dimmed out.*]

SCENE TWO

The area representing the pink villino is lighted: the light is warm gold afternoon light and striated as if coming through half-open shutters.

A cupid is lowered over the bed by a wire: there are smaller cupids on the four posts of the bed.

BLACKIE, CHRIS, *and* GIULIO *enter the narrow lighted area, the young poet limping.* GIULIO *bears the canvas sack with difficulty, muttering 'Pesante!'*

BLACKIE: Here you are, this is it. Now!

CHRIS: What?

BLACKIE: How are your legs? Mrs Goforth keeps a doctor on the place, a resident physician, and I think he ought to come here and do a proper job on those dog-bites.

CHRIS: They're not that bad, really.

BLACKIE: Have you had shots?

CHRIS: Shots?

BLACKIE: For tetanus?

CHRIS: – Yes, yes, sometime or other. I'm actually just – tired out.

BLACKIE: Giulio, see if the water's running in the bathroom. I'm sure you want to bathe before you rest, Mr Flanders. Oh, oh, no covers on the bed.

CHRIS: Don't bother about covers on it.

BLACKIE: I think, I have an idea, you're going to sleep a good while and you might as well sleep comfortably. Giulio. Covers for bed.

GIULIO: *Dovè?*

BLACKIE: *Cerca nell' armadio del bagno.*

[GIULIO *exists.* CHRIS *sits down on the foot of the narrow bed: his head falls forward.*]

Mr Flanders!

[*He pulls himself up.*]

Please try to stay awake till the bed's made up and you've bathed.

CHRIS: Your name is – ? [*He rises, unsteadily.*]

BLACKIE: Frances Black, called Blackie.

CHRIS: How do you do. Mine's Flanders, Christopher Flanders.

[GIULIO *enters.*]

GIULIO: Non c'è acqua.

BLACKIE: Well, tell your papa to turn the water on.

[GIULIO *tosses some pink silk sheets on the bed and runs back out.*]

I hope you don't mind camphor, the smell of camphor.

[*He shakes his head slightly, holding on to a bed post.*]

The water ought to be running in a minute.

CHRIS: I hope there's a shower, a tub wouldn't be safe for me. I don't think even drowning would wake me up.

BLACKIE: I'll wait here till you've bathed.

CHRIS: It's wonderful here after – yesterday in – Naples. . . .

BLACKIE: Would you please get on the other side of the bed and help me spread these sheets?

[*He staggers around the bed: They make it up.*]

CHRIS: You –

BLACKIE: What?

CHRIS: I wondered if you're related to Mrs Goforth or if you're –

BLACKIE: Not related. I'm working for Mrs Goforth: secretarial work: She's writing a sort of – all right, you can sit down, now – she's writing her memoirs and I'm helping her with it, the little, as best I – can. . . .

[*He sinks back on to the bed and drops his head in his hands.*]

Mr Flanders, the water's turned on, now.

CHRIS [*staggering up*]: Oh. Good. Thank you. This way? [*Starts off.*]

BLACKIE: I'll fill the tub for you. Do you want warm or cold water, or –

CHRIS: Cold, please. Let me do it.

BLACKIE: No, just stay on your feet till it's ready for you.

[*She crosses off: sound of running water.*]

[*He sits exhaustedly on the bed: sways: his forehead strikes newel-post which is topped by a cupid: the room is full of painted and carved cupids.*

He looks up at the cupid on the post, shakes his head with a sad, wry grimace and drops his head in his hands and slumps over again. BLACKIE *returns from the bathroom with a towel-robe. She claps her hands.*]

BLACKIE: I told you to stay on your feet.

CHRIS [*struggling up*]: Sorry. What is – I almost said 'Where am I?'

BLACKIE: Here's a towel-robe for you, you'd better just duck in and out.

[*He crosses to door.*]

CHRIS [*looking back at her from threshold*]: Is this called the Cupid Room?

BLACKIE: I don't know if it's called that but it should be.

[*He starts to enter but remains on threshold.*]

CHRIS: What a remarkable bath-tub, it's almost the size of deck-pool on a steamship.

BLACKIE [*dryly*]: Yes, Mrs Goforth thinks a bath-tub should be built for at least two people.

CHRIS [*entering*]: She must have been to Japan.

BLACKIE: Yes. She probably owns it.

[CHRIS *enters the bathroom: a splash, a loud gasp.*]

BLACKIE: Oh, I should have warned you, it's mountain spring water.

CHRIS: Does it come from a glacier?

[BLACKIE *picks up the cords of his rucksack to drag it away from the bedside. She finds it startlingly heavy.*

She kneels beside it to loosen the draw-strings, draws out a silvery section of some metal-work.

Rises guiltily as CHRIS *reappears in the towel-robe.*]

BLACKIE: You're – shivering.

CHRIS: For exercise; shivering's good exercise.

BLACKIE: I don't think you need any more exercise for a while. – How did you get this sack of yours up the mountain?

CHRIS: Carried it – from Genoa.

BLACKIE: I could hardly drag it away from the bed.

CHRIS: Yes, it's heavy with metal, I work in metal, now, I construct mobiles, but it's not the mobiles that are heavy, it's the metalsmith tools.

BLACKIE: You, uh – sell – mobiles, do you?

CHRIS: No, mostly give 'em away. Of course I –

BLACKIE: – What?

CHRIS: Some things aren't made to be sold, oh, you sell them, but they're not made for that, not for selling, they're made for –

BLACKIE: Making them?

CHRIS: Is there something buzzing in the room or is the buzz in my head? Oh, a wasp, it'll fly back out the shutters, is this a cigarette box? [*Opens box on small bedside table.*] Empty.

BLACKIE: – Have a Nazionale. [*Offers him the pack.*]

CHRIS: Thank you.

BLACKIE: I'll leave the pack here, I have more in my room. – Your hair's not dry, it's still wet.

> [*He shakes his head like a spaniel.*]
> Dry it with the towel and get right into bed, I have to get back to work now. I work here, I do secretarial work and I –

CHRIS: Don't go right away.

BLACKIE: You need to rest, right away.

CHRIS: The ice water woke me up.

BLACKIE: Just temporarily, maybe.

CHRIS: I'll rest much better if I know a bit more, such as – Did Mrs Goforth remember who I was?

BLACKIE: I don't know about that but she liked your looks, if that's any comfort to you.

CHRIS: I didn't see her. She saw me?

BLACKIE: She inspected you through a pair of military field-glasses before she had me take you to the pink villa with the – king-size bath-tub, the pink silk sheets and the cupids.

CHRIS: Do they, uh – signify something?

BLACKIE: Everything signifies something. I'll – I'll shut the shutters and you get into bed. [*Turns away from him.*]

CHRIS [*sitting on the bed*]: What is the programme for me when I wake up?

BLACKIE [*her back still toward him*]: Don't you make out your own programmes?

CHRIS: Not when I'm visiting people. I try to adapt myself as well as I can to their programmes, when I'm – visiting people.

BLACKIE: Is that much of the time?

CHRIS: Yes, that's – *most* of the time. . . .

BLACKIE: Well, I think you're in for a while, if you play your cards right. You do want to be in, don't you? After hauling that sack all the way from Genoa and up this mountain to Mrs Goforth? Or have the pink silk sheets and the cupids scared you, worse than the dogs you ran into?

CHRIS: You have a sharp tongue, Blackie.

BLACKIE: I'm sorry but I was mistaken when I thought I had strong nerves. They're finished for today if not for the season, for – years. . . . [*She starts away.*]

CHRIS: Have a cigarette with me. [*He extends the pack to her.*]

BLACKIE: You want to get some more information from me?

CHRIS: I'd sleep better if I knew a bit more.

BLACKIE: I wouldn't be too sure of *that*.

CHRIS: I've heard, I've been told, that Mrs Goforth hasn't been well lately.

[BLACKIE *laughs as if startled.*]

CHRIS: She's lucky to have you with her.

BLACKIE: – Why?

CHRIS: I can see you're – sympathetic and understanding about Mrs Goforth's – condition, but – not sentimental about it. – Aren't I right about that?

BLACKIE: I'm not understanding about it and I'm afraid I've stopped being sympathetic. Mrs Goforth is a dying monster. [*Rises.*] *Sorry: I'm talking too much!*

CHRIS: No, not enough. Go on.

BLACKIE: Why do you want to hear it?

CHRIS: I've climbed a mountain and fought off a wolf-pack to see her.

BLACKIE: – *Why?*

CHRIS: Nowhere else to go, now.

BLACKIE: Well, that's an honest admission.

CHRIS: Let's stick to honest admissions.

BLACKIE [*sitting back down by the bed*]: All right. I'll give you something to sleep on. You'll probably wish I hadn't but here it is. She eats nothing but pills: around the clock. And at night she has nightmares in spite of morphine injections. I rarely sleep a night through without an electric buzzer by

my bed waking me up. I tried ignoring the buzzer, but
found out that if I did she'd come stumbling out of her
bedroom, on to the terrace, raving into a microphone that's
connected to a tape-recorder, stumbling about and raving
her –

CHRIS: Raving?

BLACKIE: Yes, her demented memoirs, her memories of her
career as a great international beauty which she thinks she
still is. I'm here, employed here, to – take down and type up
these –

CHRIS: Memories?

BLACKIE: – That's enough for you now. Don't you think so?

CHRIS: She doesn't know she's – ?

BLACKIE: Dying? Oh no! Won't face it! Apparently never
thought that her – legendary – existence – could go on less
than forever! Insists she's only suffering from neuralgia,
neuritis, allergies and bursitis! Well? Can you still sleep?
After this – bed-time story?

CHRIS: – Blackie, I've had a good bit of experience with old
dying ladies, scared to death of dying, ladies with lives
like Mrs Goforth's behind them, which they won't think
are over, and I've discovered it's possible to give them, at
least to offer them, something closer to what they need
than what they think they still want. Yes. . . . Would you
please throw me the strings of my sack, Blackie?

[*She tosses the strings to the bedside: He hauls the rucksack over,
leans out of the bed to open it: removes a mobile.*]

– Give her this for me, Blackie. It took me six months to
make it. It has a name, a title, it's called 'The Earth Is a Wheel
in a Great Big Gambling Casino'.

[*The* HARMONIUM PLAYER, *in his dim upstage light, starts
playing softly.*]

BLACKIE: – 'The Earth Is – '?

CHRIS: 'A Wheel in a Great Big Gambling Casino'. I made it
on hinges, it has to be unfolded before it's hung up. I think
you'd better hang it up before you show it to her, if you
don't mind, and in a place where it will turn in the wind, so
it will make a – more impressive – impression. . . .

– And this is for you, this book? [*He hands a book to her.*]

BLACKIE: Poems?

CHRIS: It's a verse-adaptation I made of the writings of a Swami, a great Hindu teacher, my – teacher. Oh. One thing more. I'd like to make a phone-call to a friend, an invalid lady, in Sicily – Taormina a mountain above Taormina. – Would Mrs Goforth object if I – ?

BLACKIE: Not if she doesn't know. What's the number?

[*He gives her the number. She makes the call in Italian and is told that it will not go through for some time.*]

– There'll be a delay: is it very important?

CHRIS: Yes, it is: she's dying. – Blackie? You're the kindest person I've met in a long, long time. . . .

BLACKIE [*drawing a sheet over him*]: This sort of thing is just automatic in women.

CHRIS: Only in some of them, Blackie. [*His eyes fall shut.*]

BLACKIE: You're falling asleep.

CHRIS: – Yes, automatic – like kindness in some women . . .

[*He drops his cigarette and she picks it up and crosses to the phone.*]

BLACKIE [*into phone*]: Mariella? Bring a tray of food up to the pink villa: Better make it cold things: the guest's asleep and won't wake up for hours. [*She hangs up, looks at* CHRIS *and exits with book.*]

[*Light dims on this area and a spot of light immediately hits* MRS GOFORTH *on terrace.*

The STAGE ASSISTANTS *have set a screen before this area and light is brought up on the forestage which represents the terrace of the white villa. The* STAGE ASSISTANTS *remove a wide screen and we see* MRS GOFORTH *with two servants,* GIULIO *and* SIMONETTA. MRS GOFORTH *is preparing to take a sun-bath on the terrace. Her appearance is bizarre. She has on a silk robe covered with the signs of the zodiac, and harlequin sunglasses with purple lenses.*]

MRS GOFORTH [*in her very 'pidgin' Italian*]: Table here. Capite? Tabolo. [*Points.*] Qui. On tabolo, I want – What are you grinning at?

GIULIO [*very Neapolitan*]: Niente, niente, mascusa! [*Places table by chaise.*]

SIMONETTA [*giggling*]: Tabolo.

MRS GOFORTH: On tabolo voglio – una bottoglia d'acqua

minerale, San Pellegrino, capite, molto ghiacciato: capite?
[SIMONETTA *giggles behind her hand at* GIULIO's *antic
deference to the Signora.*

MRS GOFORTH *glares suspiciously from one to the other,
turning from side to side like a bull wondering which way to
charge.*

BLACKIE *enters the terrace area with the mobile, folded.*]

MRS GOFORTH: *Che stronze!* Both of 'em.

BLACKIE: You mustn't call them that, it has an insulting
meaning.

MRS GOFORTH: I know what it means and that's what I mean
it to mean. Generalissimo Rudy says they sleep together and
carry on together some nights right here on my terrace.

BLACKIE: They're from Naples, and –

MRS GOFORTH: What's that got to do with it?

BLACKIE: – And Generalissimo Rudy wants the girl for himself, so he –

MRS GOFORTH: WILL YOU PLEASE TELL THEM WHAT I
WANT ON THE TABLE BY THIS CHAISE. HERE?

BLACKIE: What do you want on the table?

MRS GOFORTH: I – want a cold bottle of acqua minerale,
cigarettes, matches, my Bain-Soleil, my codein and empirin
tablets, a shot of cognac on the rocks, the *Paris Herald-
Tribune, The Rome Daily American, The Wall Street Journal,
The London Times* and *Express,* the –
– Hey, what did you do with the –

BLACKIE: The visitor?

MRS GOFORTH: The beatnik trespasser, yes, and what the hell
have you got there that rattles like a string of box cars
crossing a railyard switch?

BLACKIE: The young man's in the pink villa where you told
me to put him – this is something he gave me for me to give
you. It seems he constructs mobiles.

MRS GOFORTH: Mobiles? Constructs?

BLACKIE: Yes, those metal decorations. He gives them titles:
this one's called 'The Earth is a Wheel in a Great Big
Gambling Casino'.

MRS GOFORTH: Is it a present or something he hopes he can
sell me?

BLACKIE: It's a present. He wanted me to suspend it before you saw it, but since you've already seen it – shall I hang it up somewhere?

MRS GOFORTH: No, just put it down somewhere and help me up, the sun is making me dizzy, I don't know why I came out here. What am I doing out here?

BLACKIE: I was going to remind you that Dr Rengucci warned you not to expose yourself to the sun till the chest abscess, the lesion, has healed completely.

MRS GOFORTH: I DON'T HAVE A CHEST ABSCESS! – stop putting bad mouth on me! Open the door, I'm going in the library.

[*The* STAGE ASSISTANTS *rush out and remove the screen masking that area as* MRS GOFORTH *starts toward it, lifting a hand like a Roman empress saluting the populace.*
She enters the library area.]

What did he have to say?

BLACKIE: The – ?

MRS GOFORTH: *Trespasser*, what did he have to say?

BLACKIE: About what?

MRS GOFORTH: *ME*.

BLACKIE: He wondered if you remembered him or not.

MRS GOFORTH: Oh, I might have met him somewhere, some-time or other, when I was still meeting people, interested in it, before they all seemed like the same person over and over and I got tired of the person.

BLACKIE: This young man won't seem like the same person to you.

MRS GOFORTH: That remains to be – Blackie, y'know what I need to shake off this, this – depression, what would do me more good this summer than all the shots and pills in the pharmaceutical kingdom? I need me a lover.

BLACKIE: What do you mean by 'a lover'?

MRS GOFORTH: I mean a lover! What do *you* mean by a lover, or is that word outside your Vassar vocabulary?

BLACKIE: I've only had one lover, my husband Charles, and I lost Charles last spring.

MRS GOFORTH: What beats me is how you could have a hus-band named Charles and not call him Charlie. I mean the fact that you called him Charles and not Charlie describes your whole relationship with him, don't it?

BLACKIE [*flaring*]: *Stop about my husband!*

MRS GOFORTH: The dead are dead and the living are living!

BLACKIE: Not so, I'm not dead but not living!

MRS GOFORTH: GIULIO!

[*He has entered the library area with the mineral water.*]

MRS GOFORTH: Va a villino rosa e portame qui the sack – il sacco, SACCO! – delle hospite la.

BLACKIE: Oh, no, you mustn't do that, that's too undignified of you!

[GIULIO *exits to perform this errand.*]

MRS GOFORTH: Take care of your own dignity and lemme take care of mine. It's a perfectly natural, legitimate thing to do, to go through the luggage of a trespasser on your place for – possible – weapons, and so forth.... [*Sits at desk.*] Pencil, notebook, dictation.

[BLACKIE *pays no attention to these demands: lights a cigarette behind* MRS GOFORTH'S *back as she begins dictating.*]

– Season of '24, costume ball at Cannes. Never mind the style, now, polish up later ...

– Went as Lady Godiva. All of me, gilded, my whole body painted gold, except for – green velvet fig leaves. Breasts? Famous breasts? Nude, nude completely!

– Astride a white horse, led into the ballroom by a young nigger. Correction. A Nubian – slave-boy. Appearance created a riot. Men clutched at my legs, trying to dismount me so they could *mount* me. Maddest party ever, ever imaginable in those days of mad parties. This set the record for madness. – In '29, so much ended, but not for me. I smelt the crash coming, animal instinct – very valuable asset, put everything into absolutely indestructible utilities such as – chemicals, *electric* ... minerals.

[GIULIO *enters with the rucksack.*]

GIULIO: *Ecco, il sacco!* [*Drops it before* MRS GOFORTH *with a crash that makes her gasp.*]

BLACKIE: May I be excused? I don't want to take part in this.

MRS GOFORTH: Stay here. You heard that noise, that wasn't just clothes, that was metal.

BLACKIE: Yes, I suppose he's come here to seize the mountain by force of arms.

MRS GOFORTH [*to* GIULIO]: Giulio, open, *apierte!*

[GIULIO *opens the sack and the inspection begins.*]

BLACKIE: I told you he made mobiles, the sack's full of metalsmith's tools.

MRS GOFORTH: He hauled this stuff up the mountain?

BLACKIE: It didn't fly up.

MRS GOFORTH: He must have the back of a dray horse. Tell this idiot to hold the sack upside down and empty it all on the floor, he's taking things out like it was a Christmas stocking.

BLACKIE: I'll do it. He'd break everything. [*She carefully empties the contents of the sack on to the floor*].

MRS GOFORTH: See if he's got any travellers' cheques and how much they amount to.

BLACKIE [*ignoring this order and picking up a book*]: He offered me this book, I forgot to take it.

MRS GOFORTH [*glaring at the book through her glasses*]: 'Meanings Known and Unknown'. It sounds like something religious.

BLACKIE: He says it's a verse-adaptation he did of a –

MRS GOFORTH: Swami Something. See if you can locate the little book they always carry with names and addresses in it, sometimes it gives you a clue to their backgrounds and – inclinations. Here. This is it. [*Snatches up an address book.*] – Christ. Lady Emerald Fowler, she's been in hell for ten years. – Christabel Smithers, that name rings a long ago church bell for a dead bitch, too. Mary Cole, *dead!* Laurie Emerson, *dead!* Is he a graveyard sexton? My God, where's his passport?

BLACKIE [*picking it up*]: Here.

MRS GOFORTH: Date of birth. 1928: hmmm, no chicken, Blackie. How old's that make him?

BLACKIE: – Thirty-four. [*Lights a cigarette.* MRS GOFORTH *coughs and snatches the cigarette from* BLACKIE'S *hand. She sets it on the desk and in a moment will start smoking it herself.*]

MRS GOFORTH: No travellers' cheques whatsoever. Did he have some cash on him?

BLACKIE: I don't know, I neglected to frisk him.

MRS GOFORTH: Did you get him to bathe?

BLACKIE: Yes.

MRS GOFORTH: How'd he look in the bath-tub?

BLACKIE: I'm afraid I can't give you any report on that.

MRS GOFORTH: Where's his clothes, no clothes, *niente vestiti in sacco?*

[GIULIO *produces one shirt, laundered but not ironed.*]

GIULIO: *Ecco, una cammicia, una bella cammicia!*

MRS GOFORTH: One shirt!

BLACKIE: He probably had to check some of his luggage somewhere, in order to get up the – goat path ... and the clothes he had on were demolished by Rudy's dogs.

MRS GOFORTH: Well, put a robe in his room: I know: the Samurai warrior's robe that Alex wore at breakfast, we always wore robes at breakfast in case he wanted to go back to bed right after ...

[STAGE ASSISTANT *enters with robe: sword belt attached.*]

BLACKIE: Did he keep the sword on him at breakfast?

MRS GOFORTH: Yes, he did and sometimes he'd draw it out of the scabbard and poke me with it. Ho, ho. Tickle me with the point of it, ho ho ho ho!

BLACKIE: You weren't afraid he'd – accidentally – ?

MRS GOFORTH: Sure, and it was exciting. I had me a little revolver. I'd draw a bead on him sometimes and I'd say, you are too beautiful to live and so you have to die, now, tonight – tomorrow –

[STAGE ASSISTANT *has handed the robe to* BLACKIE *who accepts it without a glance at him.*]

– put the robe in the pink villino, and then call the Witch of Capri.

BLACKIE: Which witch?

MRS GOFORTH: The one that wired me last month. 'Are you still living?' Tell her I am. And get her over for dinner, tell her it's *urgentissimo!* Everything's *Urgentissimo* here this summer....

[*Phone buzzes on desk. As* BLACKIE *starts off,* MRS GO-FORTH *answers the phone.*]

Pronto, pronto, chi parla? – Taormina? Sicilia? – I've placed no call to that place. [*Slams phone.*] – Hmmmm, the summer is coming to life! I'm coming back to life with it! [*She presses buttons on her inter-com. system: electric buzzers sound from various points on the stage as the* STAGE ASSISTANTS *cover the library area with the griffin-crested screen.*]

DIM OUT

SCENE THREE

That evening: the terrace of the white villa and a small section of MRS GOFORTH'S *bedroom, upstage left.*

In this scene, the STAGE ASSISTANTS *may double as butlers, with or without white jackets.*

At rise: two screens are lighted, one masking the small dinner table on the forestage, the other MRS GOFORTH. *A* STAGE ASSISTANT *stands beside each screen so that they can be removed simultaneously when a chord on the harmonium provides the signal.*

The middle panel of MRS GOFORTH'S *screen is topped by a gold-winged griffin to signify that she is 'in residence' behind it.*

MRS GOFORTH'S VOICE [*asthmatically*]: Simonetta, la roba.

> [SIMONETTA *rushes behind the screen with an elaborate Oriental costume.*]

Attenzione, goddam it, questa roba molto, molto valore. Va bene. Adesso, *perruga!**

SIMONETTA [*Emerging from the screen*]: La perrucha bionde?

MRS GOFORTH: *Nero, nero!*

> [*The* MUSICIAN *strikes a ready chord on the harmonium: the screens are whisked away. In the stage left area, we see* MRS GOFORTH *in the Oriental robe, on the forestage,* RUDY *in his semi-military outfit pouring himself a drink, and a small section of balustrade on which is a copper brazier, flickering with blue flame.* BLACKIE *enters, stage right, with a napkin and silver and sets a third place at the table.* RUDY *hovers behind her.*]

BLACKIE: Stop breathing down my neck.

MRS GOFORTH: Ecco!

> [*She puts on a black Kabuki wig with fantastic ornaments stuck in it. Her appearance is gorgeously bizarre.*
>
> *As she moves, now, out upon the forestage, the harmonium outlined dimly against a starry night sky, plays a bit of Oriental music.*]

Well, no comment, Blackie.

*Wig.

164 THE MILK TRAIN DOESN'T STOP HERE ANYMORE

BLACKIE: The Witch of Capri has just gotten out of the boat and is getting into the funicular.

MRS GOFORTH: You kill me, Blackie, you do, you literally kill me. I come out here in this fantastic costume and all you say is the Witch of Capri has landed.

BLACKIE: I told you how fantastic it was when you wore it last week-end when that Italian screen star didn't show up for dinner, so I didn't think it would be necessary to tell you again, but what I do want to tell you is that I wish you'd explain to Rudy that I find him resistible, and when I say resistible I'm putting it as politely as I know how.

MRS GOFORTH: What's Rudy doing to you?

BLACKIE: Standing behind me, and –

MRS GOFORTH: You want him in front of you, Blackie.

BLACKIE: I want him off the terrace while I'm on it.

MRS GOFORTH: Rudy, you'd better go check my bedroom safe. These rocks I've put on tonight are so hot they're radioactive. [*To* BLACKIE.] Guess what I'm worth on the hoof in this regalia.

BLACKIE: I'm no good at guessing the value of –

MRS GOFORTH: I can't stand anything false. Even my kidney-stones, if I had kidney-stones, would be genuine diamonds fit for a queen's crown, Blackie.

[BLACKIE *lights a cigarette.* MRS GOFORTH, *takes the cigarette from her.*]

A witch and a bitch always dress up for each other, because otherwise the witch would upstage the bitch, or the bitch would upstage the witch, and the result would be havoc.

BLACKIE: Fine feathers flying in all directions?

MRS GOFORTH: That's right. – The Witch has a fairly large collection of rocks herself, but no important pieces. [*Crosses, smoking, to the table.*] Hey. The table's set for three. Are you having dinner with us?

BLACKIE: Not this evening, thanks, I have to catch up on my typing.

MRS GOFORTH: Then who's this third place set for?

BLACKIE: The young man in the pink villa, I thought he'd be dining with you.

MRS GOFORTH: That was presumptuous of you. He's having

no meals with me till I know more about him. The Witch of
Capri can give me the low-down on him: in fact, the only
reason I asked The Witch to dinner was to get the low-down
on this mountain climber.

THE WITCH [*at a distance*]: Yoo-hoo!

MRS GOFORTH: YOOO-HOOO! She won't be here more
than a minute before she makes some disparaging comment
on my appearance. Codein, empirin, brandy, before she
gets here; she takes a morbid interest in the health of her
friends because her own's on the down-grade.

THE WITCH [*nearer*]: Yoo-hoo!

MRS GOFORTH: Yooo-hooo! Here she comes, here comes
The Witch.

[THE WITCH *of Capri, the Marquesa Constance Ridgeway-
Condotti, appears on the terrace. She looks like a creature out of a
sophisticated fairy tale, her costume like something that might
have been designed for Fata Morgana. Her dress is grey chiffon,
panelled, and on her blue-tinted head she wears a cone-shaped hat
studded with pearls, the peak of it draped with the material of
her dress, her expressive, claw-like hands a-glitter with gems. At
the sight of MRS GOFORTH, she halts dramatically, opening
her eyes very wide for a moment, as if confronted by a frightening
apparition: then she utters a dramatic little cry and extends her
arms in a counterfeit gesture of pity.*]

THE WITCH: *Sissy! Love!*

MRS GOFORTH: Connie ...

[*They embrace ritually and coolly: then stand back from each
other with sizing-up stares.*]

THE WITCH: Sissy, don't tell me we're having a Chinese
dinner.

MRS GOFORTH: This isn't a Chinese robe, it's a Kabuki
dancer's, a Japanese national treasure that Simon Willing-
ham bought me on our reconciliation trip to Japan. It's
only some centuries old. I had to sneak it through customs
– Japanese customs – by wearing it tucked up under a
chinchilla coat. Y'know I studied Kabuki, and got to be
very good at it, I was a guest artist once at a thing for
typhoon relief, and I can still do it, you see.

[*She opens her lacquered fan and executes some Kabuki dance steps, humming weirdly: the effect has a sort of grotesque beauty, but she is suddenly dizzy and staggers against the table.* THE WITCH *utters a shrill cry:* BLACKIE *rushes to catch her and the table.* MRS GOFORTH *tries to laugh it off.*]

MRS GOFORTH: — Ha, ha, too much codein, I took a little codein for my neuralgia before you got here.

THE WITCH: Well, I'm suffering, too. We're suffering together. Will you look at my arm. [*Draws up her flowing sleeves to expose a bandaged forearm.*] The sea is full of Medusas.

MRS GOFORTH: Full of what?

THE WITCH: Medusas, you know, those jelly-fish that sting, the Latins call them Medusas, and one of them got me this morning, a giant one, at the Piccola Marina. I want a martini. I've got to stay slightly drunk to bear the pain. [*She tosses her parasol to* BLACKIE *and advances to the liquor cart.*] Sissy, your view is a *meraviglia, veramenta una meraviglia!* [*Drains a martini that* BLACKIE *pours her: then swings full circle and dizzily returns to a chair at the table.*] Do we have to eat? — I'm so full of canapés from Mona's cocktail do. . . .

MRS GOFORTH: Oh, is that what you're full of? We're having a very light supper, because the smell of food after codein nauseates me, Connie.

BLACKIE: Mrs Goforth, shouldn't I take something to your house-guest since he's not dining with you?

MRS GOFORTH: No, meaning no, but you can leave us now, Blackie. Oh, excuse me, this is my secretary, Miss Black. Blackie, this is — what's your latest name, Connie?

THE WITCH: I mailed you my wedding invitation the spring before last spring to some hospital in Boston, the Leahey Clinic, and never received a word of acknowledgment from you.

MRS GOFORTH: Oh, weddings and funerals're things you show up at or you don't, according to where you are and — [*Rings bell for service: the* STAGE ASSISTANTS *appear with white towels over their forearms or coloured mess-jackets.* NOTE: *Although they sometimes take part in the action of the play, the characters in the play never appear to notice the* STAGE ASSISTANTS.] — *other* circumstances: Have a gull's egg, Connie.

THE WITCH: No, thank you, I can't stand gulls.

MRS GOFORTH: Well, eating their eggs cuts down on their population.

THE WITCH: What is this monster of the deep?

MRS GOFORTH: Dentice, dentice freddo.

THE WITCH: It has a horrid expression on its face.

MRS GOFORTH: Don't look at it, just eat it.

THE WITCH: Couldn't possibly, thank you.

MRS GOFORTH: – Are you still living on blood transfusions, Connie? That's not good, it turns you into a vampire, a pipistrella, ha ha. . . . Your neck's getting too thin, Connie. Is it true you had that sheep embryo – plantation in – Switzerland? I heard so: don't approve of it. It keys you up for a while and then you collapse, completely. The human system can't stand too much stimulation after – sixty. . . .

THE WITCH: – What did they find out at The Leahey Clinic, Sissy?

MRS GOFORTH: Oh, *that,* that was just a little – routine check-up. . . .

THE WITCH: When you called me today I was so relieved I could die: shouted 'Hallelujah' silently, to myself. I'd heard such distressing rumours about you lately, Sissy.

MRS GOFORTH: Rumours? Hell, what rumours?

THE WITCH [*crossing to bar cart for a refill*]: I can't tell you the rumours that have been circulating about you since your house-party last month. The ones you brought over from Capri came back to Capri with stories that I love you too much to repeat.

MRS GOFORTH: Repeat them, Connie, repeat them.

THE WITCH: Are you sure you feel well enough to take them? [*Returns to her chair.*] Well – they said you were, well, that you seemed to be off your rocker. They said you spent the whole night shouting over loudspeakers so nobody could sleep and that what you shouted was not to be *believed*!

MRS GOFORTH: Oh, how *nice* of them, Connie. Capri's turned into a nest of vipers, Connie – and the sea is full of Medusas? Mmm. The Medusas are spawned by the bitches. You want to know the truth behind this gossip?

Or would you rather believe a pack of malicious inventions?

THE WITCH: You know I love you, Sissy. What's the truth?

MRS GOFORTH: Not *that*. – I'll tell you the truth. [*Rises and indicates the inter-com. speaker.*] I'm writing my memoirs, this summer. I've got the whole place wired for sound, a sort of very elaborate inter-com. or walkie-talkie system, so I can dictate to my secretary, Blackie. I buzz my secretary any time of the day and night and continue dictating to her. That's the truth, the true story. [*Crosses to* THE WITCH.]

THE WITCH [*holding her hand*]: I'm so glad you told me, Sissy, love!

MRS GOFORTH: Has it ever struck you, Connie, that life is all memory except for the one present moment that goes by you so quick you hardly catch it going? It's really all memory, Connie, except for each passing moment. What I just now said to you is a memory now – recollection. Uhhummm ... [*She paces the terrace.*] – I'm up now. When I was at the table is a memory, now. [*Arrives at edge of lighted area Down Right and turns.*] – When I turned at the other end of the terrace is a memory now ...

    [THE WITCH *crosses to her.*]

Practically everything is a memory to me, now, so I'm writing me memoirs ... [*Points up.*] Shooting star: it's shot: – a memory now. Six husbands, all memory now. All lovers: all memory now.

THE WITCH: So you're writing your memoirs.

MRS GOFORTH: Devoting all of me to it and all of my time. ... At noon today, I was dictating to Blackie on a tape-recorder: the beautiful part of my life, my love with Alex, my final marriage: Alex.

THE WITCH [*crossing to bar cart*]: Oh, the young Russian dancer from the Diaghilev troupe?

MRS GOFORTH [*crossing back to her chair*]: Oh, God, no, I never married a dancer. Slept with a couple but never married a one. They're too narcissus for me, love only mirrors. Nope. Alex was a young poet with a spirit that was as beautiful as his body. Only one I married that wasn't rich as Croesus.

Alex made love without mirrors. He used my eyes for his mirrors. The only husband I've had of the six I've had that I could make love to with a bright light burning over the bed. Hundred watt bulbs overhead! To see, while we loved. . . .

THE WITCH [*also back at the table, with the pitcher of martinis*]: – Are you dictating this? Over a loudspeaker?

MRS GOFORTH: – Ah, God – Alex . . .

THE WITCH: – Are you in pain? Do you have a pain in your chest?

MRS GOFORTH: – Why?

THE WITCH: You keep touching your chest.

MRS GOFORTH: – Emotion, I've been very emotional all day. . . . At noon today, a young poet came up the goat-path from the highway just as I was in the emotional – throes – of dictating my memories of young Alex. . . .

THE WITCH: Ah-ha. [*Finishes her martini.*]

MRS GOFORTH: He came up the goat-path from the Amalfi Drive wearing lederhosen like Alex was wearing the first time I set eyes on Alex.

THE WITCH [*starts to pour another martini*]: Ahh-ha!

MRS GOFORTH [*snatching the pitcher from her and placing it on the floor*]: – Do you want to hear this story?

THE WITCH: Liquor improves my concentration. Go on. You've met a new poet. What was the name of this poet?

MRS GOFORTH: His name was on the book.

THE WITCH: Yes, sometimes they do put the author's name on a book.

MRS GOFORTH [*unamused*]: Sanders? No. Manders? No.

THE WITCH: Flanders. Christopher Flanders. [*Makes large eyes.*] Is he still in circulation?

MRS GOFORTH: I don't know if he's in circulation or not but I do know he came up here to see me and not by the boat and funicular he –

THE WITCH [*crossing to her*]: Well, God help you, Sissy.

MRS GOFORTH: Why, is something wrong with him?

THE WITCH: Not if you're not superstitious. Are you superstitious?

MRS GOFORTH: What's superstition got to do with –

THE WITCH: I've got to have a wee drop of brandy on this! [*Crosses to bar cart.*] This is really uncanny!

MRS GOFORTH: *Well, come out with it, what?*

THE WITCH [*selecting the brandy bottle*]: I think I'd rather not tell you.

MRS GOFORTH [*commandingly*]: *WHAT?*

THE WITCH: Promise me not to be frightened?

MRS GOFORTH: When've I ever been frightened? Of what? Not even that stiletto you've got for a tongue can scare me! [*Downs her own martini at a gulp.*] So what's the – ?

THE WITCH: Chris, poor Chris Flanders, he has the bad habit of coming to call on a lady just a step or two ahead of the undertaker. [*She sits.*] Last summer at Portofino he stayed with some Texas oil people and at supper one night that wicked old Duke of Parma, you know the one that we call the Parma Violet, he emptied a champagne bottle on Christopher's head and he said, I christen thee, Christopher Flanders, the 'Angel of Death'. The name has stuck to him, Sissy. Why, some people in our age bracket, we're senior citizens, Sissy, would set their dogs on him if he entered their grounds, but since you're not superstitious. – Why isn't he dining here with us?

MRS GOFORTH: I wanted some information about him before I –

THE WITCH: Let him stay here?

MRS GOFORTH: He's here on probation. [*She rings for GIULIO and crosses centre.*] I put him in the pink villa where he's been sleeping since noon, when he climbed up a goat-path to see me.

THE WITCH [*following*]: I hope he's not playing his sleeping trick on you, Sissy.

MRS GOFORTH: Trick? Sleeping?

THE WITCH: Yes, last summer when he was with that Portofino couple from Texas, they were thrown into panic when they heard his nickname, Angel of Death, and told him that night to check out in the morning. Well, that night, he swallowed some sleeping pills that night, Sissy, but of course he took the precaution of leaving an early morning

call so he could be found and revived before the pills
could –

[MRS GOFORTH *abruptly leaves.*]

– Where're you going, Sissy?

MRS GOFORTH: Follow me to the pink villa, hurry, hurry, I
better make sure he's not playing that trick on me.

[*She rushes offstage.* THE WITCH *laughs wickedly as she follows.
The* STAGE ASSISTANTS *immediately set a screen before this
acting area and it dims: then they remove a screen upstage and we
see* CHRIS *asleep in the pink villa.
Harmonium: Variation of a lullaby, perhaps Brahms!*
MRS GOFORTH *and* THE WITCH *appear just on the edge of
the small lighted area.*]

MRS GOFORTH: Everything's pink in this villa so it's called
the pink villa.

THE WITCH: I see, that's logical, Sissy. Hmmm. There he is:
sleeping.

MRS GOFORTH [*in a shrill whisper as they draw closer to the bed*]:
Can you tell if he's – ?

[THE WITCH *removes her slippers, creeps to the bedside and
touches his wrist.*]

– Well?

THE WITCH: Hush! [*Slips back to* MRS GOFORTH.] You're
lucky, Sissy. His pulse seems normal, he's sleeping nor-
mally, and he has a good colour. – Let me see if there's
liquor on his breath. [*Slips back to bed and bends her face to his.*]
No. It's sweet as a baby's.

MRS GOFORTH: Don't go to bed with him!

THE WITCH: No, that's your privilege, Sissy.

MRS GOFORTH [*moving downstage from the lighted area in a
follow spot*]: Come out here.

THE WITCH [*reluctantly following*]: You must have met him
before.

MRS GOFORTH: Oh, somewhere, sometime, when I was still
meeting people, before they all seemed like the same person
over and over and I got tired of the – person.

THE WITCH: You know his story, don't you?

[*The* STAGE ASSISTANTS *place a section of balustrade, at an
angle, beside them, and a copper brazier with the blue flame in it.*

The flame flickers eerily on THE WITCH'S *face as she tells what she knows of* CHRIS: *Harmonium plays under the stylized recitation.*]

Sally Ferguson found him at a ski lodge in Nevada where he was working as a ski instructor.

MRS GOFORTH: A poet, a ski instructor?

THE WITCH: Everything about him was like that, a contradiction. He taught Sally skiing at this Nevada lodge where Sally was trying to prove she was a generation younger than she was and thought she could get away with it. – Well, she should have stuck to the gentle slopes, since her bones had gone dry, but one day she took the ski lift to the top of the mountain, drank a hot buttered rum, and took off like a wild thing, a crazy bird, down the mountain, slammed into a tree and broke her hip bone. Well, Christopher Flanders carried her back to the ski lodge. We all thought she was done for but Chris worked a miracle on her that lasted for quite a while. He got her back on her pins after they'd pinned her broken hip together with steel pins. They travelled together, to and from Europe together, but then one time in rough weather, on the promenade deck of one of the Queen ships, the *Mary*, he suddenly let go of her, she took a spill and her old hip bone broke again, too badly for steel pins to pin her back together again, and Sally gave up her travels except from one room to another, on a rolling couch pushed by Chris. We all advised her to let Chris go like Chris had let go of her on the promenade deck of the *Mary*. Would she? Never! She called him my saint, my angel, till the day that she died. And her children contested her will so that Chris got nothing, just his poems published, dedicated to Sally. The book won a prize of some kind and *Vogue* and *Harper's Bazaar* played it up big with lovely photos of Chris looking like what she called him, an angel, a saint. . . .

MRS GOFORTH: Did he sleep with that old Ferguson bitch? Or was he just her Death Angel?

[*Phone rings on the bedside table: the area has remained softly lighted.* CHRIS *starts up: drops back, feigning sleep, as* MRS GOFORTH *rushes to the phone, snatches it up.*]

– Pronto, dica. – Taormina, Sicily? No, Spogliato!

[*Looks with angry suspicion at* CHRIS, *who murmurs as if in sleep. She notices the food tray by the bed, and snatches it up: returns to* THE WITCH, *downstage.*]

MRS GOFORTH: He's already making long-distance calls on the phone and look at this. He's had them bring him a food tray and I am going to remove it. I can't stand guests, especially not invited, that act like they're in a hotel, charging calls and calling for room service. Come on, I'm turning out the lights.

THE WITCH: My slippers.

[*She slips back to the bed and picks up her slippers: lingers over* CHRIS: *suddenly bends to kiss him on the mouth. He rolls over quickly, shielding his lower face with an arm and uttering a grunt of distaste.*]

Possum!

[*The lights dim in the area: as* THE WITCH *moves downstage:* MRS GOFORTH *has disappeared.*]

Sissy? Sissy? Yoo-hoo!

MRS GOFORTH [*at a distance*]: Yoo-hoo!

THE WITCH [*crossing into the wings*]: Yooooooooo-hoooooo. . .

[*The* STAGE ASSISTANTS *replace the screen that masked the pink villa bed. Then they fold and remove the screen before* BLACKIE'S *bed in the blue villa.*

The area remains dark till a faint dawn light appears on the cyclorama. Then BLACKIE'S *bed is lighted and we see her seated on it, brushing her dark hair with a silver-backed brush.*]

SCENE FOUR

Later that night: the terrace of the white villa. The watchman
RUDY *sweeps the audience with the beam of his flashlight. We hear a*
long, anguished 'Ahhh' from behind the screen masking MRS
GOFORTH'S *bed.* RUDY, *as if he heard the outcry, turns the flash-*
light momentarily on the screen behind which it comes. He chuckles:
sways drunkenly: then suddenly turns the light beam on the figure of
CHRIS *who has entered quietly from the wings, stage right.*

CHRIS [*shielding his eyes from the flashlight*]: Oh. Hello.
RUDY: You still prowling around here?
CHRIS [*still agreeably*]: No, I'm. Well, yes, I'm – [*His smile
    fades as* RUDY *moves in closer.*] – I just now woke up hungry. I
    didn't want to disturb anybody, so I –
RUDY: You just now woke up, huh?
CHRIS: Yes, I –
RUDY: Where'd you just now wake up?
CHRIS: In the, uh, guest-house, the –
RUDY: Looking for the dogs again, are you? [*Whistles the dogs
    awake. They set up a clamour at a distance.*]
CHRIS: I told you I just now woke up hungry: I came out to
    see if –
RUDY [*moving still closer and cutting in*]: Aw, you woke up
    hungry?
CHRIS: Yes. Famished.
RUDY: How about this, how'd you like to eat this, something
    like this, huh? [*Thrusts his stick hard into* CHRIS'S *stomach.*]
CHRIS: [*Expels his breath in a 'hah'.*]
RUDY: 'Sthat feel good on your belly? Want some more of
    that, huh?
    [*Drives the stick again into* CHRIS'S *stomach, so hard that*
    CHRIS *bends over, unable to speak.* BLACKIE *rushes on to the
    terrace in a dressing-gown, her hair loose.*]
BLACKIE: RUDY! WHAT'S GOING ON HERE?
    [*The* DOGS *have roused and have started barking at a distance.*]

This young man is a guest of Mrs Goforth. He's staying in the pink villa. Are you all right, Mr Flanders?

[CHRIS *can't speak: leans on a section of balustrade, bent over, making a retching sound.*]

Rudy, get off the terrace! – you drunk gorilla!

RUDY: [*grinning*]: He's got the dry heaves, Blackie, he woke up hungry and he's got the dry heaves.

CHRIS: Can't – catch – breath!

[*From her bed behind the griffin-crested screen,* MRS GOFORTH *cries out in her sleep, a long, anguished 'Ahhhhh!'.*

DOG *barking subsides gradually. The 'Ahhhhh' is repeated and a faint light appears behind her screen.*

BLACKIE *turns on* RUDY, *fiercely.*]

BLACKIE: I said get off the terrace, now get off it.

RUDY: You shoulda told me you –

BLACKIE: Off it, off the terrace!

RUDY [*overlapping*]: You got yourself a boy-friend up here, Blackie! You should've let me know that.

BLACKIE: Mr Flanders, I'll take you back to your place.

CHRIS [*gaspingly*]: Is there – anywhere closer – I could catch my breath?

BLACKIE: Yes. Yes, I'll – my place is closer. ...

[*She stands protectively near him as* RUDY *goes off the terrace, laughing.*

The STAGE ASSISTANTS *rush out to remove a screen masking* BLACKIE'S *bed in the blue villa, announcing 'Blackie's bedroom'.* CHRIS *straightens slowly, still gasping. The* STAGE ASSISTANTS *exit.*

Then CHRIS *and* BLACKIE *cross to her villino, represented only by a narrow blue-sheeted bed with a stand beside it that supports an inter-com. box.*]

BLACKIE: Now tell me just what happened so I can give a report to Mrs Goforth tomorrow.

CHRIS: The truth is I was looking for something to eat. I've had no food for five days, Blackie, except some oranges that I picked on the road. And you know what the acid, the citric acid in oranges, does to an empty stomach, so I – I woke up feeling as if I had a – a bushel of burning sawdust in my stomach, and I –

BLACKIE: I had food sent to your room, you didn't find it?

CHRIS: No. God, no!

BLACKIE: Then the cook didn't send it or it was taken out while you were sleeping, and I'm afraid you'll have to wait till morning for something to eat. You see the only kitchen is in Mrs Goforth's villa, it's locked up like a bank vault till Mrs Goforth wakes up and has it opened.

CHRIS: How long is it till morning?

BLACKIE: Oh, my – watch has stopped. I'm a watch-winding person but I forgot to wind it.

[*The cyclorama has lightened a little and there is the sound of church-bells at a distance.*]

CHRIS: The church-bells are waking up on the other mountains.

BLACKIE: Yes, it's, it must be near morning, but morning doesn't begin on Mrs Goforth's mountain till she sleeps off her drugs and starts pressing buttons for the sun to come up. So –

CHRIS: – What?

[*The inter-com. box comes alive with a shrill electric buzz.*]

BLACKIE: Oh, God, she's awake, buzzing for me!

CHRIS: Oh, then, could you ask her to open the kitchen? A glass of milk, just some milk, is all I –

BLACKIE: Mrs Goforth isn't buzzing for morning, she's buzzing for me to take dictation and, Oh, God, I don't think I can do it. I haven't slept tonight and I just couldn't take it right now, I –

CHRIS: Let me take it for you.

BLACKIE: No. I'll have to answer myself or she'll come stumbling raving out and might fall off the cliff. [*She presses a button on the inter-com. box.*] Mrs Goforth? Mrs Goforth?

[*The* STAGE ASSISTANTS *remove the screen masking* MRS GOFORTH'S *bed, up stage left. We see her through the gauze curtains enclosing the bed. She pulls a cord opening the curtains and speaks hoarsely into a microphone.*]

MRS GOFORTH: *Blackie? It's night, late night!*

BLACKIE: Yes, it's late, Mrs Goforth.

MRS GOFORTH: Don't answer: this is dictation. Don't interrupt me, this is clear as a vision. The death of Harlon

Goforth, just now – clearly – remembered, clear as a vision. It's night, late night, without sleep. He's crushing me under the awful weight of his body. Then suddenly he stops trying to make love to me. He says, Flora, I have a pain in my head, a terrible pain in my head. And silently to myself, I say, Thank God, but out loud I say something else: 'Tablets, you want your tablets?' He answers with the groan of – I reach up and turn on the light, and I see – death in his eyes! I see, I know. He has death in his eyes, and something worse in them, terror. I see terror in his eyes. I see it, I feel it, myself, and I get out of the bed, I get out of the bed as if escaping from quicksand! I don't look at him again, I move away from the bed. . . .

[*We see her rising from the bed, the microphone gripped in her hand.*]

I move away from death, terror! I don't look back, I go straight to the door, the door on to the terrace! [*She moves downstage with the microphone.*] It's closed, I tear it open, I leave him alone with his death, his –

BLACKIE: She's out of bed, she's going out on the – [*She rushes into the wings: light dims on the blue villa bed.*]

MRS GOFORTH [*dropping the microphone as she moves out on the white villa terrace*]: I've gone out, now, I'm outside, I'm on the terrace, twenty-five stories over the high, high city of Goforth, I see lights blazing as bright as the blaze of terror that I saw in his eyes! [*She staggers to the edge of the forestage.*] Wind, cold wind, clean, clean! Release! Relief! Escape from – [*She reaches the edges of the orchestra pit. A wave crashes loudly below.*] I'm lost, blind, dying! I don't know where I –

BLACKIE [*rushing out behind her*]: Mrs Goforth! Don't move! You're at the edge of the cliff!

MRS GOFORTH [*stopping, her hands over her eyes*]: Blackie! [*She sways:* BLACKIE *rushes forward to catch her.*] Blackie, don't leave me alone!

THE STAGE IS BLACKED OUT: INTERMISSION

SCENE FIVE

The terrace of the white villa the following morning: MRS GO-
FORTH *is standing on the terrace while dictating to* BLACKIE,
*who sits at a small table. Above the table and about the balustrade are
cascades of bougainvillaea: coins of gold light, reflected from the sea
far below, flicker upon the playing area, which is backed by fair sky.
There has been a long, reflective pause in the dictation.*

*   MRS GOFORTH stands glaring sombrely out at the sea.*

MRS GOFORTH: *Blackie, I want to begin this chapter on a more
    serious note.* [*She moves around right of the table. Then emphatically
    and loudly.*] MEANING OF LIFE!
BLACKIE: Dictation?
MRS GOFORTH: Not yet, wait, don't rush me. [*Repeats in a
    softer tone: 'meaning of Life . . .'*]
        [CHRIS *appears at a far end of the terrace. He wears the Samurai
        robe.* BLACKIE *sees him but* MRS GOFORTH *doesn't:*
        BLACKIE *indicates by gesture that he should not approach yet.*]
Yes, I feel this chapter ought to begin with a serious comment
    on the meaning of life, because, y'know, sooner or later, a
    person's obliged to face it.
BLACKIE: Dictating, now, Mrs Goforth?
MRS GOFORTH: No, no, thinking – reflecting, I'll raise my
    hand when I begin the dictation.
        [*She raises a jewelled hand to demonstrate the signal that she will
        use.*]
BLACKIE: Begin now?
        [CHRIS *smiles at her tone of voice:* BLACKIE *shrugs and closes
        her notebook: rises quietly and goes up to* CHRIS *for a smoke.*]
MRS GOFORTH: One time at Flora's Folly which was the
    name of the sixteenth-century coach-house, renovated, near
    Paris where I had my salon, my literary evenings, I brought
    up that question, 'What is the meaning of Life?' And do
    you know they treated it like a joke? Ha ha, very funny,
    Sissy can't be serious! – but she *was*, she *was*. . . .

CHRIS: I think she's started dictating. Is there something to eat?

BLACKIE: Black coffee and saccharine tablets.

CHRIS: That's *all*?!

BLACKIE: Soon as I get a chance I'll raid the kitchen for you.

MRS GOFORTH [*almost plaintively*]: Why is it considered ridiculous, bad taste, *mauvais goût,* to seriously consider and discuss the possible meaning of life and only stylish to assume it's just – what?

[*The* STAGE ASSISTANTS *have come out of the wings.*]

ONE: Charade. Game.

TWO [*tossing a spangled ball to his partner*]: Pastime.

ONE [*tossing the ball back*]: Flora's Folly.

ONE [*same action*]: Accident of atoms.

TWO [*same action*]: Resulting from indiscriminate copulation.

[BLACKIE *tosses her cigarette away and returns to her former position. The* STAGE ASSISTANTS *withdraw.*]

MRS GOFORTH: I've often wondered but I've wondered *more* lately: meaning of *life.*

[*The* STAGE ASSISTANTS *reappear with a small table and two chairs: wait in the wings for the moment to place them.*]

– Sometimes I think, I suspect, that everything that we do is a way of – *not* thinking about it. Meaning of life, and meaning of death, too ... WHAT IN HELL ARE WE DOING? [*Raises her jewelled hand.*] Just going from one goddam frantic distraction to another, till finally one too many goddam frantic distractions leads to disaster, and black out? Eclipse of, total of, sun? [*She keeps staring out from the terrace, her head turning slowly right and left, into the swimming gold light below her, murmuring to herself, nodding a little, then shaking her head a little: her small jewelled hands appear to be groping blindly for something: she coughs from time to time.*] – There's a fog coming in. See it over there, that fog coming in?

BLACKIE: No. It's perfectly clear in all directions this morning.

MRS GOFORTH: When I woke up this morning, I said to myself –

BLACKIE: Dictation?

MRS GOFORTH: Shut up – I said to myself, Oh, God, not

morning again, oh, no, no, I can't bear it. But I *did,* I bore it.
– You really don't see that mist coming in out there?

BLACKIE [*closing her notebook*]: – Mrs Goforth, the young man
in the pink villa, Mr Flanders, is waiting out here to see
you. He has on the Samurai robe you gave him to wear while
his clothes are being repaired and it's very becoming to him.

MRS GOFORTH: Call him over.

BLACKIE: Mr Flanders!

MRS GOFORTH: Hay, Samurai! *Bonzei!*

[*Approaching, he ducks under a brilliant cascade of bougainvillaea vine.*]

BLACKIE: You certainly had a long sleep.

CHRIS: Did I ever!

MRS GOFORTH: DID he ever, ho ho. He slept round the
clock but still has romantic shadows under his eyes! There
was a chorus girl in the Follies – I used to be in the Follies,
before my first marriage – when she'd show up with circles
under her eyes, she'd say, 'The blackbirds kissed me last
night' meaning she's been too busy to sleep that night,
ho ho. . . .

CHRIS: I was busy sleeping, just sleeping. [*He bends over her
hand.*]

MRS GOFORTH: No, no, none of that stuff. Old Georgia
swamp-bitches don't go in for hand-kissing but – setzen sie
doon, and – Are you coming out here for battle with that
sword on?

CHRIS: Oh. No, but – I ran into a pack of wild dogs on the
mountain, yesterday, when I climbed up here.

MRS GOFORTH: Yes, I heard about your little misunderstanding with the dogs. You don't seem much the worse for it.
You're lucky they didn't get at – [*grins wickedly*] – your *face.*

CHRIS: I'm sorry if it disturbed you, but their bite was worse
than their bark.

MRS GOFORTH: The Italians call them Lupos which means
wolves, these watchdogs: they're necessary for the protection of estates like this, but – didn't you notice the
'Private Property' sign in English and Italian, and the
'Beware of Dogs' sign when you started up that goat-path
from the highway?

CHRIS: I don't think I noticed a reference to dogs, no, I don't remember any mention of dogs, in English or Italian.

BLACKIE [*quickly*]: Naturally not, the 'Beware of Dogs' sign was put up *after* Mr Flanders' 'little misunderstanding with the dogs'.

MRS GOFORTH: Blackie, that is not so.

BLACKIE: Yes, it *is* so, I heard you ordering the sign put up after, just after the –

MRS GOFORTH [*trembling with fury*]: Blackie! You have *work* to do, don't you?

BLACKIE: I've never taken a job that called for collusion in – falsehood!

MRS GOFORTH [*mocking her*]: Oh, what virtue, what high moral character, Blackie.

CHRIS [*cutting in quickly*]: Mrs Goforth, Miss Black, I obviously *did* enter and trespass on private property at my own risk.

MRS GOFORTH: If that statement's typed up – Blackie, type it up. – Would you be willing to sign it, Mr Flanders?

CHRIS: Certainly, yes, of course, but let me write it up in my own handwriting and sign it right now. I'd hate for you to think I'd –

BLACKIE: He was attacked again last night.

MRS GOFORTH: Again, by dogs?

BLACKIE: Not by dogs, by a dog, your watchman, Rudy, attacked him because he woke up hungry and came outside to –

MRS GOFORTH [*rising*]: BLACKIE, GET OFF THE TERRACE!

BLACKIE: I want to get off this mountain gone mad with your madness! I try to help you, I try to feel sorry for you because you're –

MRS GOFORTH: WHAT? WHAT AM I?

CHRIS: Please. [*Tears a page out of* BLACKIE'*s notebook and says to her quietly.*] It's all right. Go in.

MRS GOFORTH: What did you say to that woman?

CHRIS: I said you're very upset, I said you're trembling.

MRS GOFORTH: *I've been up here surrounded by traitors all summer!* [*Staggers.*] *Ahhhhh!*

 [*He helps her into her chair.*]

– God! God. . . .

CHRIS: Now. [*Scribbles rapidly on the sheet of paper.*] Here. 'I, Christopher Flanders, entered a gate marked Private at my own risk and am solely responsible for a – misunderstanding with – dogs.' – Witnesses? Of the signature?

MRS GOFORTH: Can you unscrew this bottle? [*She has been trying to open her codein bottle.*]

CHRIS [*taking it from her and removing the cap*]: One?

MRS GOFORTH: Two. – Thank you. – Brandy on that – [*Indicates liquor cart.*]

CHRIS: Courvoisier?

MRS GOFORTH: Remy-Martin. – Thank you.

CHRIS: Welcome. [*He resumes his seat and smiles at her warmly.*] Let me hold that glass for you.

[*She has spilled some of the brandy, her hand is shaking so violently.*]

MRS GOFORTH: Thank you.

[*He sits back down and resumes his smile, with a quick, friendly nod.*]

– Ahh . . . [*Draws a deep breath: begins to recover herself.*] –You have nice teeth. – Are they capped?

[CHRIS *shakes his head, smiling more.*]

Well, you got beautiful teeth, in that respect nature's been favourable to you.

CHRIS: Thank you.

MRS GOFORTH: Don't thank me, thank your dentist. [*She's putting on lipstick and dabbing her nostrils with a bit of disposable tissue.*]

CHRIS: I've never been to a dentist: honestly not.

MRS GOFORTH: Well, then, thank the Lord for the calcium that you got from your mother's milk. Well, I have a pretty wonderful set of teeth myself. In fact, my teeth are so good people think they are false. But look, look here! [*She takes her large incisors between thumb and forefinger to demonstrate the firmness of their attachment.*] See? Not even a bridge. – In my whole mouth I've had exactly three fillings which are still there, put in there ten years ago! See them? [*She opens her mouth wide to expose its interior to him.*] – This tooth here was slightly chipped when my daughter's third baby struck me in the mouth with the butt of a water pistol at Murray Bay. I told my daughter that girl would turn to a problem child and it sure as hell did. – A little pocket-size bitch, getting bigger! I'm allergic to bitches. Although some people regard me as one myself ... Sometimes *with* some justification. Want some coffee, Mr Trojan Horse Guest?

CHRIS: Thanks, yes: – why do you call me that, a Trojan Horse Guest?

MRS GOFORTH: Because you've arrived here without invitation, like the Trojan Horse got into Troy. [*She has risen shakily to pour him a cup of coffee from a silver urn on the smaller upstage table.*]

CHRIS: Don't you remember our meeting and conversation at the Ballet Ball, some years ago, quite a few when you asked me to come whenever I was in Europe?

MRS GOFORTH: Passports expire and so do invitations. They've got to be renewed every couple of years.

CHRIS: Has my invitation expired?

MRS GOFORTH: Coffee. We'll see about that, that remains to be seen.

[NOTE: *While she was pouring the coffee, he may have quietly crumpled the sheet of paper and thrown it into the orchestra pit, such an action being in line with the ambiguity of his character.*]

Don't you smoke with your coffee?

CHRIS: Usually, but I –

[*He indicates he has no cigarettes.* MRS GOFORTH *smiles knowingly and opens a cigarette box on the table.*]

CHRIS: How does it feel, Mrs Goforth, to be a legend in your own lifetime?

MRS GOFORTH [*pleased*]: If that's a serious question, I'll give it a serious answer. A legend in my own lifetime, yes, I reckon I am. Well, I had certain advantages, endowments to start with, a face people naturally noticed and a figure that was not just sensational, but very durable, too. Some women my age, or younger, 've got breasts that look like a couple of mules hangin' their heads over the top rail of a fence. [*Touches her bosom.*] This is natural, not padded, not supported: and nothing's ever been lifted. Hell, I was born between a swamp and the wrong side of the tracks in One

Street, Georgia, but not even that could stop me in my tracks, wrong side or right side or no side. Hit show-biz at fifteen when a carnival show, I mean the manager of it, saw me and dug me on that One Street in One Street, Georgia. I was billed as the Dixie Doxey, was just supposed to move my anatomy but was smart enough to keep my tongue moving, too, and the verbal comments I made on my anatomical motions while in motion were a public delight. So I breezed through show-biz like a tornado, rising from one-week 'gigs' in the sticks to star-billing in 'The Follies' while still in m'teens, ho ho ... and I was still in my teens when I married Harlon Goforth, a marriage into the Social Register and Dun-and-Bradstreet's, both. Was barely out of my teens when I became his widow. Scared to make out a will, he died intestate so everything went to me.

CHRIS: Marvellous. Amazing.

MRS GOFORTH: That's right, all my life was and still *is* except here lately I'm a little run-down, like a race-horse that's been entered in just one race too many, even for me. . . . How do *you* feel about being a legend in your own life-time? Huh?

CHRIS: Oh, *me!* I don't feel like a – mythological – griffin with gold wings, but this strong fresh wind's reviving me like I'd had a – terrific breakfast!

MRS GOFORTH: Griffin, what's a griffin?

CHRIS: A force in life that's almost stronger than death. [*Springs up, turns to the booming sea.*] The sea's full of white race-horses today. May I, would you mind if I, suggested a programme for us? A picnic on the beach, rest on the rocks in the sun till nearly sundown, then we'd come back up here revitalized for whatever the lovely evening had to offer?

MRS GOFORTH: What do you think it would have to offer?

CHRIS: Dinner on the terrace with the sea still booming? How is that for a programme? Say, with music, a couple of tarantella dancers brought up from the village, and –

[*RUDY appears on the terrace.*]

RUDY: Miss Goforth, I've taken care of that for you, they're going, on the way out.

MRS GOFORTH: No trouble?

RUDY: Oh, yeah, sure, they want to see the Signora.

MRS GOFORTH: No, no, no. I won't see them!

[*But 'they' are appearing upstage: her* KITCHEN STAFF *discharged.*]

Here they come, hold them back!

[*She staggers up, turns her back on them. They cry out to her in Italian.* RUDY *rushes upstage and herds them violently off. A wave crashes.*]

CHRIS [*quietly*]: Boom. – What was their – ?

MRS GOFORTH: What?

CHRIS: – Transgression?

MRS GOFORTH: They'd been robbing me blind, he caught them at it, we had – an inventory and discovered that – they'd been robbing me blind like I was – blind. . . .

CHRIS [*his back to her, speaking as if to himself*]: When a wave breaks down there, it looks as delicate as a white lace fan, but I bet if it hit you, it would knock you against the rocks and break your bones. . . .

MRS GOFORTH: What?

CHRIS: – I said it's so wonderful here, after yesterday in Naples. . . .

MRS GOFORTH: What was wrong with yesterday in Naples? Were you picked up for vagrancy in Naples?

CHRIS: I wasn't picked up for anything in Naples.

MRS GOFORTH: That's worse than being picked up for vagrancy, baby. [*She chuckles: he grins agreeably.*]

CHRIS: Mrs Goforth, I'm going to tell you the truth.

MRS GOFORTH: The truth is all you could tell me that I'd believe so tell me the truth, Mr Flanders.

CHRIS: I'll go back a little further than Naples, Mrs Goforth. I'd drawn out all my savings account to come over here this summer on a Yugoslavian freighter that landed at Genoa.

MRS GOFORTH: You're leading up to financial troubles, aren't you?

CHRIS: Not so much that as – something harder, much harder, for me to deal with, a state of – Well, let me put it this way. Everybody has a sense of *reality* of some kind or other, some kind of sense of things being real or not real in his, his – particular – world. . . .

MRS GOFORTH: I know what you mean: go on.

CHRIS: I've lost it lately: this sense of reality in my particular world. We don't all live in the same world, you know, Mrs Goforth, oh, we all see the same things – sea, sun, sky, human faces and inhuman faces, but – they're different in *here*! [*Touches his forehead.*] And one person's sense of reality can be another person's sense of – Well, of madness! – Chaos! – And, and –

MRS GOFORTH: Go on: I'm still with you.

CHRIS: And when one person's sense of reality, or loss of sense of reality, disturbs another one's sense of reality – I know how mixed up this –

MRS GOFORTH: Not a bit, clear as a bell, so keep on, y'haven't lost my attention.

CHRIS: Being able to talk: wonderful! – When one person's sense of reality seems too – disturbingly different from another person's, uh –

MRS GOFORTH: Sense of reality: Continue.

CHRIS: Well, he's – avoided! Not welcome! It's – *that simple.* . . . And – yesterday in Naples, I suddenly realized that I was in that situation. [*Turns to the booming sea and says 'Boom'.*] I found out that I was now a – *leper*!

MRS GOFORTH: Leopard?

CHRIS: LEPER! – BOOM!

[*She ignores the 'boom'.*]

Yes, you see, they hang labels, tags of false identification, on people that disturb their own sense of reality too much, like the bells that used to be hung on the necks of – *lepers*! – BOOM!

– The lady I'd come over to visit who lives in a castle on the top of Ravello, sent me a wire to Naples. I walked to Naples on foot to pick it up, and picked it up at American Express in Naples, and what it said was: 'Not yet, not ready for you, dear – Angel of – Death . . .'

[MRS GOFORTH *regards him a bit uncomfortably. He smiles very warmly at her, she relaxes.*]

MRS GOFORTH: – Ridiculous!

CHRIS: Yes, and inconvenient since I'd –

MRS GOFORTH: Invested all your remaining capital in this standing invitation that had stopped standing, collapsed, ho, ho, ho!

CHRIS: – Yes . . .

MRS GOFORTH: Who's this bitch at Ravello?

CHRIS: I'd rather forget her name, now.

MRS GOFORTH: But you see you young people, well, you *reasonably* young people who used to be younger, you get in the habit of being sort of – professional house-guests, and as you get a bit older, and who doesn't get a bit older, some more than just a *bit* older, you're still professional house-guests, and –

CHRIS: Yes?

MRS GOFORTH: Oh, you have charm, all of you, you still have your good looks and charm and you all do something creative, such as writing but not writing and painting but not painting, and that goes fine for a time but –

CHRIS: You've made your point, Mrs Goforth.

MRS GOFORTH: No, not yet, quite yet. Your case is special. You've gotten a special nickname, 'Dear Angel of Death'. – And it's lucky for you I couldn't be less superstitious, deliberately walk under ladders, think a black cat's as lucky as a white cat, am only against the human cats of this world of which there's no small number. So! What're you looking around for, Angel of Death, as they call you?

CHRIS: I would love to have some buttered toast with my coffee.

MRS GOFORTH: Oh, no toast with my coffee, buttered, un-buttered, no toast. For breakfast I have only black coffee. Anything solid takes the edge off my energy and it's the time after breakfast when I do my best work.

CHRIS: What are you working on?

MRS GOFORTH: My memories, my memoirs, night and day, to meet the publishers' deadlines. The pressure has brought on a sort of nervous breakdown, and I'm enjoying every minute of it because it has taken the form of making me absolutely frank and honest with people, no more pretences, although I was always frank and honest with people:

comparatively: but now much more so. No more pretences at all. . . .

CHRIS: It's wonderful.

MRS GOFORTH: What?

CHRIS: That you and I have happened to meet at just this time because I have reached the same point in my life as you say you have come to in yours.

MRS GOFORTH [*suspiciously*]: What? Which? Point?

CHRIS: The point you mentioned, the point of no more pretences.

MRS GOFORTH: You say you've reached that point, too?

[CHRIS *nods, smiling warmly.*]

Hmmmm.

[*The sound is sceptical and so is the look she gives him.*]

CHRIS: It's *true*, I *have*, Mrs Goforth.

MRS GOFORTH: I don't mean to call you a liar or even a fantasist, but I don't see how you could afford to arrive at the point of no more pretences, Chris.

CHRIS: I probably couldn't afford to arrive at this point any more than I could afford to travel this summer.

MRS GOFORTH: Hmmm. I see. But you travelled?

CHRIS: Yes, mostly on foot, Mrs Goforth – since – Genoa.

MRS GOFORTH [*rises and crosses near balustrade*]: One of the reasons I took this place here is because it's supposed to be inaccessible except from the sea. Between here and the highway, there's just a goat-path, hardly possible to get down, and I thought impossible to get up. Hmmm. Yes. Well. But you got yourself up.

CHRIS [*pours last of the coffee*]: I had to. I had to get up it.

MRS GOFORTH [*crossing back to him and sitting*]: Let's play the truth game: do you know the truth game?

CHRIS: Yes, but I don't like it. I've always made excuses to get out of it when it's played at parties because I think the truth is too delicate and, well, *dangerous* a thing to be played with at parties, Mrs Goforth. It's nitro-glycerine, it has to be handled with the – the carefulest care, or somebody hurts somebody and gets hurt back and the party turns to a – devastating explosion, people crying, people screaming, people even fighting and throwing things at each other. I've seen it happen, and there's no truth in it – that's true.

MRS GOFORTH: But you say you've reached the same point that I have this summer, the point of no more pretences, so why can't we play the truth game together, huh, Chris?

CHRIS: – Why don't we put it off till – say, after – supper?

MRS GOFORTH: You play it better on a full stomach, do you?

CHRIS: Yes, you have to be physically fortified for it as well as – morally fortified for it.

MRS GOFORTH: And you like to stay for supper? You don't have any other engagement for supper?

CHRIS: I have no engagements of any kind now, Mrs Goforth.

MRS GOFORTH: Well, I don't know about supper. Sometimes I don't want any.

CHRIS: How about after – ?

MRS GOFORTH: – What?

CHRIS: After lunch?

MRS GOFORTH: Oh, sometimes I don't have lunch, either.

CHRIS: You're not on a healthful régime. You know, the spirit has to live in the body and so you have to keep the body in a state of repair because it's the home of the – spirit. . . .

MRS GOFORTH: – Hmmm. Are you talking about your spirit and body or mine?

CHRIS: Yours.

MRS GOFORTH: One long ago meeting between us, and you expect me to believe you care more about my spirit and body than your own? Mr Flanders?

CHRIS: Mrs Goforth, some people, some people, most of them, get panicky when they're not cared for by somebody, but I get panicky when I have no one to care for.

MRS GOFORTH: Oh, you seem to be setting yourself up as a – as a saint of some kind. . . .

CHRIS: All I said is I need somebody to care for. I don't say that – [He has finished his coffee and crosses to the warmer for more.] I'm playing the truth game with you. Caring for somebody gives me the sense of being – sheltered, protected. . . .

MRS GOFORTH: 'Sheltered, protected' from what?

CHRIS [*standing above her*]: – Unreality! – lostness? – Have you ever seen how two little animals sleep together, a pair of kittens or puppies? All day they seem so secure in the house of their master, but at night, when they sleep, they don't seem sure of their owner's true care for them: then they draw close together: they curl up against each other, and now and then, if you watch them, you notice they nudge each other a little with their heads or their paws, exchange little signals between them. The signals mean: we're not in danger ... sleep: we're close: – it's safe here. – Their owner's house is never a sure protection, a reliable shelter. – Everything going on in it is mysterious to them, and no matter how hard they try to please, how do they know if they please? – They hear so many sounds, voices, and see so many things they can't comprehend! – Oh, it's ever so much better than the pet shop window but what's become of their mother? – who warmed them and sheltered them and fed them until they were snatched away from her, for no reason they know. We're all of us living in a house we're not used to – too. .... A house full of – voices, noises, objects, strange shadows, light that's even stranger – we can't understand. We bark and jump around and try to – be – *pleasingly playful* in this big mysterious house but – in our hearts we're all very frightened of it: don't you think so? – Then it gets to be dark. – We're left alone with each other: we have to creep close to each other and give those gentle little nudges with our paws and our muzzles before we can slip into – sleep and – rest for the next day's – playtime ... and the next day's mysteries. [*He lights a cigarette for her as* THE WITCH *enters dramatically still on terrace.*]

THE WITCH: The next day's mysteries. Ecco, sono qui.

MRS GOFORTH: My Lord, are you still here? [*With unconcealed displeasure.* CHRIS *turns.*]

THE WITCH [*as if amazed*]: Christopher! Flanders!

CHRIS: How do you do, Mrs – Oh, I started to say Mrs Ridgeway but that isn't it, now, is it?

THE WITCH: What a back number you are!

[*He draws back from her and crosses away.*]

CHRIS: Yes.

MRS GOFORTH: How'd you miss your return trip to Capri last night, I thought you'd gone back there last night? I had the boatman waiting up for you last night.

THE WITCH: Oh, last night! What confusion! [*She puts down her hat and follows* CHRIS.] When was the last time I saw you?

MRS GOFORTH: If you don't know why should he?

THE WITCH: Oh, at the wedding banquet those Texas oil people gave me in Portofino, oh, yes, you were staying with them, and so depressed over the loss of –

CHRIS [*cutting in*]: Yes. [*He moves again toward the balustrade.*]

THE WITCH: You'd taken such beautiful care of that poor old ridiculous woman but couldn't save her, and, oh, the old Duke of Parma did such a wicked thing to you, poured champagne on your head and – called you – what did he call you?

MRS GOFORTH: Let him forget it, Connie.

[THE WITCH *gives her a glance and moves to* CHRIS.]

THE WITCH: Something else awful happened and you were involved in some way but I can't remember the details.

CHRIS: Yes, it's better forgotten, Mrs Goforth is right, some of the details are much better forgotten if you'll let me – forget them. . . .

[MRS GOFORTH *rises and starts upstage.*]

THE WITCH: Are you leaving us, Sissy?

MRS GOFORTH: I'm going to phone the boat-house t'make sure there's a boat ready for your trip back to Capri, because I know you want back there soon as possible, Connie. [*She crosses into the library and out the door.*]

THE WITCH [*crossing now to the table*]: Chris, you're not intending to STAY here!?

CHRIS: Yes, if I'm invited: I would like to.

THE WITCH: Don't you know, can't you tell? Poor Sissy's going, she's gone. The shock I got last night when I – I had to drink myself blind! – when I saw her condition! [*She crosses closer.*] You don't want to be stuck with a person in her appalling condition. You're young, have fun. Oh, Chris, you've been foolish too long, the years you devoted to that old Ferguson bitch, and what did you get?

CHRIS [*lighting a cigarette*]: Get?

THE WITCH: Yes, get? She *had* you, you were *had*! – *left* you? *Nothing!* – I bet, or why would you be here?

CHRIS: Please don't make me be rude: we don't understand each other, which is natural, but don't make me say things to you that I don't want to say.

THE WITCH: What can you say to me that I haven't heard said?

CHRIS: Have you heard this said to your face about you, that you're the heart of a world that has no heart, the heartless world you live in, has anyone said that to you, Mrs Ridgeway?

THE WITCH: Condotti, Marquessa Ridgeway-Condotti, Mr Death Angel Flanders.

CHRIS: Yes, we both have new titles.

THE WITCH [*throwing back her head*]: Sally! Laurie! Sissy! It's time for death, old girls, beddy-bye! [*Less shrilly*] Beddy-bye, old girls, the Death Angel's coming, no dreams....

[*Meanwhile in the library area:* MRS GOFORTH *enters, followed by* BLACKIE *with a notebook.*]

MRS GOFORTH: Ah, God.... What in Hell's going on here?

BLACKIE: I wish I knew, Mrs Goforth.

MRS GOFORTH [*circling the desk*]: I call, I buzz, no one answers!

BLACKIE: I was in the kitchen when you –

MRS GOFORTH: Why in the kitchen?

BLACKIE: The new kitchen staff had arrived and I was explaining the kitchen equipment to them.

MRS GOFORTH [*cutting in*]: Never mind that, let that go, just call the boat-house and have them have a boat ready to take the Capri Witch back to Capri.

[BLACKIE *moves to phone.*]

She's still here, spent the night here. Why didn't you get her away when – Look! Look!

[THE WITCH *has crossed toward* CHRIS, *who turns.*]

CHRIS: I'm sorry you forced me to say what I feel about you.

THE WITCH: Oh, that. My heart pumps blood that isn't my own blood, it's the blood of anonymous blood donors, and as for the world I live in, you know it as well as I know it. – Come to Capri, it's a mountain, too.

CHRIS [*again moving away*]: You're not afraid of the nickname I've been given?

THE WITCH: No, I think it's a joke that you take seriously, Chris. You've gotten too solemn. [*She follows him.*] Let me take that curse off you. Come to Capri, and I'll give you a party, decorated with your mobiles, and—

MRS GOFORTH [*to* BLACKIE]: See? *She's out there putting the make on*—

[BLACKIE *exits as* MRS GOFORTH *crosses out of the library.*]

THE WITCH [*cutting into* FLORA'S *speech*]: You're pale, you look anaemic, you look famished, you need someone to put you back in the picture, the social swim. Capri?

[MRS GOFORTH *has come back out on the terrace: she advances behind* CHRIS *and* THE WITCH.]

MRS GOFORTH: What picture? What swim? Capri?

THE WITCH: It's marvellous there this season.

MRS GOFORTH: The sea is full of Medusas. Didn't you tell me the sea is full of Medusas and a giant one got you?

THE WITCH [*crossing to her*]: Oh, they'll wash out, they'll be washed out by tomorrow.

MRS GOFORTH: When are *you* going to wash out? I thought you'd washed out last night—I've ordered a boat to take you back to Capri.

THE WITCH: I can't go back to Capri in a dinner gown before sundown. [*She sits at the table and stares at* CHRIS.]

MRS GOFORTH: Well, try my hot sulphur baths or just look the place over, it's worth it. It's worth looking over. Me, I'm about to start work so I can't talk to you right now. [*She gets* THE WITCH'S *hat and brings it to her.*] I'm right on the edge of breaking through here today, I'm on a strict discipline, Connie, as I explained last night to you, and—[*She coughs: falls into her chair.*]

THE WITCH: Sissy, I don't like that cough.

MRS GOFORTH: Hell, do you think I like it? Neuralgia, nerves, overwork, but I'm going to beat it, it isn't going to beat *me* or it'll be the first thing that ever *did* beat me!

THE WITCH [*rising and crossing to her*]: Be brave, Sissy—'Snothing more necessary.

MRS GOFORTH: Leave me alone, go, Connie, it'll do you in,

too. [*She crosses away for a tissue.* THE WITCH *looks, wide-eyed, at* CHRIS *and crosses to him.*]

THE WITCH: Watch out for each other! – Chris, give her the Swami's book you translated. Ciao! [*She throws him a kiss and moves off, calling back.*] *Qu'este veramente* una meraviglia … – *Ciao, arrivedeei* … Amici! [THE WITCH *goes out of the lighted area down the goat-path.* CHRIS *crosses to table and sits, looking about.*]

MRS GOFORTH: What are you looking for now?

CHRIS: I was just looking for the cream and sugar.

MRS GOFORTH: Never touch it, y'want a saccharine tablet?

CHRIS: Oh, no, thanks, I – don't like the chemical taste.

MRS GOFORTH [*crossing down to table*]: Well, it's black coffee or else, I'm afraid, Mr what? – Chris!

CHRIS: You have *three* villas here?

MRS GOFORTH: One villa and two villinos. Villino means a small villa. I also have a little grass hut, very Polynesian – [*Crossing a little below the table.*] down on my private beach too. I have a special use for it, and a funny name for it, too.

CHRIS: Oh?

MRS GOFORTH: Yes, I call it 'The Oubliette'. Ever heard of the Oubliette?

CHRIS: A place where people are put to be forgotten?

MRS GOFORTH: That's right, Chris. You've had some education along that line. [*She crosses above the table, closer to him.*]

CHRIS: Yes, quite a lot, Mrs Goforth, especially lately.

MRS GOFORTH: As for the use of it, well, I've been plagued by imposters lately, the last few summers, the continent has been overrun by imposters of celebrities, writers, actors, and so forth. I mean they arrive and say, like I am Truman Capote. Well, they look a bit like him so you are taken in by the announcement, I am Truman Capote and you receive him cordially only to find out later it isn't the true Truman Capote it's the false Truman Capote. Last summer I had the false Truman Capote and the year before that I had the false Mary McCarthy. That's before I took to checking the passports of sudden visitors. Well, – [*She crosses to the other chair and sits opposite him.*] – as far as I know they're still down there in that little grass hut on the beach where undesirables are transferred to when the villas are over-crowded. The oubliette. A medieval institution that I think personally was discarded too soon. It was a dungeon, where people were put for keeps to be forgotten. You say you know about it?

[CHRIS *stares straight at her, not answering by word or gesture: his look is gentle, troubled.*]

So that's what I call my little grass shack on the beach, I call it the oubliette from the French verb 'oublier' which means to forget, to forget, to put away and –

CHRIS: – forget . . .

MRS GOFORTH: And I do really forget 'em. Maybe you think I'm joking but it's the truth. Can't stand to be made a Patsy. Understand what I mean?

[*He nods.*]

This is nothing personal. You came with your book – [*She picks up his book of poetry.*] – with a photograph of you on it which still looks like you just, well, ten years younger, but still unmistakably you. You're not the false Chris Flanders, I'm sure about that.

CHRIS: Thank you. I try not to be.

MRS GOFORTH: However, I don't keep up with the new per-sonalities in the world of art like I used to. Too much a waste of vital energy, Chris. Of course you're not exactly a new personality in it: would you say so?

[CHRIS *smiles: shakes his head slightly.*]

You're almost a veteran in it. I said a veteran, I didn't say a 'has been' – [*She sneezes violently.*] I'm allergic to something around here. I haven't found out just what, but when I do, oh, brother, watch it go!

CHRIS [*who has risen and brought her a clean tissue*]: I hope it isn't the bougainvillaea vines.

MRS GOFORTH: No, it isn't the bougainvillaea, but I'm having an allergy specialist flown down here from Rome to check me with every goddam plant and animal on the place, and whatever it is has to go.

CHRIS: Have you tried breathing sea water?

MRS GOFORTH: Oh, you want to drown me?

CHRIS [*crossing back to his chair and sitting*]: Ha ha, no, I meant have you tried snuffing it up your nostrils to irrigate your nasal passages, Mrs Goforth, it's sometimes a very effective treatment for –

MRS GOFORTH: Aside from this allergy and a little neuralgia, sometimes more than a little, I'm a healthy woman. Know how I've kept in shape, my body the way it still is?

CHRIS: – Exercise?

MRS GOFORTH: Yes! In bed! Plenty of it, still going on! ... but there's this worship of youth in the States, this Whistler's Mother complex, you know what I mean, this idea that at a certain age a woman ought to resign herself to being a sweet old thing in a rocker. Well, last week-end, a man, a *young* man, came in my bedroom and it wasn't too easy to get him out of it. I had to be very firm about it.

[BLACKIE *appears on the terrace with a plate of food for* CHRIS – MRS GOFORTH *rises*.]

– What've you got there, Blackie?

BLACKIE: Mr Flanders' breakfast, I'm sure he would like some.

MRS GOFORTH: Aw, now, isn't that thoughtful. Put it down there.

[*As* BLACKIE *starts to put it down on the table,* MRS GOFORTH *indicates the serving table*.]

I said down there, and get me my menthol inhaler and Kleenex. I have run out.

[BLACKIE *sets the plate on the serving table and retires from the lighted area*.]

Simonetta!

[MRS GOFORTH *rings and hands the tray to* SIMONETTA *who has entered*.]

Take this away. I can't stand the smell of food now.

[SIMONETTA *exits*.]

CHRIS [*who has moved toward the serving table, stands stunned*]: Mrs Goforth, I feel that I have, I must have disturbed you, annoyed you – disturbed you because I – [*He crosses back to the table*.]

MRS GOFORTH: Don't reach for a cigarette till I offer you one.

CHRIS: May I have one, Mrs Goforth?

MRS GOFORTH: Take one. Be my Trojan Horse Guest. Wait. [*She moves down beside him.*] Kiss me for it.

[*CHRIS doesn't move.*]

Kiss me for it, I told you.

CHRIS [*putting the cigarette away*]: Mrs Goforth, there are moments for kisses and moments not for kisses.

MRS GOFORTH: This is a 'not for kiss' moment?

[*He turns away and she follows and takes his arm.*]

I've shocked *you* by my ferocity, have I? Sometimes I shock myself by it.

[*They move together towards the balustrade.*]

Look: a coin has two sides. On one side is an eagle but on the other side is – something else. . . .

CHRIS: Yes, something else: usually some elderly potentate's profile.

[*She laughs appreciatively at his* riposte *. . . touches his shoulder: he moves a step away from her.*]

MRS GOFORTH: Why didn't you grab the plate and run off with it?

CHRIS: Like a dog grabs a bone?

MRS GOFORTH: Sure! Why not? It might've pleased me to see you show some fight.

CHRIS: I can fight if I have to, but the fighting style of dogs is not my style.

MRS GOFORTH: *Grab, fight, or go hungry!* – nothing else works.

CHRIS: How is it possible for a woman of your reputation as a patron of arts and artists, to live up here, with all this beauty about you, and yet be –

MRS GOFORTH: A bitch, a swamp-bitch, a devil? Oh, I see it, the view, but it makes me feel ugly this summer for some reason or other: – bitchy, a female devil.

CHRIS: You'd like the view to be ugly to make you superior to it?

MRS GOFORTH [*turning to him*]: Why don't we sing that old church hymn,

'From Greenland's icy mountains to India's coral isle
Everything is beautiful' . . .

CHRIS: 'Man alone is vile.'

MRS GOFORTH: – Hmm. – Devils can be driven out of the heart by the touch of a hand on a hand or a mouth on a mouth. Because, like Alex said once, 'Evil isn't a person: evil is a thing that comes sneaky-snaking into the heart of a person, and takes it over: a mean intruder, a *squatter*!'

CHRIS [*crossing to her*]: May I touch your hand, please?

MRS GOFORTH [*as he does*]: Your hand's turned cold, I've shocked the warm blood out of it. Let me rub it back in.

CHRIS: Your hand's cold, too, Mrs Goforth.

MRS GOFORTH: Oh, that's just – nervous tension, never mind that. – I'll tell you something, Chris, you came here at a time unusually favourable to you. Now we're going to talk turkey, at least, I'm going to talk turkey, you can talk ducks and geese but I am going to talk turkey, cold turkey. You've come here at a time when I'm restless, bored and shocked by the news of deaths of three friends in the States, one, two, three, like fire-crackers going off, right together almost, like rat-a-tat-tat blindfolded against the wall. – Well, you see I – [*She moves down to the lower terrace.*] – I had a bad scare last winter. I was visiting relatives I'd set up on a grand estate on Long Island when some little psychosomatic symptom gave me a scare. They made a big deal of it, had me removed by a seaplane to the East River where they had an ambulance waiting for me, and whisked me off to a – Know what I said when I was advised to go under the knife the next day? Ha, I'll tell you, ha ha! – Called my law firm and dictated a letter cutting them off with one dollar apiece in my will. . . .

CHRIS [*who has come down to her*]: Mrs Goforth, are you still afraid of – [*He hesitates.*]

MRS GOFORTH: Death – never even think of it.

[*She takes his arm and they move down to a bench and sit.*]

CHRIS: Death is one moment and life is so many of them.

MRS GOFORTH: A million billion of them if you think in terms of a lifetime as rich as mine's been, Chris.

CHRIS: Yes, life is something, death's nothing. . . .

MRS GOFORTH: Nothing, nothing, but nothing – I've had to refer to many deaths in my memoirs, – Oh, I don't think I'm immortal. I still go to sleep every night wondering if I'll

– wake up the next day ... [*Coughs: gasps for breath.*] – face that angry old lion.

CHRIS: Angry old – ?

MRS GOFORTH: – Lion!

CHRIS: The sun? You think it's angry?

MRS GOFORTH: Naturally, of course; looking down on – ? – well, you know what it looks down on. ...

CHRIS: It seems to accept and understand things today. ...

MRS GOFORTH: It's just a big fire-ball that toughens the skin, including the skin of the heart.

CHRIS: – How lovely the evenings must be here – when the fishing boats go out on the Gulf of Salerno with their little lamps shining.

MRS GOFORTH: Well, they call this coast the *Divina Costiera* that means the divine coast, you know.

CHRIS: Yes, I know – I suppose ...

MRS GOFORTH: You suppose what?

CHRIS: I suppose you dine on the terrace about the time the fishing boats go out with their little lamps and the stars come out of the –

MRS GOFORTH: Firmament, call it the firmament, not the sky, it's much more classy to call it the firmament, baby. How about spring? You write about spring and live in it, you write about love in the spring, haven't you written love-poems for susceptible – patrons? – Well! How many books of poems have you come out with?

CHRIS: Just the one that I brought you.

MRS GOFORTH: You mean you burnt out as a poet?

CHRIS: – Pardon?

MRS GOFORTH: You mean you burnt out as a poet?
    [CHRIS *laughs uncomfortably.*]
Why're you laughing? I didn't say anything funny.

CHRIS: I didn't know I was laughing. Excuse me, Mrs Goforth. But you are very – direct.

MRS GOFORTH: Is that shocking?

CHRIS: No. – No, not really. In fact I like that about you.

MRS GOFORTH: Each time you give that little embarrassed laugh like I'd made you uncomfortable.

CHRIS: My nerves are –

MRS GOFORTH: Gone through like your list of suckers.
[MRS GOFORTH *sneezes and crosses away for another tissue.*]

CHRIS [*standing*]: Mrs Goforth – if you want me to go –

MRS GOFORTH: That depends.

CHRIS: – What does it depend on?

MRS GOFORTH: – Frankly, I'm very lonely up here this summer.

CHRIS: – I can understand that.

MRS GOFORTH: Now you're not stupid. You're attractive to me. You know that you are. You've deliberately set out to be attractive to me and you are. So don't be a free-loader.
[*Pause.*]

CHRIS: Mrs Goforth, I think you've been exposed to the wrong kind of people and –

MRS GOFORTH [*cutting in*]: I'm sick of moral blackmail! You know what that is. People imposing on you by the old, old trick of making you feel it would be unkind of you not to permit them to do it. In their hearts they despise you. So much they can't quite hide it. It pops out in sudden little remarks and looks they give you. Busting with malice – Because you have what they haven't. You know what some writer called it? 'A robust conscience, and the Viking spirit in life!'

CHRIS [*crossing back on terrace*]: Oh? Is that what he called it?

MRS GOFORTH [*following*]: He called it that, and I have it! I give away nothing, I sell and I buy in my life, and I've always wound up with a profit, one way or another. You came up that hill from the highway with an old book of poems that you got published ten years ago, by playing on the terrible, desperate loneliness of a rich old broken-hipped woman, who, all she could do, was pretend that someone still loved her.

CHRIS: You're talking about Mrs Ferguson.

MRS GOFORTH: Yes, I am.

CHRIS [*moving up away from her*]: I made her walk again. She published my poems.

MRS GOFORTH: How long after she published your poems did you let go of her arm so she fell on the deck of a steamship and her hip broke again?

CHRIS: – I didn't let her go. She broke away from me,

[MRS GOFORTH *laughs uproariously.*]

if you'll allow me to make a minor correction in the story. We were walking very slowly about the promenade deck of the *Queen Mary*, eight summers ago, more than a year after my poems were published. A young man called to her from a deck-chair that we'd just passed, and she wheeled around and broke away from my hand, and slipped and fell and her hip was broken again. Of course some malicious 'friends' blamed me, but – I wouldn't leave her.

MRS GOFORTH: No? She was still your meal-ticket?

CHRIS: Not at all.

MRS GOFORTH: Who *was*?

CHRIS [*sitting*]: – I was fashionable, then.

MRS GOFORTH: Do you sit down while a lady is standing?

CHRIS [*springs up with a rather ferocious smile*]: Sorry, won't you sit down!

[*His tone is so commanding, abruptly, that she does sit down in the chair he jerks out for her.*]

– May I tell you something about yourself? It may seem presumptuous of me to tell you this but I'm going to tell you this: you're suffering more than you need to.

MRS GOFORTH: I am –

CHRIS [*cutting through her protest*]: You're suffering from the worst of all human maladies, all afflictions, and I don't mean one of the body, I mean the thing people feel when they go from room to room for no reason, and then they go back from room to room for no reason, and then they go *out* for no reason and come back *in* for no reason –

MRS GOFORTH: You mean I'm alone here, don't you?

[CHRIS *takes hold of her hand.*]

MRS GOFORTH [*snatching her hand away from him*]: I'm WORK-ING up here this summer, WORKING! EVER HEARD OF IT?

[*A* STAGE ASSISTANT *appears in the wings as if she had shouted for him. He hands her a letter.*]

This morning's mail brought me this! My London publisher's letter! 'Darling Flora: Your book of memoirs, *Facts and a Figure* – will, in my opinion, rank with and possibly – [*Squints in the glare, unable to decipher the letter further.*

He removes it from her trembling, jewelled hand, and completes
the reading.]

CHRIS: '– rank with and possibly even out-rank the great
Marcel Proust's *Remembrance of Things Past* as a social
documentation of two continents in three decades. . . .'

MRS GOFORTH: *Well?*

CHRIS: A letter like this should fall on a higher mountain.

MRS GOFORTH: Huh?

CHRIS: A letter like this should be delivered above the snow-
line of an Alpine peak because it's snow, a snow-job.

[*She snatches it back from him.*]

MRS GOFORTH [*raging*]: For you, a blond beatnik, coming
from Naples on foot up a goddam goat-path, wearing at
this table a Japanese robe because dogs tore your britches, I
think your presumption is not excusable, Mister. It lacks
the excuse of much youth, you're not young enough for
your moxey. This publisher's not a lover, a lover might
snow me but this man's a business associate and they don't
snow you, not ME, not SISSY GOFORTH! They
don't snow me – SNOW me! They don't get up that early
in the morning –

[*Her agitation somehow touches him: His smile turns warm again.*]
– that they could – [*laughs.*] – snow me. . . .

[*The STAGE ASSISTANTS lean whispering together as they
retire from the stage.*]

CHRIS: Of course without having your publisher's advantage
of knowing *Facts and a Figure* –

MRS GOFORTH: Nothing, not a word of it!

CHRIS: No, not a word, but what I was going to say was that
I think you need *companionship*: not just employees about
you, up here, but – how often do you see old friends or new
friends this summer, Mrs Goforth? Often or not so often?

MRS GOFORTH: Hell, all I have to do is pick up a phone to
crowd this mountain with –

CHRIS: CROWDS? Is it that easy this summer? You're proud.
You don't want to ask people up here that might not come,
because they're pleasure-seekers, frantic choosers of silly
little distractions, and – and –

MRS GOFORTH: 'and and' WHAT?

CHRIS: Your condition, the terrible strain of your work, makes you seem – eccentric, disturbing! – To those sea-level, those lower than sea-level people. . . .

MRS GOFORTH: GET TO WHATEVER YOU'RE LEADING UP TO, WILL YOU!

CHRIS: I notice you have trouble reading. I've been told I have a good reading voice.

MRS GOFORTH: Most human voices are very monotonous to me. Besides, I'm more interested in producing literature this summer than having it read to me.

CHRIS: Mmm, but you do need some agreeable companion-ship.

MRS GOFORTH: Right you are about *that*, but how do I know your idea of agreeable companionship is the same as mine? You purr at me like a cat, now, but a cat will purr at you one minute and scratch your eyes out the next.

[*He leans back, smiling, working the sword up and down in its scabbard.*]

I think you'd better take off that old sword-belt.

CHRIS: There's no buttons on the robe so without the belt on it –

MRS GOFORTH: Take it off you!

CHRIS: The *robe*?

MRS GOFORTH: The *sword*-belt. You grin and fiddle with the hilt – the sword like you had – evil – intentions.

CHRIS: Oh. You suspect I'm a possible assassin?

MRS GOFORTH: *Take it off, give it here!*

CHRIS: All right: formal surrender, *unconditional* . . . *nearly.* [*Takes the sword-belt off and hands it to her.*]

MRS GOFORTH: *O K. Robert E. Lee!: At Appomatox . . .* [*Hurls the sword-belt to the terrace tiles behind her.*]

[*A* STAGE ASSISTANT *darts out of the wings to remove it: the other* ASSISTANT *laughs offstage.*]

CHRIS: Now what can I use for a sash to keep things proper?

MRS GOFORTH: See if this goes around you, if being proper's so important to you. [*Hands him a brilliant scarf she wore about her throat.*]

[*He turns upstage to tie the scarf about him.*
A phone is heard ringing, off.

BLACKIE *appears from behind the library screen.*]

MRS GOFORTH: Who's calling, my broker again, with the closing quotations?

BLACKIE: The call's for *Mr Flanders*.

CHRIS: *Me*, for *me*? But who could know I'm up here!

MRS GOFORTH: Cut the bull, you got a call up here last night; business is picking up for you.

CHRIS: This is – mystifying!

BLACKIE: The phone's in the library.

CHRIS: Excuse me. [*Crosses quickly behind the library screen.*]

[MRS GOFORTH *crosses toward it but remains, listening, outside it.*]

CHRIS'S VOICE [*behind screen*]: *Pronto, sono pronto. – Madelyn!* – How are you, how's your dear mother? – Oh, my God! – I meant to come straight down there but – was it, uh, what they call *peaceful*? Oh, I'm so glad, I prayed so hard that it *would* be! And I'm so relieved that it *was*. I did so long to be with you but had to stop on the way. And you? Will you be all right? – Yes, I know, expected, but still I could be some use in making the necessary arrangements? I'm at Flora Goforth's place, but if you could send a car to pick me up I could – Oh? – Well, Madelyn, all I can say is *accept* it. – Bless you, goodbye: *accept* it.

[MRS GOFORTH *is shaken: she moves back to the table as if she had received a personal shock.*

CHRIS *comes back out: at the same moment, church-bells ring in a village below the mountain.*]

CHRIS: – Church-bells? In the village?

MRS GOFORTH: Yes, appropriate, aren't they? Ringing right on a dead cue. . . .

CHRIS: – I just received news that's – *shocked* me. . . .

MRS GOFORTH: Another name you have to scratch off the list?

CHRIS: – Did you say 'list'?

[MRS GOFORTH *smiles at him cunningly, fiercely.*]

MRS GOFORTH: – I went to a spiritualist once. She said to me, 'I hear many dead voices calling, Flora, Flora.' I knew she was a fake, then, since all my close friends call me Sissy. I said, 'Tell them to mind their own business, play their gold harps and mind their own harp-playing, Sissy Goforth's not ready to go forth yet and won't go forth till she's ready....'

[*The bell stops ringing.*

CHRIS *extends a hand to her.*]

MRS GOFORTH: What are you reaching out for?

CHRIS: Your hand, if I may, Mrs Goforth. [*He has taken hold of it.*]

MRS GOFORTH: Hold it but don't squeeze it, the rings cut my fingers.

CHRIS: I'm glad we've talked so frankly, so quickly today. The conversation we had at the ball at the Waldorf in 1950 was a long conversation but not as deep as this one.

MRS GOFORTH: Who said anything deep? I don't say anything deep in a conversation, not this summer, I save it for my memoirs. Did you say anything deep, in your opinion? If you did, it escaped me, escaped my notice completely. Oh, you've known Swanees. Excuse me: Swamis. You've been exposed to the – the intellectual scene and it's rubbed off on you a little, but only skin-deep, as deep as your little blond beard....

CHRIS: Perhaps I used the wrong word.

[*She places a cigarette in her mouth and waits for him to light it. He turns deliberately away from her and places a foot on the low balustrade, facing seaward.*]

– This 'wine-dark sea', it's the oldest sea in the world....

MRS GOFORTH: What deep remark was that?

CHRIS: Only the sea down there has said anything deep: *boom!* – that's deep. Looking down there, do you know what I see?

MRS GOFORTH: The sea.

CHRIS: Yes, and a fleet of Roman triremes, those galleys with three banks of oars, rowed by slaves, commanded by commanders headed for conquests. Out for loot. *Boom!* Out for conquering, pillaging and collecting more slaves. *Boom!* Here's where the whole show started, it's the oldest sea in the Western world, Mrs Goforth, this sea called the Mediterranean Sea, which means the middle of earth, was the cradle of life, not the grave but the cradle of pagan and

Christian – civilizations, this sea, and its connecting river, that old water-snake, the Nile.

MRS GOFORTH: I've been on the Nile. No message. Couple of winters ago I stayed at the Mena House, that hotel under the pyramids. I could see the pyramids, those big – big calcified fools-caps from my breakfast balcony. No message. Rode up to 'em on a camel so I could say I'd done the whole bit.

CHRIS: No message?

MRS GOFORTH: No message except you can get seasick on a camel, yep, you can get mighty seasick on the hump of a camel. Went inside those old king-size tombstones.

CHRIS: No message inside them, either?

MRS GOFORTH: No message except the Pharaohs and families had the idiotic idea they were going to wake up hungry and thirsty and had provided themselves with breakfasts which had gone very stale and dry and the Pharaohs and families were still sound asleep, ho ho. . . .

[*He still had his back to her: she is obviously annoyed by his lost attention to her.*]

And if you look this way you'll notice I've got a cigarette in my mouth and I'm waiting for you to light it. Didn't that old Sally Ferguson bitch teach you to light a cigarette for a lady?

CHRIS [*facing her*]: She wasn't a bitch unless all old dying ladies are bitches. She was dying, and scared to death of dying, which made her a little – eccentric. . . .

[*He has picked up* MRS GOFORTH'S *diamond-studded lighter. He lights her cigarette but doesn't return the lighter to the table: tosses it in the palm of his hand.*]

MRS GOFORTH: Thanks. Now put it down.

[*He sits down, smiling, on the low balustrade: there has been a marked change in his surface attitude toward her: the deferential air has gone completely.*]

I meant my Bulgari lighter, not your – *backside!*

[*He studies the lighter as if to calculate its value. Pause.*]

– If you don't put that lighter back down on the table I'm going to call for Rudy! You know Rudy, you've made his acquaintance, I think.

CHRIS: If I don't put it down on the table but in my pocket

and if I ran down the goat-path with it – how fast can Rudy run?

MRS GOFORTH: How fast can *you* run? Could you out-run the dogs. Yesterday you didn't out-run the dogs.

CHRIS: That was – up-hill, on the other side of your mountain. I think I could get down this side, yes, by the – funicular, I could operate it.

MRS GOFORTH: Can you out-run a bullet?

CHRIS: Oh, would you have Rudy shoot at me for this lighter?

MRS GOFORTH: You bet I would. That's a very valuable lighter.

[CHRIS *laughs and tosses the lighter on the table.*]

CHRIS: – Hmmm. – On a parapet over the Western world's oldest sea, the lady that owns it had a gangster –

MRS GOFORTH: The bodyguard of a syndicate gangster!

CHRIS: Yes, the lady that owns it had her bodyguard shoot down a – what? – burnt-out poet who had confiscated a diamond-studded lighter because he was unfed and hungry, he'd been on a five-day fast for – non-secular reasons and it had upset his reason.

[MRS GOFORTH *rings the bell on the table.*

CHRIS *seizes her hand and wrests the bell away from it.*

She rises from the table and shouts: 'RUDY!']

CHRIS [louder]: *RUDY!*

MRS GOFORTH: You couldn't get away with it!

CHRIS: Oh, yes, I could: if I wanted. [*He tosses the lighter back on the table with a mocking grin.*]

MRS GOFORTH: What a peculiar – puzzlesome young man you are! You came out here like a dandy, kissed my hand, and now you're coming on like a young hood all of a sudden, and I don't like the change, it makes me nervous with you, and now I don't know if I want you around here or not, or if I'm – not superstitious. See? You've made me shaky.

CHRIS: You didn't know I was teasing?

MRS GOFORTH: No. You're too good at it.

CHRIS [*turning seaward again*]: I see it, your oubliette on the beach, it looks attractive to me.

MRS GOFORTH: – Help me into my bedroom. [*Tries to rise: falls back into the chair.*] – It's time for my siesta.

CHRIS: Could I stay there, a while?

MRS GOFORTH: Later maybe: now now: I need to rest.

CHRIS: I meant the grass hut on the beach, not your bedroom.

MRS GOFORTH: Be still, she's coming back out, my secretary, and I'm not sure I trust her.

CHRIS: Do you trust anybody?

MRS GOFORTH: Nobody human, just dogs. All except poodles, I never trusted a poodle. . . .

    [BLACKIE *comes on to the terrace.*]

In again, out again, Finnegan! What's it *this* time, Blackie?

BLACKIE: Is it true you've discharged the kitchen staff, Mrs Goforth?

MRS GOFORTH: Yes, it's true. . . . Haven't you heard about the inventory?

BLACKIE: What inventory, inventory of what?

MRS GOFORTH: I had an intuition that things were disappearing and had Rudy check my list of fabulous china, my Sèvres, Limoges, Lowenstoff, against what was still on the mountain. Half of it gone, decimated! And my Medici silver, banquet silver used by the Medicis hundreds of years ago, GONE! – That's what the inventory disclosed!

BLACKIE: Mrs Goforth, is it possible you don't remember –

MRS GOFORTH: WHAT?

BLACKIE: You had it removed to a storage house in Naples, in an armoured truck.

MRS GOFORTH: ME?

BLACKIE: YOU!

MRS GOFORTH: NOT TRUE!

BLACKIE: Mrs Goforth, when people are very ill and taking drugs for it, they get confused, their memories are confused, they get delusions.

MRS GOFORTH: THIS MOUNTAIN HAS BEEN SYSTEMATI-CALLY PILLAGED! – That's what the inventory –

BLACKIE: An inventory made by the bodyguard of a syndicate gangster?

MRS GOFORTH: *How dare you suggest – I have a guest at the table!*

BLACKIE: *I will always dare to say what I know to be true!*

MRS GOFORTH: *Go in, find my cheque-book and write out a cheque for yourself for whatever's coming to you, and bring it out here and I'll sign it for cash, at the Naples branch of my bank! You wanted out, now you got it, so TAKE IT! TAKE IT!*

BLACKIE: *Gladly! Gladly!*

MRS GOFORTH: Mutually *gladly! GO IN!*

[BLACKIE *starts off:* MRS GOFORTH'S *shouting has brought on a coughing spasm. She covers her mouth with her hands and rushes, in a crouched position, toward the upstage area of the library.*]

CHRIS: – *Boom* . . .

BLACKIE: *Release!*

CHRIS: Blackie? Look! – [*Points at the terrace pavement.*] – Blood, she's bleeding. . . .

MRS GOFORTH'S VOICE [*offstage, hoarsely*]: DOTTORE, CHIAME LO DOTTORE! GIULIO, SIMON-ETTA!

CHRIS: You'd better go in there with her.

BLACKIE: I can't yet. They'll get the doctor for her. [*She moves downstage, gasping.*] You see, she's made me *inhuman!*

[GIULIO *and* SIMONETTA *explode on to the forestage.*]

SIMONETTA: *Signorina, la Signora e molto, molto malatta!*

BLACKIE [*crossing to her*]: *Dov'é la Signora, in camera da letto?*

SIMONETTA: *No, nella libreria, con il dottore!* [*She sits on a bench and sobs hysterically.*]

BLACKIE: Well, I'd better go in there.

CHRIS: What shall I do? Anything?

BLACKIE: Yes, stay here, don't go.

[*Then to* SIMONETTA *who is now crying theatrically.*]
Ferma questa – commedia.

[SIMONETTA *stops and begins straightening up the table. To* CHRIS] Call the hospital in Rome, Salvatore Mundi, and ask for Dr Rengucci. Tell him what's happening here and a nurse is needed at once. Then come in there, the library, and we'll –

[GIULIO *rushes out.*]

GIULIO: *Signora Goforth vuol vedere il Signore, presto, molto presto!*

BLACKIE: She's calling for *you*. – I'd better go in first. Make the call and then come to the library.

[*She exits one way:* CHRIS *the other.*]

GIULIO [*To* SIMONETTA]: She's dying?

SIMONETTA: No one's paid this week, who will pay us if she dies today?

GIULIO: *Guarda!* [*He displays a gold bracelet.*]

[SIMONETTA *snatches at it.* GIULIO *pockets it with a grin and starts off as she follows.*]

SCENE DIMS OUT

SCENE SIX

A while later, toward sundown. The interiors of the white villa are screened and the terrace is lighted more coolly.

BLACKIE is seated at the downstage table, jotting memoranda in a notebook, of things to be done before leaving.

The STAGE ASSISTANTS stand by the flag-staff ready to lower the banner of MRS GOFORTH.

ONE: Cable her daughter that the old bitch is dying.

TWO: The banner of the Griffin is about to be lowered.

BLACKIE [*as if translating their speech into a polite paraphrase*]: Cable Mrs Goforth's daughter at Point Goforth, Long Island, that her mother is not expected to survive the night: and I'm waiting for – immediate – instructions.

ONE: Fireworks tonight at Point Goforth, Long Island.

TWO: A champagne fountain.

TOGETHER: Death: Celebration.

BLACKIE: Call police in Amalfi to guard the library safe till Rudy has gone.

ONE: Rudy's root-a-toot-tooting through that safe right now.

TWO: He's disappointed to discover that the old bitch still has on her most important jewels.

ONE: And she's still conscious; fiercely.

BLACKIE: Contact mortuary. Amalfi.

TWO: That Blackie's a cool one.

[*CHRIS comes on to the terrace, now wearing his repaired lederhosen and a washed but unironed white shirt.*]

CHRIS: Blackie?

BLACKIE [*glancing up*]: Oh. I'm making out a list of things to do before leaving.

CHRIS: You're not leaving right away, are you?

BLACKIE: Soon as I get instructions from her daughter.

CHRIS: I called the Rome doctor and told him what had happened. He said he's expected it sooner and there's nothing more to be done that can't be done by the doctor on the place.

BLACKIE: The little doctor, Lullo, has given her a strong shot of adrenalin which was a mistake, I think. She won't go to bed, keeps pressing electric buzzers for Simonetta who's run away, and she's put on all her rings so they won't be stolen: she's more afraid of being robbed of her jewellery than her life. What time would it be in the States?

CHRIS: What time is it here?

BLACKIE: Sundown, nearly.

CHRIS: About seven-thirty here would make it – about two-thirty there.

BLACKIE: Maybe a phone-call would get through before a cable.

> [*Rises; one of the* STAGE ASSISTANTS *brings a phone from the table by the chaise-longue, a little upstage.*
> *Taking the phone.*]

Try her daughter's husband at *Goforth, Faller and Rush, In-corporated*, Plaza 1-9000, while I – [*She gives* CHRIS *the phone and pours herself a brandy.*]

> [RUDY *comes out with a stong box from the safe.*]

BLACKIE: Who's that? Oh! YOU! What are you taking out?

RUDY: Just what I was told to take out.

BLACKIE: Well, take it out, but don't forget that everything's been listed.

RUDY: I don't forget nothing, Blackie. [*Goes off.*]

STAGE ASSISTANT ONE [*removing the crested screen*]: Her bed-room in the white villa.

TWO: The griffin is staring at death, and trying to out-stare it.

> [*We see* MRS GOFORTH *seated: she wears a majestic ermine-trimmed robe to which she has pinned her 'most important jewels', and rings blaze on her fingers that clench the chair-arms.*]

ONE: Her eyes are bright as her diamonds.

TWO: Until she starts bleeding again, she'll give no ground to any real or suspected adversary. . . .

ONE: And *then?*

> [*During this exchange between the* ASSISTANTS, *who back into the wings, now, on their soundless shoes,* BLACKIE *has made*

several other notations: now, without looking up at CHRIS, *she asks him –*]

BLACKIE: You're still very hungry, aren't you?

CHRIS: Yes, very.

BLACKIE: The new kitchen staff has arrived. I've put a bottle of milk in your rucksack and your rucksack is in the library. You'd better just have the milk now: we'll have dinner later together.

CHRIS: Blackie, I've seen her grass hut on the beach, her oubliette, as she calls it. And –

BLACKIE: (?)

CHRIS: I wonder how long I could stay down there before I'd be discovered and – evicted?

BLACKIE: Long as you want to, indefinitely, I guess, but how would you live down there with the villas all closed?

CHRIS: On, on – *frutta de mare:* shell-fish. – And I'd make a spear for spear-fishing.

BLACKIE: There's no fresh water down there, just the sea water.

CHRIS: I know how to make fresh water out of sea-water.

BLACKIE: Why would you want to stay down there?

CHRIS [*as a wave crashes under the mountain*]: BOOM! I'd like to make a mobile; I'd call it BOOM. The sea and the sky are turning the same colour, dissolving into each other. Wine-dark sea and wine-dark sky. In a little while the little fishing boats with their lamps for night fishing will make the sea look like the night sky turned upside down, and you and I will have a sort of valedictory dinner on the terrace.

BLACKIE: Yes, it sounds very peaceful. . . .

[*The bedroom of the white villa is brightened:* MRS GOFORTH *staggers from her chair, knocking it over. The* STAGE AS-SISTANTS *dart out to snatch the small chair up and move it further upstage, as she leans on a bed-post, gasping. Then she draws herself up: advances to the chair's new position a little further upstage. She reaches out for it. The* ASSISTANTS *draw it further upstage. She staggers dizzily after it. The* ASSISTANTS *exchange inquiring looks at each other: silently agree to allow her the chair: back out of the area. She sits down with a cry of fury and resumes her fierce contest with death: a*

*reserve of power, triggered by the adrenalin, begins to re-animate
her: she rises and drags the chair to a small boudoir table and
calls out –.]*

MRS GOFORTH: CHRIS? CHRIS?

BLACKIE: That's her, she's calling for you. – Can you stand to
go in there?

CHRIS: Sure I can – It's a professional duty.

[*As he turns upstage the* STAGE ASSISTANTS *remove the screen
masking the library: he enters that area: one of the* STAGE
ASSISTANTS *turns the screen perpendicular to the proscenium
so that it represents a wall-division between bedroom and library.*]

BOOM!

Mrs Goforth?

MRS GOFORTH: Oh, you've finally got here. Stay out there,
don't come in here right away. The doctor gave me a shot
that's made me a little dizzy, I'll call you in – in a minute....
[*She staggers up from the chair, knocking it over.*]

CHRIS: – Are you all right, Mrs Goforth? [*He discovers his sack:
removes and opens the milk bottle.*]

MRS GOFORTH: Just a little unsteady after the shot, the
doctor said. The bleeding was from a little blood-vessel at
the back of my throat. But he thinks I ought to lay off the
work for a while, just wind up this volume and save the
rest for – sequels....

[CHRIS *opens the milk bottle and sips the milk as if it were
sacramental wine.*]

– Don't you think that's better, since it's such a strain on me?

CHRIS: Yes, I do, I think it's a – [*Drinks milk.*] – a wise
decision.... [*He catches some drops of milk that have run down
his chin: licks them almost reverently off the palm of his hand.*]

[MRS GOFORTH *enters the library.*]

MRS GOFORTH: All that work, the pressure, was burning me
up, it was literally burning me up like a house on fire.

[*He assists her to the desk chair.*]

CHRIS: Yes, we – all live in house on fire, no fire-department
to call; no way out, just the upstairs windows to look out of
while the fire burns the house down with us trapped,
locked in it.

MRS GOFORTH: What do you mean by – what windows?

CHRIS [*touching his forehead*]: These upstairs windows, not wide enough to crawl out of, just wide enough to lean out of and look out of, and – look and look and look, till we're almost nothing but looking, nothing, almost, but *vision*. . . .

MRS GOFORTH: Hmmm. – Yes. – It isn't as cool out here as it was in my bedroom and this robe I've put on is too heavy. So come on in. We can talk in my bedroom. [*She retires behind bedroom screen.*]

MRS GOFORTH'S VOICE [*from behind her screen*]: Talking between rooms is a strain on the ears and the vocal cords – so come in, now: I'm ready.

[*He crosses to the screens: stops short.*]

CHRIS: Oh. Sorry. [*He turns away from the screens.*] I'll wait till you've –

MRS GOFORTH'S VOICE: Modesty? *Modesty?* I wouldn't expect you to suffer from modesty, Chris. I never was bothered with silliness of that kind. If you've got a figure that's pleasing to look at, why be selfish with it?

CHRIS: Yes, it *was* a pleasure, Mrs Goforth.

MRS GOFORTH'S VOICE: Then why'd you retreat, back away? In my bedroom, in here, I almost never, if ever, wear a stitch of clothes, in summer. I like to feel cool air on my bare skin in summer. Don't you like that? Cool air and cool water on the bare skin in summer's the nicest thing about summer. Huh? Don't you think so, too?

CHRIS: I've found my duffle-bag. It wandered in here, for some reason.

MRS GOFORTH'S VOICE: I had it brought there so I could get your passport for the local police. They want a look at the passport of anyone just arrived.

CHRIS: I see.

MRS GOFORTH'S VOICE: You'll get it back when you go, you know, there's no hurry, is there?

CHRIS: I'm not sure about that. [*Finds passport.*] Anyway, it's already been returned.

MRS GOFORTH: We've just been getting acquainted. The preliminaries of a friendship, or any kind of relationship, are the most difficult part, and our talk on the terrace was just a – *preliminary*.

CHRIS [*wryly, beneath her hearing*]: Sometimes the preliminaries are rougher than the main bout. [*He is rearranging the articles in the rucksack.*]

MRS GOFORTH: I didn't catch that. What was that?

CHRIS [*to himself*]: I didn't mean you to catch it.

MRS GOFORTH: Stop mumbling and fussing with that metal stuff in the sack, the fussing drowns out the mumbling. D'ya want me to break another blood vessel in my throat talking to you from here?

CHRIS: Are you dressed now, Mrs Goforth?

MRS GOFORTH: Hell, I told you I'm never dressed in my bedroom.

CHRIS: You said 'rarely if ever' – not never. [*He sighs and crosses to the door again.*] – You have a beautiful body, Mrs Goforth. It's a privilege to be permitted to admire it. It makes me think of one of those great fountain figures in Scandinavian countries.

MRS GOFORTH: Yeah, well, baby, a fountain figure is a stone figure, and my body isn't a stone figure, although it's been sculpted by several world-famous sculptors, it's still a flesh and blood figure. And don't think it's been easy to keep it the way it still is. I'm going to lie down and rest now on this cool bed, mmm, these sheets are so cool, come on in. Why are you standing there paralysed in that door?

CHRIS: I'm – silent on a peak in – *Darien*. . . . [*Turns away from the door.*] I came here hoping to be your friend, Mrs Goforth, but –

MRS GOFORTH'S VOICE: You said 'but' something, but what?

CHRIS: I wouldn't have come here unless I thought I was able to serve some purpose or other, in return for a temporary refuge, a place to rest and work in, where I could get back that sense of reality I've been losing lately, as I tried to explain on the terrace, but – [*He has removed the large mobile under her desk: he climbs on the desk to attach the mobile to the chandelier above it.*] – You knew I was hungry but it was 'black coffee or else'.

MRS GOFORTH: Is that why you won't come in here?

CHRIS: It would just be embarrassing for us both if I did. [*He jumps off the desk.*]

MRS GOFORTH: *What's that, what're you doing?*

CHRIS: I hung up a gift I brought you, a mobile called 'The Earth is a Wheel in a Great Big Gambling Casino'. And now I think I should leave, I have a long way to go.

MRS GOFORTH: Just a minute. I'm coming back out there to see this mobile of yours. [*She comes from behind the screen, pulling the regal white robe about her.*] Well, where is it?

CHRIS: Right over your head.

[*She looks up, staggering against the desk.*]

MRS GOFORTH: It doesn't move, doesn't go.

CHRIS: It will, when it's caught by the wind.

[*The mobile begins to turn, casting faint flickers of light.*]
There now, the wind's caught it, it's turning. [*He picks up his canvas sack as if preparing to leave.*]

MRS GOFORTH [*picking up the phone, suddenly*]: Kitchen, cucina, cucina! – Cucina? Uno momento! [*She thrusts phone toward* CHRIS.] Tell the cook what you would like for supper.

CHRIS: Anything, Mrs Goforth.

MRS GOFORTH [*into the phone*]: O K – Cucina? Senta – Pranza questa sera. – Pastini in brodo, per commencare. Capish? – SI! – Poi, una grade pesca, si si, una grandissima pescha, anche – carne freddo, si, si, carne freddo – *ROAST BEEF, BIF, BEEEEEEF!* [*Gasps, catches her breath.*] Prosciutto, Legume, tutte, tutte legume. Capito? Poi, ua insalata verde. No, mista! Insalata mista, MISTA! – they don't know their own language.... – Poi, dulce, zuppe Inglesa, frutta, fromaggio, tutte fromagio, e vino, vino, bianco e rosa, una bottiglia de Soave e una bottiglia de – [*Gasps for breath again.*] – Valpolicella. – Hanh? – va bene. ... [*Hangs up.*] This new cook sounds like a – Mau-mau.... She'll probably serve us long pig with – shrunk heads on toothpicks stuck in it.... [*Tries to laugh: coughs. Hanging up phone.*] Now, then, you see you're not just going to be fed, you're going to be wined and dined in high style tonight on the terrace. But meanwhile, we're going to enjoy a long siesta together in the cool of my bedroom which is full of historical treasures, including myself! [*She crosses to the bedroom doors, beckons him commandingly.*]

[*He doesn't move.*]

– *Well?!*

CHRIS: I'm afraid I came here too late to accept these – invitations.

MRS GOFORTH: Who else has invited you somewhere?

CHRIS: I've passed the point where I wait for invitations but I think I'll be welcomed by the elderly spinster lady whose mother died in Taormina today.

MRS GOFORTH: Not if she's heard your nickname. And Sicily's an island. How'll you get there, can you walk on water?

CHRIS: Your discharged secretary gave me a bottle of milk with some ten thousand lire notes attached to it with a – rubber band. So – goodbye, Mrs Goforth. [*He bends to hoist his rucksack over his shoulder.*]

MRS GOFORTH: Mr Flanders, you have the distinction, the dubious distinction, of being the first man that wouldn't come in my bedroom when invited to enter.

CHRIS: I'm sorry.

MRS GOFORTH: Man bring this up road, huh?

CHRIS: No, I –

MRS GOFORTH: What else? Your book of poems, your calling card? Y'must be running short of 'em, here, take it back! [*She hurls it off her desk to his feet.*] I haven't read it but I can imagine the contents. *Facile sentiment!* TO BE good a poem's got to be tough and to write a good, tough poem you've got to cut your teeth on the marrow-bone of this world: I think you're still cutting your milk teeth, Mr Flanders.

CHRIS: I know you better than you know me. I admire you: admire you so much that I almost like you: *almost*. I think if that old Greek explorer, Pytheas, hadn't beat you to it by centuries, you would've sailed up through the Gates of Hercules to map out the Western world, and you would have sailed up further and mapped it out better than he did, no storm could've driven you back or changed your course, oh, no, you're nobody's fool, but you're a fool, Mrs Goforth, if you don't know that finally, sooner or later, you need somebody or something to mean God to you, even if it's a cow on the streets of Bombay, or carved rock on the Easter Islands or –

MRS GOFORTH: You came here to bring me *God*, did you?

CHRIS: I didn't say God, I said someone or something to –

MRS GOFORTH: I heard what you said, you said *God*, my eyes are out of focus but not my ears! Well, *bring* him, I'm ready to lay out a red carpet for him, but how do you bring Him? Whistle? Ring a bell for him? [*She snatches a bell off her desk and rings it fiercely.*] HUH? HOW? WHAT? [*She staggers back against the desk, gasping.*]

CHRIS: I've failed, I've disappointed, some people in what they wanted or thought they wanted from me, Mrs Goforth, but sometimes, once in a while, I've given them what they needed even if they didn't know what it was. I brought it up the road to them, and that's how I got the name that's made me unwelcome this summer.

STAGE ASSISTANT: Tell her about the first time!

TOGETHER: Tell her, tell her, the first time!

[*They draw back to the wings.*

The HARMONIUM PLAYER *begins to play softly.*]

CHRIS: – I was at Mrs Ferguson's mountain over Palm Springs, the first time. I wasn't used to her world of elegant bitches and dandies.... Early one morning I went down the mountain and across the desert on a walking trip to a village in Baja, California, where a great Hindu teacher had gathered a group of pupils, disciples, about him. Along the road I passed a rest-home that looked like a grand hotel, and just a little further along, I came to an inlet, an estuary of the ocean, and I stopped for a swim off the beach that was completely deserted, swam out in the cool water till my head felt cool as the water: then turned and swam back in, but the beach wasn't deserted completely any longer. There was a very old gentleman on it. He called 'Help!' to me, as if he was in the water drowning, and I was on shore. I swam in and asked him how I could help him and he said this, he said: 'Help me out there, I can't make it alone, I've gone past pain I can bear.' – I could see it was true. He was elegantly dressed but emaciated, cadaverous. I gave him the help he wanted, I led him out in the water, it wasn't easy. Once he started to panic, I had to hold on to him tight as a lover till he got back his courage and said, All right, the tide took him as light as a leaf. But just before I did that, and this is the oddest thing, he took out his wallet and thrust all the money in it into my hand. Here take this, he said to me. And I –

MRS GOFORTH: Took it, did you, you took it?

CHRIS: The sea had no use for his money. The fish in the sea had no use for it, either, so I took it and went on where I was going.

MRS GOFORTH: How much were you paid for this – service?

CHRIS: It was a very special difficult service: I was well paid for it.

MRS GOFORTH: Did you tell the old Hindu, the Swami, when you got to his place, that you'd killed an old man on the way and –

CHRIS: I told him that I had helped a dying old man to get through it.

MRS GOFORTH: What did he say about that?

CHRIS [*reflectively*]: What did he say: – He said, You've found your vocation: and he smiled. It was a beautiful smile in spite of showing bare gums, and – he held out his hand for the money: the hand was beautiful too in spite of being dry skin pulled tight as a glove over bones.

MRS GOFORTH: Did you give him the money?

CHRIS: Yes, they needed the money: I didn't: I gave it to them.

MRS GOFORTH: I *bet* you did.

CHRIS: I *did*.

MRS GOFORTH: Did he say thank you for it?

CHRIS: I don't know if he did. You see, they – No, I guess you don't see. – They had a belief in believing that too much is said when feeling, quiet feelings – enough. – Says *more*. . . .

And he had a gift for gesture. You couldn't believe how a hand that shrivelled and splotched could make such a beautiful gesture of holding out the hand to be helped from the ground. It made me, so quickly, peaceful. That was important to me, that sudden feeling of quiet, because I'd come there, all the way down there, with the – the spectre of lunacy at my heels all the way. – He said: Stay. – We sat about a fire on the beach that night: Nobody said anything.

MRS GOFORTH: No message, he didn't have any message?

CHRIS: Yes, that night it was silence, it was the meaning of silence.

MRS GOFORTH: Silence? Meaning?

CHRIS: Acceptance.

MRS GOFORTH: What of?

CHRIS: Oh, many things, everything, nearly. Such as how to live and to die in a way that's more dignified than most of us know how to do it. And of how not to be frightened of not knowing what isn't meant to be known, acceptance of not knowing anything but the moment of still existing until we stop existing, and acceptance of that moment, too.

MRS GOFORTH: How do you know he wasn't just an old faker?

CHRIS: How do you know that I am not just a young one?

MRS GOFORTH: I don't. You *are* what they call you!

[*He takes hold of her hand.*]

CHRIS: As much as anyone is what anyone calls him.

MRS GOFORTH: A butcher is called a butcher, and that's what he is. A baker is called a baker, and he's a baker. A –

CHRIS: Whatever they're called, they're *men*, and being men, they're not known by themselves or anyone else.

[*She presses a button that shrills on the stage.*]

MRS GOFORTH: Rudy? Rudy!

CHRIS: Your bodyguard's gone, Mrs Goforth.

[*She goes on pressing the button.*]

He left with the contents of your strong-box, your safe.

MRS GOFORTH: – I've got on me all my important jewels, and if Rudy's gone, I want you to go, too. Go on to your next appointment. You've tired me, you've done me in. This day has been the most awful day of my life. . . .

CHRIS: I know: that's why you need me here a while longer.

[*He places his arm about her.*]

MRS GOFORTH: *Don't, don't* you – *scare* me!

CHRIS: Let me take you into your bedroom, now, and put you to bed, Mrs Goforth.

MRS GOFORTH: *No, no* GO, *let me* GO!!

[*He releases her: picks up his canvas sack.*]

Hey!

[*He pauses with his back to her.*]

– Did somebody tell you I was dying this summer? Yes, isn't that why you came here, because you imagined that I'd be ripe for a soft touch because I'm dying this summer? Come on, for once in your life be honestly frank, be frankly honest with someone! You've been tipped off that old Flora Goforth is about to go forth this summer.

CHRIS: – Yes, that's why I came here.

MRS GOFORTH: – Well, I've escorted four husbands to the eternal threshold and come back alone without them, just with the loot of *three* of them, and, ah, God, it was like I was building a shell of bone round my heart with their goddam loot, their loot the material for it. – It's my turn, now, to go forth, and I've got no choice but to do it. But I'll do it alone. I don't want to be escorted, I want to go forth alone. But you, you counted on touching my heart because you'd heard I was dying, and old dying people are your speciality, your vocation. But you miscalculated with this one. This milk train doesn't stop here anymore. I'll give you some practical advice. Go back to Naples. Walk along Santa Lucia, the bay-front. Yesterday, there, they smelt the smell of no money, and treated you like a used, discarded used person. It'll be different this time. You'll probably run into some Americans at a sidewalk table along there, a party that's in for some shopping from the islands. If you're lucky, they'll ask you to sit down with them and say, 'Won't you have something, Chris?' – Well, *have* something, Chris! and if you play your cards right, they might invite you to go back to an island with them. Your best bet is strangers, I guess. Don't work on the young ones or anybody attractive. They're not ripe to be taken, and not the old ones, either, they been taken too often. Work on the middleage drunks, that's who to work on, Chris, work on them, sometimes the old milk train still comes to a temporary stop at their crazy station, so concentrate on the middleage drunks in Naples.

CHRIS: This isn't the time for such – practical advice. ...

[*She makes a gasping sound and presses a tissue to her mouth, turning upstage.*]

MRS GOFORTH [*turning front*]: – A paper rose ... [*The tissue is dyed red with blood.*] – Before you go, help me into my bedroom, I can't make it alone. ...

[*He conducts her to the screen between the two rooms as the* STAGE ASSISTANTS *advance from the wings to remove it.*]

– It's full of historical treasures. The chandelier, if the dealer that sold it to me wasn't a liar, used to hang in Versailles, and the bed, if he wasn't lying, was the bed of Countess Walewska, Napoleon's Polish mistress, it's a famous old bed, for a famous old body. ...

[*The* STAGE ASSISTANTS *remove the screen masking the bed.*]

CHRIS: Yes, it looks like the catafalque of an empress. [*He lifts her on to the bed, and draws a cover over her.*]

MRS GOFORTH: *Don't leave me alone till –*

CHRIS: I never leave till the end.

[*She stretches out her blind, jewelled hand, He takes it.*]

MRS GOFORTH: – *Not so tight, the –*

CHRIS: I know, the rings cut your fingers.

[*He draws a ring off a finger. She gasps. He draws off another. She gasps again.*]

MRS GOFORTH: Be here, when I wake up.

[*Then the* STAGE ASSISTANTS *place before her the bed screen with the gold-winged griffin cresting its middle panel. Light dims out on that area and is brought up on the turning mobile.*
Music seems to come from the turning mobile that casts very delicate gleams of light on the stage.

   BLACKIE *appears on the forestage as the* STAGE AS-SISTANTS *bring out a dinner-table and rapidly set two places. Then they cross to the flag-staff by the right wings and begin to slowly lower the flag.*]

ONE: Flag-lowering ceremony on the late Mrs Goforth's mountain.

TWO: Bugle?

[*A muted bugle is heard, as if from a distance.*]

– That's not Taps, that's Reveille.

ONE: It's Reveille always, Taps never, for the gold griffin.

TWO [*Snapping his fingers*]: Let's go.

> [*Exeunt with folded banner.*

>> CHRIS *comes from behind the bedroom screen, on to the terrace where* BLACKIE *sits coolly waiting.*

>> *The* STAGE ASSISTANTS *reappear in mess-jackets bearing a small table set for supper on the terrace: they place it before* BLACKIE: *she rises and pours wine into a medieval goblet as she speaks to* CHRIS.]

BLACKIE: – Is it – is she – ?

> [CHRIS *nods as he moves out on to the forestage.*]

BLACKIE: Was it what they call 'peaceful'?

> [CHRIS *nods again.*]

With all that fierce life in her?

CHRIS: You always wonder afterwards where it's gone, so far, so quickly. You feel it must be still around somewhere, in the air. But there's no sign of it.

BLACKIE: Did she say anything to you before she – ?

CHRIS: She said to me: 'Be here when I wake up.' – After I'd taken her hand and stripped the rings off her fingers.

BLACKIE: What did you do with – ?

CHRIS [*giving her a quick look that might suggest an understandable shrewdness*]: – Under her pillow like a pharaoh's breakfast waiting for the pharaoh to wake up hungry. . . .

> [*She comes up beside him on the forestage and offers him the wine-goblet. The sea is heard under the mountain.*]

BLACKIE: The sea is saying the name of your next mobile.

CHRIS: BOOM!

BLACKIE: What does it mean?

CHRIS: It says 'Boom' and that's what it means: no translation, no explanation, just 'BOOM'.

> [*He drinks from the goblet and passes it back to her as* –]

THE CURTAIN FALLS SLOWLY

THE END

The Night of the Iguana

The Night of the Iguana was presented at the Royale Theater in New York on 28 December 1961 by Charles Bowden, in association with Violla Rubber. It was directed by Frank Corsaro; the stage setting was designed by Oliver Smith; lighting by Jean Rosenthal; costumes by Noel Taylor; audio effects by Edward Beyer. The cast, in order of appearance, was as follows:

MAXINE FAULK	*Bette Davis*
PEDRO	*James Farentino*
PANCHO	*Christopher Jones*
REVEREND SHANNON	*Patrick O'Neal*
HANK	*Theseus George*
HERR FAHRENKOPF	*Heinz Hohenwald*
FRAU FAHRENKOPF	*Lucy Landau*
WOLFGANG	*Bruce Glover*
HILDA	*Laryssa Lauret*
JUDITH FELLOWES	*Patricia Roe*
HANNAH JELKES	*Margaret Leighton*
CHARLOTTE GOODALL	*Lane Bradbury*
JONATHAN COFFIN (NONNO)	*Alan Webb*
JAKE LATTA	*Louis Guss*

Production owned and presented by 'The Night of the Iguana' Joint Venture (the joint venture consisting of Charles Bowden and Two Rivers Enterprises, Inc.)

The play takes place in the summer of 1940 in a rather rustic and very Bohemian hotel, the Costa Verde, which, as its name implies, sits on a jungle-covered hilltop overlooking the 'caleta', or 'morning beach' of Puerto Barrio in Mexico. But this is decidedly not the Puerto Barrio of today. At that time – twenty years ago – the west coast of Mexico had not yet become the Las Vegas and Miami Beach of Mexico. The villages were still predominantly primitive Indian villages, and the still-water morning beach of Puerto Barrio and the rain forests above it were among the world's wildest and loveliest populated places.

The setting for the play is the wide verandah of the hotel. This roofed verandah, enclosed by a railing, runs around all four sides of the somewhat dilapidated, tropical-style frame structure, but on the stage we see only the front and one side. Below the verandah, which is slightly raised above the stage level, are shrubs with vivid trumpet-shaped flowers and a few cactus plants, while at the sides we see the foliage of the encroaching jungle. A tall coconut palm slants upward at one side, its trunk notched for a climber to chop down coconuts for rum-cocos. In the back wall of the verandah are the doors of a line of small cubicle bedrooms which are screened with mosquito-net curtains. For the night scenes they are lighted from within, so that each cubicle appears as a little interior stage, the curtains giving a misty effect to their dim inside lighting. A path which goes down through the rain forest to the highway and the beach, its opening masked by foliage, leads off from one side of the verandah. A canvas hammock is strung from posts on the verandah and there are a few old wicker rockers and rattan lounging chairs at one side.

ACT ONE

As the curtain rises, there are sounds of a party of excited female tourists arriving by bus on the road down the hill below the Costa Verde Hotel. MRS MAXINE FAULK, *the proprietor of the hotel, comes round the turn of the verandah. She is a stout, swarthy woman in her middle forties – affable and rapaciously lusty. She is wearing a pair of levis and a blouse that is half unbuttoned. She is followed by* PEDRO, *a Mexican of about twenty – slim and attractive. He is an employee in the hotel and also her casual lover.* PEDRO *is stuffing his shirt under the belt of his pants and sweating as if he had been working hard in the sun.* MRS FAULK *looks down the hill and is pleased by the sight of someone coming up from the tourist bus below.*

MAXINE [*calling out*]: Shannon! [*A man's voice from below answers:* 'Hi!'] Hah! [MAXINE *always laughs with a single harsh, loud bark, opening her mouth like a seal expecting a fish to be thrown to it.*] My spies told me that you were back under the border! [*to* PEDRO] Anda, hombre, anda!
　　[MAXINE'S *delight expands and vibrates in her as* SHANNON *labours up the hill to the hotel. He does not appear on the jungle path for a minute or two after the shouting between them starts.*]
MAXINE: Hah! My spies told me you went through Saltillo last week with a busload of women – a whole busload of females, all females, hah! How many you laid so far? Hah!
SHANNON [*from below, panting*]: Great Caesar's ghost ... stop ... shouting!
MAXINE: No wonder your ass is draggin', hah!
SHANNON: Tell the kid to help me up with this bag.
MAXINE [*shouting directions*]: Pedro! Anda – la maléta. Pancho, no seas flojo! Va y trae el equipaje del señor.
　　[PANCHO, *another young Mexican, comes around the verandah and trots down the jungle path.* PEDRO *has climbed up a coconut tree with a machete and is chopping down nuts for rum-cocos.*]
SHANNON [*shouting, below*]: Fred? Hey, Fred!

MAXINE [*with a momentary gravity*]: Fred can't hear you, Shannon. [*She goes over and picks up a coconut, shaking it against her ear to see if it has milk in it.*]

SHANNON [*still below*]: Where is Fred – gone fishing?

> [MAXINE *lops the end off a coconut with a machete, as* PANCHO *trots up to the verandah with Shannon's bag – a beat-up Gladstone covered with travel stickers from all over the world. Then* SHANNON *appears, in a crumpled white linen suit. He is panting, sweating, and wild-eyed. About thirty-five,* SHANNON *is 'black Irish'. His nervous state is terribly apparent; he is a young man who has cracked up before and is going to crack up again – perhaps repeatedly.*]

MAXINE: Well! Lemme look at you!

SHANNON: Don't look at me; get dressed!

MAXINE: Gee, you look like you had it!

SHANNON: You look like you been having it, too. Get dressed!

MAXINE: Hell, I'm dressed. I never dress in September. Don't you know I never dress in September?

SHANNON: Well, just, just – button your shirt up.

MAXINE: How long you been off it, Shannon?

SHANNON: Off what?

MAXINE: The wagon ...

SHANNON: Hell, I'm dizzy with fever. Hundred and three this morning in Cuernavaca.

MAXINE: Whatcha got wrong with you?

SHANNON: Fever ... fever ... Where's Fred?

MAXINE: Dead.

SHANNON: Did you say *dead*?

MAXINE: That's what I said. Fred is dead.

SHANNON: How?

MAXINE: Less'n two weeks ago, Fred cut his hand on a fish-hook, it got infected, infection got in his blood stream, and he was dead inside of forty-eight hours. [*To Pancho*] Vete!

SHANNON: Holy smoke....

MAXINE: I can't quite realize it yet....

SHANNON: You don't seem – inconsolable about it.

MAXINE: Fred was an old man, baby. Ten years older'n me. We hadn't had sex together in ...

SHANNON: What's that got to do with it?

MAXINE: Lie down and have a rum-coco.

SHANNON: No, no. I want a cold beer. If I start drinking rum-cocos now I won't stop drinking rum-cocos. So Fred is dead? I looked forward to lying in this hammock and talking to Fred.

MAXINE: Well, Fred's not talking now, Shannon. A diabetic gets a blood infection, he goes like that without a decent hospital in less'n a week. [*A bus horn is heard blowing from below.*] Why don't your busload of women come on up here? They're blowing the bus horn down there.

SHANNON: Let 'em blow it, blow it. . . . [*He sways a little.*] I got a fever. [*He goes to the top of the path, divides the flowering bushes and shouts down the hill to the bus.*] Hank! Hank! Get them out of the bus and bring 'em up here! Tell 'em the rates are O.K. Tell 'em the. . . . [*His voice gives out, and he stumbles back to the verandah, where he sinks down on to the low steps, panting.*] Absolutely the worst party I've ever been out with in ten years of conducting tours. For God's sake, help me with 'em because I can't go on. I got to rest here a while. [*She gives him a cold beer.*] Thanks. Look and see if they're getting out of the bus. [*She crosses to the masking foliage and separates it to look down the hill.*] Are they getting out of the bus or are they staying in it, the stingy – daughters of – bitches. . . . Schoolteachers at a Baptist Female College in Blowing Rock, Texas. Eleven, eleven of them.

MAXINE: A football squad of old maids. . . .

SHANNON: Yea, and I'm the football. Are they out of the bus?

MAXINE: One's gotten out – she's going into the bushes.

SHANNON: Well, I've got the ignition key to the bus in my pocket – this pocket – so they can't continue without me unless they walk.

MAXINE: They're still blowin' that horn.

SHANNON: Fantastic. I can't lose this party. Blake Tours has put me on probation because I had a bad party last month that tried to get me sacked and I am now on probation with Blake Tours. If I lose this party I'll be sacked for sure . . . Ah, my God, are they still all in the bus? [*He heaves himself off the steps and staggers back to the path, dividing the foliage to look*

down it, then shouts] Hank! Get them out of the busssss!
Bring them up heeee-re!

HANK'S VOICE [*from below*]: They wanta go back in tooooo-
wwwwn.

SHANNON: They *can't* go back in tooowwwwn! – Whew
– Five years ago this summer I was conducting round-the-
world tours for Cook's. Exclusive groups of retired Wall
Street financiers. We travelled in fleets of Pierce Arrows
and Hispano Suizas. – Are they getting out of the bus?

MAXINE: You're going to pieces, are you?

SHANNON: No! Gone! Gone! [*He rises and shouts down the
hill again.*] Hank! come up here! Come on up here a minute!
I wanta talk to you about this situation! – Incredible, fantastic ... [*He drops back on the steps, his head falling into his
hands.*]

MAXINE: They're not getting out of the bus. – Shannon ...
you're not in a nervous condition to cope with this party,
Shannon, so let them go and you stay.

SHANNON: You know my situation: I lose this job, what's
next? There's nothing lower than Blake Tours, Maxine
honey. – Are they getting out of the bus? Are they getting
out of it now?

MAXINE: Man's comin' up the hill.

SHANNON: Aw. Hank. You gotta help me with him.

MAXINE: I'll give him a rum-coco.

[HANK *comes grinning on to the verandah.*]

HANK: Shannon, them ladies are not gonna come up here,
so you better come on back to the bus.

SHANNON: Fantastic. – I'm not going down to the bus and
I've got the ignition key to the bus in my pocket. It's going
to stay in my pocket for the next three days.

HANK: You can't get away with that, Shannon. Hell, they'll
walk back to town if you don't give up the bus key.

SHANNON: They'd drop like flies from sunstrokes on that
road.... Fantastic, absolutely fantastic ... [*Panting and
sweating, he drops a hand on Hank's shoulder.*] Hank, I want
your cooperation. Can I have it? Because when you're
out with a difficult party like this, the tour conductor –
me – and the guide – you – have got to stick together to

control the situations as they come up against us. It's a
test of strength between two men, in this case, and a busload of old wet *hens*. You know that, don't you?

HANK: Well.... [*He chuckles.*] There's this kid that's crying
on the back seat all the time, and that's what's rucked up the
deal. Hell, I don't know if you did or you didn't, but they
all think that you did 'cause the kid keeps crying.

SHANNON: *Hank? Look!* I don't care what they think. A tour
conducted by T. Lawrence Shannon is in his charge, completely – where to go, when to go, every detail of it. Otherwise I resign. So go on back down there and get them out of
that bus before they suffocate in it. Haul them out by force
if necessary and herd them up here. Hear me? Don't give
me any argument about it. Mrs Faulk, honey? Give him a
menu, give him one of your sample menus to show the
ladies. She's got a Chinaman cook here, you won't believe
the menu. The cook's from Shanghai, handled the kitchen
at an exclusive club there. I got him here for her, and he's a
bug, a fanatic about – whew! – continental cuisine ... can
even make beef Strogonoff and thermidor dishes. Mrs Faulk,
honey? Hand him one of those – whew! – one of those fantastic sample menus. [MAXINE *chuckles, as if perpetrating a
practical joke, and she hands him a sheet of paper.*] Thanks. Now,
here. Go on back down there and show them this fantastic
menu. Describe the view from the hill, and ... [HANK
accepts the menu with a chuckling shake of the head.] And have a
cold Carta Blanca and ...

HANK: You better go down with me.

SHANNON: I can't leave this verandah for at least forty-eight
hours. *What in blazes is this?* A little animated cartoon by
Hieronymus Bosch?

[*The German family which is staying at the hotel, the*
FAHRENKOPFS, *their daughter and son-in-law, suddenly
make a startling, dreamlike entrance upon the scene. They troop
around the verandah, then turn down into the jungle path. They
are all dressed in the minimal concession to decency and all are
pink and gold like baroque cupids in various sizes – Rubensesque,
splendidly physical. The bride,* HILDA, *walks astride a big in-
flated rubber horse which has an ecstatic smile and great winking*

*eyes. She shouts 'Horsey, horsey, giddap!' as she waddles
astride it, followed by her Wagnerian-tenor bridegroom,*
WOLFGANG, *and her father,* HERR FAHRENKOPF, *a
tank manufacturer from Frankfurt. He is carrying a portable
shortwave radio, which is tuned in to the crackle and guttural
voices of a German broadcast reporting the Battle of Britain.*
FRAU FAHRENKOPF, *bursting with rich, healthy fat and
carrying a basket of food for a picnic at the beach, brings up the
rear. They begin to sing a Nazi marching song.*]

SHANNON: Aw – Nazis. How come there's so many of them
down here lately?

MAXINE: Mexico's the front door to South America – and
the back door to the States, that's why.

SHANNON: Aw, and you're setting yourself up here as a
receptionist at both doors, now that Fred's dead?
[MAXINE *comes over and sits down on him in the hammock.*]
Get off my pelvis before you crack it. If you want to crack
something, crack some ice for my forehead. [*She removes a
chunk of ice from her glass and massages his forehead with it.*] –
Ah, God. . . .

MAXINE [*chuckling*]: Ha, so you took the young chick and the
old hens are squawking about it, Shannon?

SHANNON: The kid asked for it, no kidding, but she's seventeen – less, a month less'n seventeen. So it's serious, it's very
serious, because the kid is not just emotionally precocious,
she's a musical prodigy, too.

MAXINE: What's that got to do with it?

SHANNON: Here's what it's got to do with it, she's travelling
under the wing, the military escort, of this, this – butch
vocal teacher who organizes little community sings in the
bus. Ah, God! I'm surprised they're not singing now, they
must've already suffocated. Or they'd be singing some
morale-boosting number like 'She's a Jolly Good Fellow' or
'Pop goes the Weasel'. – Oh, God. . . . [MAXINE *chuckles
up and down the scale.*] And each night after supper, after the
complaints about the supper and the check-up on the checks
by the math instructor, and the vomiting of the supper by
several ladies, who have inspected the kitchen – then the
kid, the canary, will give a vocal recital. She opens her

mouth and out flies Carrie Jacobs Bond or Ethelbert Nevin. I mean after a day of one indescribable torment after another, such as three blowouts, and a leaking radiator in Tierra Caliente.... [*He sits up slowly in the hammock as these recollections gather force.*] And an evening climb up sierras, through torrents of rain, around hairpin turns over gorges and chasms measureless to man, and with a thermos-jug under the driver's seat which the Baptist College ladies think is filled with ice-water but which I know is filled with iced tequila – I mean after such a day has finally come to a close, the musical prodigy, Miss Charlotte Goodall, right after supper, before there's a chance to escape, will give a heartbreaking and earsplitting rendition of Carrie Jacobs Bond's 'End of a Perfect Day' – with absolutely no humour....

MAXINE: Hah!

SHANNON: Yeah, 'Hah!' Last night – no, night before last, the bus burned out its brake linings in Chilpancingo. This town has a hotel ... this hotel has a piano, which hasn't been tuned since they shot Maximilian. This Texas songbird opens her mouth and out flies 'I Love You Truly', and it flies straight at *me*, with *gestures*, all right at *me*, till her chaperon, this Diesel-driven vocal instructor of hers, slams the piano lid down and hauls her out of the mess-hall. But as she's hauled out Miss Bird-Girl opens her mouth and out flies, 'Larry, Larry, I love you, I love you truly!' That night, when I went to my room, I found that I had a roommate.

MAXINE: The musical prodigy had moved in with you?

SHANNON: The *spook* had moved in with me. In that hot room with one bed, the width of an ironing board and about as hard, the spook was up there on it, sweating, stinking, grinning up at me.

MAXINE: Aw, the spook. [*She chuckles.*] So you've got the spook with you again.

SHANNON: That's right, he's the only passenger that got off the bus with me, honey.

MAXINE: Is he here now?

SHANNON: Not far.

MAXINE: On the verandah?

SHANNON: He might be on the other side of the verandah. Oh, he's around somewhere, but he's like the Sioux Indians in the Wild West fiction, he doesn't attack before sundown, he's an after-sundown shadow. . . .

[SHANNON *wriggles out of the hammock as the bus horn gives one last, long protesting blast.*]

MAXINE:

> I have a little shadow
> That goes in and out with me,
> And what can be the use of him
> Is more than I can see.
> He's very, very like me,
> From his heels up to his head,
> And he always hops before me
> When I hop into my bed.

SHANNON: That's the truth. He sure hops in the bed with me.

MAXINE: When you're sleeping alone, or . . .?

SHANNON: I haven't slept in three nights.

MAXINE: Aw, you will tonight, baby.

[*The bus horn sounds again.* SHANNON *rises and squints down the hill at the bus.*]

SHANNON: How long's it take to sweat the faculty of a Baptist Female College out of a bus that's parked in the sun when it's hundred degrees in the shade?

MAXINE: They're staggering out of it now.

SHANNON: Yeah, I've won *this* round, I reckon. What're they doing down there. Can you see?

MAXINE: They're crowding around your pal Hank.

SHANNON: Tearing him to pieces?

MAXINE: One of them's slapped him, he's ducked back into the bus, and she is starting up here.

SHANNON: Oh, Great Caesar's ghost, it's the butch vocal teacher.

MISS FELLOWES [*in a strident voice, from below*]: Shannon! Shannon!

SHANNON: For God's sake, help me with her.

MAXINE: You know I'll help you, baby, but why don't you

lay off the young ones and cultivate an interest in normal grown-up women?

MISS FELLOWES [*her voice coming nearer*]: Shannon!

SHANNON [*shouting down the hill*]: Come on up, Miss Fellowes, everything's fixed. [*To Maxine*] Oh, God, here she comes chargin' up the hill like a bull elephant on a rampage!

[MISS FELLOWES *thrashes through the foliage at the top of the jungle path.*]

SHANNON: Miss Fellowes, never do that! Not at high noon in a tropical country in summer. Never charge up a hill like you were leading a troop of cavalry attacking an almost impregnable . . .

MISS FELLOWES [*panting and furious*]: I don't want advice or instructions, I want the *bus* key!

SHANNON: Mrs Faulk, this is Miss Judith Fellowes.

MISS FELLOWES: Is this man making a deal with you?

MAXINE: I don't know what you –

MISS FELLOWES: Is this man getting a *kick-back* out of you?

MAXINE: Nobody gets any kick-back out of me. I turn away more people than –

MISS FELLOWES [*cutting in*]: This isn't the Ambos Mundos. It says in the brochure that in Puerto Barrio we stay at the Ambos Mundos in the heart of the city.

SHANNON: Yes, on the plaza – tell her about the plaza.

MAXINE: What about the plaza?

SHANNON: It's hot, noisy, stinking, swarming with flies. Pariah dogs dying in the –

MISS FELLOWES: How is this place better?

SHANNON: The view from this verandah is equal and I think better than the view from Victoria Peak in Hong Kong, the view from the roof-terrace of the Sultan's palace in –

MISS FELLOWES [*cutting in*]: I want the view of a clean bed, a bathroom with plumbing that works, and food that is eatable and digestible and not contaminated by filthy –

SHANNON: *Miss Fellowes!*

MISS FELLOWES: Take your hand off my arm.

SHANNON: Look at this sample menu. The cook is a Chinese imported from Shanghai by *me*! Sent here by *me*, year before last, in nineteen thirty-eight. He was the chef at the Royal Colonial Club in –

MISS FELLOWES [*cutting in*]: You got a telephone here?

MAXINE: Sure, in the office.

MISS FELLOWES: I want to use it – I'll call collect. Where's the office?

MAXINE [*to Pancho*]: Llevala al telefono!

[*With* PANCHO *showing her the way,* MISS FELLOWES *stalks off around the verandah to the office.* SHANNON *falls back, sighing desperately, against the verandah wall.*]

MAXINE: Hah!

SHANNON: Why did you have to . . . ?

MAXINE: Huh?

SHANNON: Come out looking like this! For you it's funny, but for me it's . . .

MAXINE: This is how I *look*. What's wrong with how I *look*?

SHANNON: I told you to button your shirt. Are you so proud of your boobs that you won't button your shirt up? – Go in the office and see if she's calling Blake Tours to get me fired.

MAXINE: She better not unless she pays for the call.

[*She goes around the turn of the verandah.*]

[MISS HANNAH JELKES *appears below the verandah steps and stops short as* SHANNON *turns to the wall, pounding his fist against it with a sobbing sound in his throat.*]

HANNAH: Excuse me.

[SHANNON *looks down at her, dazed.* HANNAH *is remark-able-looking – ethereal, almost ghostly. She suggests a Gothic cathedral image of a medieval saint, but animated. She could be thirty, she could be forty: she is totally feminine and yet androgy-nous-looking – almost timeless. She is wearing a cotton print dress and has a bag slung on a strap over her shoulder.*]

HANNAH: Is this the Costa Verde Hotel?

SHANNON [*suddenly pacified by her appearance*]: Yes. Yes, it is.

HANNAH: Are you . . . you're not, the hotel manager, are you?

SHANNON: No. She'll be right back.

HANNAH: Thank you. Do you have any idea if they have two vacancies here? One for myself and one for my grandfather who's waiting in a taxi down there on the road. I didn't

want to bring him up the hill – till I'd made sure they have
rooms for us first.

SHANNON: Well, there's plenty of room here out-of-season –
like now.

HANNAH: Good! Wonderful! I'll get him out of the taxi.

SHANNON: Need any help?

HANNAH: No, thank you. We'll make it all right.

> [*She gives him a pleasant nod and goes back off down the path
> through the rain forest. A coconut plops to the ground; a parrot
> screams at a distance.* SHANNON *drops into the hammock and
> stretches out. Then* MAXINE *reappears.*]

SHANNON: How about the call? Did she make a phone
call?

MAXINE: She called a judge in Texas – Blowing Rock, Texas.
Collect.

SHANNON: She's trying to get me fired and she is also trying
to pin on me a rape charge, a charge of statutory rape.

MAXINE: What's 'statutory rape'? I've never known what
that was.

SHANNON: That's when a man is seduced by a girl under
twenty. [*She chuckles.*] It's not funny, Maxine honey.

MAXINE: Why do you want the young ones – or think that
you do?

SHANNON: I don't want any, any – regardless of age.

MAXINE: Then why do you take them, Shannon? [*He swallows
but does not answer.*] – Huh, Shannon.

SHANNON: People need human contact, Maxine honey.

MAXINE: What size shoe do you wear?

SHANNON: I don't get the point of that question.

MAXINE: These shoes are shot and if I remember correctly,
you travel with only one pair. Fred's estate included one
good pair of shoes and your feet look about his size.

SHANNON: I loved ole Fred, but I don't want to fill his shoes,
honey.

> [*She has removed Shannon's beat-up, English-made oxfords.*]

MAXINE: Your socks are shot. Fred's socks would fit you,
too, Shannon. [*She opens his collar.*] Aw-aw, I see you got on
your gold cross. That's a bad sign, it means you're thinkin'
again about goin' back to the Church.

SHANNON: This is my last tour, Maxine. I wrote my old
Bishop this morning a complete confession and a complete
capitulation.

[*She takes a letter from his damp shirt pocket.*]

MAXINE: If this is the letter, baby, you've sweated through it,
so the old bugger couldn't read it even if you mailed it to
him this time.

[*She has started around the verandah, and goes off as* HANK
reappears up the hill-path, mopping his face. SHANNON's
relaxed position in the hammock aggravates HANK *sorely.*]

HANK: Will you get your ass out of that hammock?

SHANNON: No, I will not.

HANK: Shannon, git out of that hammock! [*He kicks at
Shannon's hips in the hammock.*]

SHANNON: Hank, if you can't function under rough circumstances, you are in the wrong racket, man. I gave you
instructions; the instructions were simple. I said get them
out of the bus and . . .

[MAXINE *comes back with a kettle of water, a towel and other
shaving equipment.*]

HANK: Out of the hammock, Shannon! [*He kicks Shannon
again, harder.*]

SHANNON [*warningly*]: That's enough, Hank. A little familiar-
ity goes a long way, but not as far as you're going.
[MAXINE *starts lathering his face.*] What's this, what are
you . . .

MAXINE: Haven't you ever had a shave-and-haircut by a lady
barber?

HANK: The kid has gone into hysterics.

MAXINE: Hold still, Shannon.

SHANNON: Hank, hysteria is a natural phenomenon, the
common denominator of the female nature. It's the big
female weapon, and the test of a man is his ability to cope
with it, and I can't believe you can't. If I believe that you
couldn't, I would not be able —

MAXINE: Hold still!

SHANNON: I'm holding still. [*To Hank*] No, I wouldn't be
able to take you out with me again. So go on back down
there and —

HANK: You want me to go back down there and tell them you're getting a shave up here in a hammock?

MAXINE: Tell them that Reverend Larry is going back to the Church, so they can go back to the Female College in Texas.

HANK: I want another beer.

MAXINE: Help yourself, piggly-wiggly; the cooler's in my office right around there. [*She points around the corner of the verandah.*]

SHANNON [*as* HANK *goes off*]: It's horrible how you got to bluff and keep bluffing even when hollering 'Help!' is all you're up to, Maxine. *You cut me!*

MAXINE: You didn't hold still.

SHANNON: Just trim the beard a little.

MAXINE: I know. Baby, tonight we'll go night-swimming, whether it storms or not.

SHANNON: Ah, God ...

MAXINE: The Mexican kids are wonderful night-swimmers. ... Hah, when I found 'em they were taking the two-hundred-foot dives off the Quebrada, but the Quebrada Hotel kicked 'em out for being over-attentive to the lady guests there. That's how I got hold of them.

SHANNON: Maxine, you're bigger than life and twice as unnatural, honey.

MAXINE: No one's bigger than life-size, Shannon, or even ever that big, except maybe Fred. [*She shouts* 'Fred?' *and gets a faint answering echo from an adjoining hill.*] Little Sir Echo is all that answers for him now, Shannon, but ... [*She pats some bay rum on his face.*] Dear old Fred was always a mystery to me. He was so patient and tolerant with me that it was insulting to me. A man and a woman have got to challenge each other; y'know what I mean. I mean I hired those diving-boys from the Quebrada six months before Fred died, and did he care? Did he give a damn when I started night-swimming with them? No. He'd go night-*fishing*, all night, and when I got up the next day, he'd be preparing to go out fishing again, but he just caught the fish and threw them back in the sea.

[HANK *returns and sits drinking his beer on the steps.*]

SHANNON: The mystery of old Fred was simple. He was just

cool and decent; that's all the mystery of him. . . . Get your pair of night-swimmers to grab my ladies' luggage out of the bus before the vocal-teacher gets off the phone and stops them.

MAXINE [*shouting*]: Pedro! Pancho! Muchachos! Trae las maletas al anejo! Pronto! [*The Mexican boys start down the path.* MAXINE *sits in the hammock beside Shannon.*] You I'll put in Fred's old room, next to me.

SHANNON: You want me in his socks and his shoes and in his room next to you? [*He stares at her with a shocked surmise of her intentions towards him, then flops back down in the hammock with an incredulous laugh.*] Oh no, honey. I've just been hanging on till I could get in this hammock on this verandah over the rain-forest and the still-water beach; that's all that can pull me through this last tour in a condition to go back to my . . . original . . . vocation.

MAXINE: Hah, you still have some rational moments when you face the fact that churchgoers don't go to church to hear atheistical sermons.

SHANNON: Goddamit, I never preached an atheistical sermon in a church in my life, and . . .

[MISS FELLOWES *has charged out of the office and round the verandah to bear down on* SHANNON *and* MAXINE, *who jumps up out of the hammock.*]

MISS FELLOWES: I've completed my call, which I made collect to Texas.

[MAXINE *shrugs, going by her around the verandah.* MISS FELLOWES *runs across the verandah.*]

SHANNON [*sitting up in the hammock*]: Excuse me, Miss Fellowes, for not getting out of this hammock, but I . . . Miss Fellowes? Please sit down a minute. I want to confess something to you.

MISS FELLOWES: *That* ought to be int'restin'! *What?*

SHANNON: Just that – well, like everyone else, at some point or other in life, my life has cracked up on me.

MISS FELLOWES: How does that compensate *us?*

SHANNON: I don't think I know what you mean by *compensate*, Miss Fellowes. [*He props himself up and gazes at her with the gentlest bewilderment, calculated to melt a heart of stone.*]

I mean I've just confessed to you that I'm at the end of my rope, and you say, 'How does that compensate *us*?' Please, Miss Fellowes. Don't make me feel that any adult human being puts personal compensation before the dreadful, bare fact of a man at the end of his rope who still has to try to go on, to continue, as if he'd never been better or stronger in his whole existence. No, don't do that; it would . . .

MISS FELLOWES: It would *what*?

SHANNON: Shake if not shatter everything left of my faith in essential . . . human . . . *goodness*!

MAXINE [*returning, with a pair of socks*]: Hah!

MISS FELLOWES: Can you sit there, I mean lie there – yeah, I mean *lie* there . . .! and talk to me about –

MAXINE: Hah!

MISS FELLOWES: 'Essential human goodness?' Why, just plain human decency is beyond your imagination, Shannon, so lie there, lie there and *lie* there, we're *going*!

SHANNON [*rising from the hammock*]: Miss Fellowes, I thought that I was conducting this party, not you.

MISS FELLOWES: You? You just now *admitted* you're incompetent, as well as . . .

MAXINE: Hah!

SHANNON: Maxine, will you –

MISS FELLOWES [*cutting in with cold, righteous fury*]: *Shannon*, we girls have worked and slaved all year at Baptist Female College for this Mexican tour, and the tour is a cheat!

SHANNON [*to himself*]: Fantastic!

MISS FELLOWES: Yes, *cheat*! You haven't stuck to the schedule and you haven't stuck to the itinerary advertised in the brochure which Blake Tours put out. Now, either Blake Tours is cheating us or you are cheating Blake Tours, and I'm putting wheels in motion – I don't care *what* it costs me – I'm . . .

SHANNON: Oh, Miss Fellowes, isn't it just as plain to you as it is to me that your hysterical insults, which are not at all easy for any born and bred gentleman to accept, are not . . . *motivated, provoked* by . . . anything as *trivial* as the, the . . . the motivations that you're, you're . . . *ascribing* them to? Now can't we talk about the *real, true* cause of . . .

MISS FELLOWES: Cause of *what*?

[CHARLOTTE GOODALL *appears at the top of the hill.*]

SHANNON: — Cause of your *rage*, Miss Fellowes, your —

MISS FELLOWES: *Charlotte!* Stay down the hill in the *bus!*

CHARLOTTE: Judy, they're —

MISS FELLOWES: *Obey me! Down!*

[CHARLOTTE *retreats from view like a well-trained dog.* MISS FELLOWES *charges back to* SHANNON, *who has got out of the hammock. He places a conciliatory hand on her arm.*]

MISS FELLOWES: *Take your hand off my arm!*

MAXINE: Hah!

SHANNON: *Fantastic.* Miss Fellowes, please! No more shouting? Please? Now I really must ask you to let this party of ladies come up here and judge the accommodations for themselves and compare them with what they saw passing through town. Miss Fellowes, there is such a thing as charm and beauty in some places, as much as there's nothing but dull, ugly imitation of highway motels in Texas and —

[MISS FELLOWES *charges over to the path to see if* CHARLOTTE *has obeyed her.* SHANNON *follows, still propitiatory.* MAXINE *says 'Hah,' but she gives him an affectionate little pat as he goes by her. He pushes her hand away as he continues his appeal to* MISS FELLOWES.]

MISS FELLOWES: I've taken a look at those rooms and they'd make a room at the 'Y' look like a suite at the Ritz.

SHANNON: Miss Fellowes, I am employed by Blake Tours and so I'm not in a position to tell you quite frankly what mistakes they've made in their advertising brochure. They just don't know Mexico. I do. I know it as well as I know five out of all six continents on the —

MISS FELLOWES: *Continent! Mexico?* You never even studied geography if you —

SHANNON: My degree from Sewanee is *Doctor of Divinity*, but for the past ten years geography's been my *speciality,* Miss Fellowes, honey! Name any tourist agency I haven't worked for! You couldn't! I'm only, now, with Blake Tours because I —

MISS FELLOWES: Because you *what*? Couldn't keep your hands off innocent, under-age girls in your —

SHANNON: Now, Miss Fellowes. . . . [*He touches her arm again.*]

MISS FELLOWES: Take your hand off my arm!

SHANNON: For days I've known you were furious and unhappy, but —

MISS FELLOWES: *Oh!* You think it's just *me* that's unhappy! Hauled in that stifling bus over the byways, off the highways, shook up and bumped up so you could get your rakeoff, is that what you —

SHANNON: What I know is, all I know is, that you are the *leader of the insurrection*!

MISS FELLOWES: All of the girls in this party have dysentery!

SHANNON: That you can't hold me to blame for.

MISS FELLOWES: I *do* hold you to blame for it.

SHANNON: Before we entered Mexico, at New Laredo, Texas, I called you ladies together in the depot on the Texas side of the border and I passed out mimeographed sheets of instructions on what to eat and what *not* to eat, what to drink, what *not* to drink in the —

MISS FELLOWES: It's not *what* we ate but *where* we ate that gave us dysentery!

SHANNON [*shaking his head like a metronome*]: It is not dysentery.

MISS FELLOWES: The result of eating in places that would be condemned by the Board of Health in —

SHANNON: Now wait a minute —

MISS FELLOWES: For disregarding all rules of sanitation.

SHANNON: It is not dysentery, it is not amoebic, it's nothing at all but —

MAXINE: Montezuma's Revenge! That's what we call it.

SHANNON: I even passed out pills. I passed out bottles of Enteroviaform because I knew that some of you ladies would rather be victims of Montezuma's Revenge than spend cinco centavos on bottled water in stations.

MISS FELLOWES: You sold those pills at a profit of fifty cents per bottle.

MAXINE: Hah-hah! [*She knocks off the end of a coconut with the machete, preparing a rum-coco.*]

SHANNON: Now fun is fun, Miss Fellowes, but an accusation like that —

MISS FELLOWES: I *priced* them in *pharmacies*, because I suspected that —

SHANNON: Miss Fellowes, I am a gentleman, and as a gentleman I can't be insulted like this. I mean I can't accept insults of that kind even from a member of a tour that I am conducting. And Miss Fellowes, I think you might also remember, you might try to remember, that you're speaking to an ordained minister of the Church.

MISS FELLOWES: *De*-frocked! But still trying to pass himself off as a minister!

MAXINE: How about a rum-coco? We give a complimentary rum-coco to all our guests here. [*Her offer is apparently unheard. She shrugs and drinks the rum-coco herself.*]

SHANNON: — Miss Fellowes? In every party there is always one individual that's discontented, that is not satisfied with all I do to make the tour more ... unique — to make it different from the ordinary, to give it a personal thing, the Shannon touch.

MISS FELLOWES: The gyp touch, the touch of a defrocked minister.

SHANNON: Miss Fellowes, don't, don't, don't ... do what ... you're doing! [*He is on the verge of hysteria, he makes some incoherent sounds, gesticulates with clenched fists, then stumbles wildly across the verandah and leans panting for breath against a post.*] Don't! Break! *Human! Pride!*

VOICE FROM DOWN THE HILL [*a very Texan accent*]: Judy? They're taking our luggage!

MISS FELLOWES [*shouting down the hill*]: Girls! Girls! Don't let those boys touch your luggage. Don't let them bring your luggage in this dump!

GIRL'S VOICE [*from below*]: Judy! We can't stop them!

MAXINE: Those kids don't understand English.

MISS FELLOWES [*wild with rage*]: Will you please tell those boys to take that luggage back down to the bus? [*She calls to the party below again.*] Girls! Hold on to your luggage; don't let them take it away! We're going to drive back to A-cap-ul-co! *You hear?*

GIRL'S VOICE: Judy, they want a swim, first!

MISS FELLOWES: I'll be right back. [*She rushes off, shouting at the Mexican boys.*] You! Boys! Muchachos! *You carry that luggage back down!*

[*The voices continue, fading.* SHANNON *moves brokenly across the verandah.* MAXINE *shakes her head.*]

MAXINE: Shannon, give 'em the bus key and let 'em go.

SHANNON: And me do what?

MAXINE: Stay here.

SHANNON: In Fred's old bedroom — yeah, in Fred's old bedroom.

MAXINE: You could do worse.

SHANNON: Could I? Well, then, I'll do worse, I'll ... do worse.

MAXINE: Aw now, baby.

SHANNON: If I could do worse, I'll do worse.... [*He grips the section of railing by the verandah steps and stares with wide lost eyes. His chest heaves like a spent runner's and he is bathed in sweat.*]

MAXINE: Give me that ignition key. I'll take it down to the driver while you bathe and rest and have a rum-coco, baby.

[SHANNON *simply shakes his head slightly. Harsh bird cries sound in the rain forest. Voices are heard on the path.*]

HANNAH: Nonno, you've lost your sun glasses.

NONNO: No. Took them off. No sun.

[HANNAH *appears at the top of the path, pushing her grand-father,* NONNO, *in a wheel-chair. He is a very old man, but has a powerful voice for his age and always seems to be shouting something of importance.* NONNO *is a poet and a showman. There is a good kind of pride and he has it, carrying it like a banner wherever he goes. He is immaculately dressed — a linen suit, white as his thick poet's hair; a black string tie; and he is holding a black cane with a gold crook.*]

NONNO: Which way is the sea?

HANNAH: Right down below the hill, Nonno. [*He turns in the wheel-chair and raises a hand to shield his eyes.*] We can't see it from here. [*The old man is deaf, and she shouts to make him hear.*]

NONNO: I can feel it and smell it. [*A murmur of wind sweeps through the rain forest.*] It's the cradle of life. [*He is shouting, too.*] Life began in the sea.

MAXINE: These two with your party?

SHANNON: No.

MAXINE: They look like a pair of loonies.

SHANNON: Shut up.

[SHANNON *looks at Hannah and Nonno steadily, with a relief of tension almost like that of someone going under hypnosis. The old man still squints down the path, blindly, but* HANNAH *is facing the verandah with a proud person's hope of acceptance when it is desperately needed.*]

HANNAH: How do you do.

MAXINE: Hello.

HANNAH: Have you ever tried pushing a gentleman in a wheel-chair uphill through a rain forest?

MAXINE: Nope, and I wouldn't even try it *downhill*.

HANNAH: Well, now that we've made it, I don't regret the effort. What a view for a painter! [*She looks about her, panting, digging into her shoulder-bag for a handkerchief, aware that her face is flushed and sweating.*] They told me in town that this was the ideal place for a painter, and they weren't – *whew* – exaggerating!

SHANNON: You've got a scratch on your forehead.

HANNAH: Oh, is that what I felt.

SHANNON: Better put iodine on it.

HANNAH: Yes, I'll attend to that – *whew* – later, thank you.

MAXINE: Anything I can do for you?

HANNAH: I'm looking for the manager of the hotel.

MAXINE: Me – speaking.

HANNAH: Oh, *you're* the manager, *good*! How do you do, I'm Hannah Jelkes, Mrs ...

MAXINE: Faulk, Maxine Faulk. What can I do for you folks? [*Her tone indicates no desire to do anything for them.*]

HANNAH [*turning quickly to her grandfather*]: Nonno, the manager is a *lady* from the States.

[NONNO *lifts a branch of wild orchids from his lap, ceremonially, with the instinctive gallantry of his kind.*]

NONNO [*shouting*]: Give the lady these – botanical curiosities! – you picked on the way up.

HANNAH: I believe they're wild orchids, isn't that what they are?

SHANNON: Laelia tibicina.

HANNAH: Oh!

NONNO: But tell her, Hannah, tell her to keep them in the icebox till after dark; they draw bees in the sun! [*He rubs a sting on his chin with a rueful chuckle.*]

MAXINE: Are you all looking for rooms here?

HANNAH: Yes, we are, but we've come without reservations.

MAXINE: Well, honey, the Costa Verde is closed in September – except for a few special guests, so . . .

SHANNON: They're special guests, for God's sake.

MAXINE: I thought you said they didn't come with your party.

HANNAH: Please let us be special guests.

MAXINE: *Watch out!*

[NONNO *has started struggling out of the wheel-chair.* SHANNON *rushes over to keep him from falling.* HANNAH *has started towards him, too, then, seeing that* SHANNON *has caught him, she turns back to Maxine.*]

HANNAH: In twenty-five years of travel this is the first time we've ever arrived at a place without advance reservations.

MAXINE: Honey, that old man ought to be in a hospital.

HANNAH: Oh, no, no, he just sprained his ankle a little in Tasco this morning. He just needs a good night's rest; he'll be on his feet tomorrow. His recuperative powers are absolutely amazing for someone who is ninety-seven years *young.*

SHANNON: Easy, Grampa. Hang on. [*He is supporting the old man up to the verandah.*] Two steps. One! Two! Now you've made it, Grampa.

[NONNO *keeps chuckling breathlessly as* SHANNON *gets him on to the verandah and into a wicker rocker.*]

HANNAH [*breaking in quickly*]: I can't tell you how much I appreciate your taking us in here now. It's – providential.

MAXINE: Well, I can't send that old man back down the hill – right now – but, like I told you, the Costa Verde's practically closed in September. I just take in a few folks as a special accommodation and we operate on a special basis this month.

NONNO [*cutting in abruptly and loudly*]: Hannah, tell the lady

that my perambulator is temporary. I will soon be ready to
crawl and then to toddle and before long I will be leaping
around here like an – old – mountain goat, ha-ha-ha-
ha. . . .

HANNAH: Yes, I explained that, Grandfather.

NONNO: I don't like being on wheels.

HANNAH: Yes, my grandfather feels that the decline of the
western world began with the invention of the wheel.

[*She laughs heartily, but* MAXINE'S *look is unresponsive.*]

NONNO: And tell the manager . . . the, uh, lady . . . that I
know some hotels don't want to take dogs, cats, or monkeys
and some don't even solicit the patronage of infants in their
late nineties who arrive in perambulators with flowers
instead of rattles . . . [*He chuckles with a sort of fearful, slightly
mad quality.* HANNAH *perhaps has the impulse to clap a hand
over his mouth at this moment, but must stand there smiling and
smiling and smiling.*] . . . and a brandy flask instead of a
teething ring, but tell her that these, uh, concessions to
man's seventh age are only temporary, and . . .

HANNAH: Nonno, I told her the wheel-chair's because of a
sprained ankle, Nonno!

SHANNON [*to himself*]: Fantastic.

NONNO: And after my siesta, I'll wheel it back down the hill,
I'll kick it back down the hill, right into the sea, and tell
her . . .

HANNAH: Yes? What, Nonno? [*She has stopped smiling now.
Her tone and her look are frankly desperate.*] What shall I tell
her now, Nonno?

NONNO: Tell her that if she'll forgive my disgraceful long-
evity and this . . . temporary decrepitude . . . I will present
her with the last signed . . . compitty [*he means 'copy'*]
of my first volume of verse, published in . . . when,
Hannah?

HANNAH [*hopelessly*]: The day that President Ulysses S. Grant
was inaugurated, Nonno.

NONNO: *Morning Trumpet!* Where is it – you have it, give it to
her right now.

HANNAH: Later, a little later! [*Then she turns to Maxine and
Shannon.*] My grandfather is the poet Jonathan Coffin. He is

ninety-seven years *young* and will be ninety-eight years *young* the fifth of next month, October.

MAXINE: Old folks are remarkable, yep. The office phone's ringing – excuse me, I'll be right back. [*She goes around the verandah.*]

NONNO: Did I talk too much?

HANNAH [*quietly, to Shannon*]: I'm afraid that he did. I don't think she's going to take us.

SHANNON: She'll take you. Don't worry about it.

HANNAH: Nobody would take us in town, and if we don't get in here, I would have to wheel him back down through the rain forest, and then *what*, then *where*? There would just be the road, and no direction to move in, except out to sea – and I doubt that we could make it divide before us.

SHANNON: That won't be necessary. I have a little influence with the patrona.

HANNAH: Oh, then, do use it. Please. Her eyes said *no* in big blue capital letters.

[SHANNON *pours some water from a pitcher on the verandah and hands it to the old man.*]

NONNO: What is this – libation?

SHANNON: Some ice-water, Grampa.

HANNAH: Oh, that's kind of you. Thank you. I'd better give him a couple of salt tablets to wash down with it. [*Briskly she removes a bottle from her shoulder-bag.*] Won't you have some? I see you're perspiring, too. You have to be careful not to become dehydrated in the hot seasons under the Tropic of Cancer.

SHANNON [*pouring another glass of water*]: Are you a little *financially* dehydrated, too?

HANNAH: That's right. Bone-dry, and I think the patrona suspects it. It's a logical assumption, since I pushed him up here myself, and the patrona has the look of a very logical woman. I am sure she knows that we couldn't afford to hire the taxi-driver to help us up here.

MAXINE [*calling from the back*]: Pancho?

HANNAH: A woman's practicality when she's managing something is harder than a man's for another woman to cope with, so if you have influence with her, please do use it. Please try to convince her that my grandfather will be on his feet tomorrow, if not tonight, and with any luck whatsoever, the money situation will be solved just as quickly. Oh, here she comes back, do help us!

[*Involuntarily,* HANNAH *seizes hold of Shannon's wrist as* MAXINE *stalks back on to the verandah, still shouting for* PANCHO. *The Mexican boy reappears, sucking a juicy peeled mango – its juice running down his chin on to his throat.*]

MAXINE: Pancho, run down to the beach and tell Herr Fahrenkopf that the German Embassy's waiting on the phone for him. [PANCHO *stares at her blankly until she repeats the order in Spanish.*] Dile a Herr Fahrenkopf que la embajada alemana lo llama al telefono. Corre, corre! [PANCHO *starts indolently down the path, still sucking noisily on the mango.*] I said *run!* Corre, corre! [*He goes into a leisurely loping pace and disappears through the foliage.*]

HANNAH: What graceful people they are!

MAXINE: Yeah, they're graceful like cats, and just as dependable, too.

HANNAH: Shall we, uh ... *register* now?

MAXINE: You all can register later but I'll have to collect six dollars from you first if you want to put your names in the pot for supper. That's how I've got to operate here out of season.

HANNAH: Six? Dollars?

MAXINE: Yeah, three each. In season we operate on the continental plan, but out of season like this we change to the modified American plan.

HANNAH: Oh, what is the, uh ... modification of it? [*She gives Shannon a quick glance of appeal as she stalls for time, but his attention has turned inward as the bus horn blows down the hill.*]

MAXINE: Just two meals are included instead of all three.

HANNAH [*moving closer to Shannon and raising her voice*]: Breakfast and dinner?

MAXINE: A continental breakfast and a cold lunch.

SHANNON [*aside*]: Yeah, very cold – cracked ice – if you crack it yourself.

HANNAH [*reflectively*]: Not dinner.

MAXINE: No! Not dinner.

HANNAH: Oh, I see, uh, but ... we, uh, operate on a special basis ourselves. I'd better explain it to you.

MAXINE: How do you mean 'operate', — on what 'basis'?

HANNAH: Here's our card. I think you may have heard of us. [*She presents the card to Maxine.*] We've had a good many write-ups. My grandfather is the oldest living and practising poet. *And* he gives recitations. I ... paint ... watercolours and I'm a 'quick sketch artist'. We travel together. We pay our way as we go by my grandfather's recitations and the sale of my watercolours and quick sketches in charcoal or pastel.

SHANNON [*to himself*]: I have fever.

HANNAH: I usually pass among the tables at lunch and dinner in a hotel. I wear an artist's smock – picturesquely dabbled with paint – wide Byronic collar and flowing silk tie. I don't push myself on people. I just display my work and smile at them sweetly and if they invite me to do so sit down to make a quick character sketch in pastel or charcoal. If not? Smile sweetly and go on.

SHANNON: What does Grandpa do?

HANNAH: We pass among the tables together slowly. I introduce him as the world's oldest living and practising poet. If invited, he gives a recitation of a poem. Unfortunately, all of his poems were written a long time ago. But do you know, he has started a new poem? For the first time in twenty years he's started another poem!

SHANNON: Hasn't finished it yet?

HANNAH: He still has inspiration, but his power of concentration has weakened a little, of course.

MAXINE: Right now he's not concentrating.

SHANNON: Grandpa's catchin' forty winks. Grampa? Let's hit the sack.

MAXINE: Now wait a minute. I'm going to call a taxi for these folks to take them back to town.

HANNAH: Please don't do that. We tried every hotel in town and they wouldn't take us. I'm afraid I have to place myself at your ... mercy.

[*With infinite gentleness* SHANNON *has roused the old man and*

[*is leading him into one of the cubicles back of the verandah. Distant cries of bathers are heard from the beach. The afternoon light is fading very fast now, as the sun has dropped behind an island hilltop out to sea.*]

MAXINE: Looks like you're in for one night. Just one.

HANNAH: Thank you.

MAXINE: The old man's in number 4. You take 3. Where's your luggage – no luggage?

HANNAH: I hid it behind some palmettos at the foot of the path.

SHANNON [*shouting to Pancho*]: Bring up her luggage. Tu, flojo ... las maletas ... baja las palmas. Vamos! [*The Mexican boys rush down the path.*] Maxine honey, would you cash a post-dated cheque for me?

MAXINE [*shrewdly*]: Yeah – mañana, maybe.

SHANNON: Thanks – generosity is the cornerstone of your nature.

[MAXINE *utters her one-note bark of a laugh as she marches around the corner of the verandah.*]

HANNAH: I'm dreadfully afraid my grandfather had a slight stroke in those high passes through the sierras. [*She says this with the coolness of someone saying that it may rain before nightfall. An instant later, a long, long sigh of wind sweeps the hillside. The bathers are heard shouting below.*]

SHANNON: Very old people get these little 'cerebral accidents', as they call them. They're not regular strokes, they're just little cerebral ... incidents. The symptoms clear up so quickly that sometimes the old people don't even know they've had them.

[*They exchange this quiet talk without looking at each other. The Mexican boys crash back through the bushes at the top of the path, bearing some pieces of ancient luggage fantastically plastered with hotel and travel stickers indicating a vast range of wandering. The boys deposit the luggage near the steps.*]

SHANNON: How many times have you been around the world?

HANNAH: Almost as many times as the world's been around the sun, and I feel as if I had gone the whole way on foot.

SHANNON [*picking up her luggage*]: What's your cell number?

HANNAH [*smiling faintly*]: I believe she said it was cell number 3.

SHANNON: She probably gave you the one with the leaky roof. [*He carries the bags into the cubicle.* MAXINE *is visible to the audience only as she appears outside the door to her office on the wing of the verandah.*] But you won't find out till it rains and then it'll be too late to do much about it but swim out of it. [HANNAH *laughs wanly. Her fatigue is now very plain.* SHANNON *comes back out with her luggage.*] Yep, she gave you the one with the leaky roof so you take mine and . . .

HANNAH: Oh, no, no, Mr Shannon, I'll find a dry spot if it rains.

MAXINE [*from around the corner of the verandah*]: Shannon!

[*A bit of pantomime occurs between* HANNAH *and* SHANNON. *He wants to put her luggage in cubicle number 5. She catches hold of his arm, indicating by gesture towards the back that it is necessary to avoid displeasing the proprietor.* MAXINE *shouts his name louder.* SHANNON *surrenders to* HANNAH'S *pleading and puts her luggage back in the leaky cubicle number 3.*]

HANNAH: Thank you so much, Mr Shannon. [*She disappears behind the mosquito netting.* MAXINE *advances to the verandah angle as* SHANNON *starts towards his own cubicle.*]

MAXINE [*mimicking Hannah's voice*]: 'Thank you so much, Mr Shannon.'

SHANNON: Don't be bitchy. Some people say thank you sincerely. [*He goes past her and down the steps from the end of the verandah.*] I'm going down for a swim now.

MAXINE: The water's blood temperature this time of day.

SHANNON: Yeah; well, I have a fever, so it'll seem cooler to me. [*He crosses rapidly to the jungle path leading to the beach.*]

MAXINE [*following him*]: Wait for me. I'll . . .

[*She means she will go down with him, but he ignores her call and disappears into the foliage.* MAXINE *shrugs angrily and goes back on to the verandah. She faces out, gripping the railings tightly and glaring into the blaze of the sunset as if it were a personal enemy. Then the ocean breathes a long, cooling breath up the hill, as* NONNO'S *voice is heard from his cubicle.*]

NONNO:

> How calmly does the orange branch
> Observe the sky begin to blanch.
> Without a cry, without a prayer.
> With no expression of despair. . . .

[*And from a beach cantina in the distance a marimba band is heard playing a popular song of that summer of 1940, 'Palabras de Mujer' – which means 'Words of Women'.*]

SLOW DIM OUT AND SLOW CURTAIN

ACT TWO

Several hours later: near sunset.
The scene is bathed in a deep golden, almost coppery light; the heavy tropical foliage gleams with wetness from a recent rain.

> [MAXINE *comes around the turn of the verandah. To the for-malities of evening she has made the concession of changing from levis to clean white cotton pants, and from a blue work shirt to a pink one. She is about to set up the folding card-tables for the evening meal, which is served on the verandah. All the while she is talking, she is setting up tables, etc.*]

MAXINE: Miss Jelkes?

> [HANNAH *lifts the mosquito net over the door of cubicle number 3.*]

HANNAH: Yes, Mrs Faulk?

MAXINE: Can I speak to you while I set up these tables for supper?

HANNAH: Of course, you may. I wanted to speak to you, too.
[*She comes out. She is now wearing her artist's smock.*]

MAXINE: Good.

HANNAH: I just wanted to ask you if there's a tub-bath Grandfather could use. A shower is fine for me – I prefer a shower to a tub – but for my grandfather there is some dan-ger of falling down in a shower and at his age, although he says he is made out of indiarubber, a broken hip-bone would be a very serious matter, so I . . .

MAXINE: What I wanted to say is I called up the Casa de Huéspedes about you and your Grampa, and I can get you in there.

HANNAH: Oh, but we don't want to *move*!

MAXINE: The Costa Verde isn't the right place for you. Y'see, we cater to folks that like to rough it a little, and – well, frankly, we cater to younger people.

> [HANNAH *has started unfolding a card-table.*]

HANNAH: Oh yes . . . uh . . . well . . . the, uh, Casa de Hués-pedes, that means a, uh, sort of a rooming-house, Mrs Faulk?

MAXINE: Boarding-house. They feed you, they'll even feed you on credit.

HANNAH: Where is it located?

MAXINE: It has a central location. You could get a doctor there quick if the old man took sick on you. You got to think about that.

HANNAH: Yes, I – [*She nods gravely, more to herself than Maxine.*] – I *have* thought about that, but . . .

MAXINE: What are you doing?

HANNAH: Making myself useful.

MAXINE: Don't do that. I don't accept help from guests here. [*HANNAH hesitates, but goes on setting the tables.*]

HANNAH: Oh, please, let me. Knife and fork on one side, spoon on the . . . ? [*Her voice dies out.*]

MAXINE: Just put the plates on the napkins so they don't blow away.

HANNAH: Yes, it is getting breezy on the verandah. [*She continues setting the table.*]

MAXINE: Hurricane winds are already hitting up coast.

HANNAH: We've been through several typhoons in the Orient. Sometimes *outside* disturbances like that are an almost welcome distraction from *inside* disturbances, aren't they? [*This is said almost to herself. She finishes putting the plates on the paper napkins.*] When do you want us to leave here, Mrs Faulk?

MAXINE: The boys'll move you in my station wagon tomorrow – no charge for the service.

HANNAH: That is very kind of you. [*MAXINE starts away.*] Mrs Faulk?

MAXINE [*turning back to her with obvious reluctance*]: Huh?

HANNAH: Do you know jade?

MAXINE: Jade?

HANNAH: Yes.

MAXINE: Why?

HANNAH: I have a small but interesting collection of jade pieces. I asked if you know jade because in jade it's the craftsmanship, the carving of the jade, that's most important about it. [*She has removed a jade ornament from her blouse.*] This one, for instance – a miracle of carving. Tiny as it is, it

has two figures carved on it – the legendary Prince Ahk and
Princess Angh, and a heron flying above them. The artist
that carved it probably received for this miraculously delicate workmanship, well, I would say perhaps the price of a
month's supply of rice for his family, but the merchant
who employed him sold it, I would guess, for at least three
hundred pounds sterling to an English lady who got tired
of it and gave it to me, perhaps because I painted her not as
she was at that time, but as I could see she must have looked
in her youth. Can you see the carving?

MAXINE: Yeah, honey, but I'm not operating a hock-shop
here. I'm trying to run a hotel.

HANNAH: I know, but couldn't you just accept it as security
for a few days' stay here?

MAXINE: You're completely broke, are you?

HANNAH: Yes, we are – completely.

MAXINE: You say that like you're proud of it.

HANNAH: I'm not proud of it or ashamed of it either. It just
happens to be what's happened to us, which has never happened before in all our travels.

MAXINE [*grudgingly*]: You're telling the truth, I reckon, but I
told you the truth, too, when I told you, when you came
here, that I had just lost my husband and he'd left me in such
a financial hole that if living didn't mean more to me than
money, I'd might as well have been dropped in the ocean
with him.

HANNAH: Ocean?

MAXINE [*peacefully philosophical about it*]: I carried out his
burial instructions exactly. Yep, my husband, Fred Faulk,
was the greatest game fisherman on the West Coast of
Mexico – he'd racked up unbeatable records in sailfish, tar-
pon, kingfish, barracuda – and on his deathbed, last week,
he requested to be dropped in the sea, yeah, right out there
in that bay, not even sewed up in canvas, just in his fisherman's outfit. So now old Freddie the Fisherman is feeding
the fish – fishes' revenge on old Freddie. How about that, I
ask you?

HANNAH [*regarding Maxine sharply*]: I doubt that he regrets
it.

MAXINE: I do. It gives me the shivers.

[*She is distracted by the German party singing a marching song on the path up from the beach.* SHANNON *appears at the top of the path, a wet beachrobe clinging to him.* MAXINE's *whole concentration shifts abruptly to him. She freezes and blazes with it like an exposed power line. For a moment the 'hot light' is concentrated on her tense, furious figure.* HANNAH *provides a visual counterpoint. She clenches her eyes shut for a moment, and when they open, it is on a look of stoical despair of the refuge she has unsuccessfully fought for. Then* SHANNON *approaches the verandah and the scene is his.*]

SHANNON: Here they come up, your conquerors of the world, Maxine honey, singing 'Horst Wessel'. [*He chuckles fiercely, and starts towards the verandah steps.*]

MAXINE: Shannon, wash that sand off you before you come on the verandah.

[*The Germans are heard singing the 'Horst Wessel' marching song. Soon they appear, trooping up from the beach like an animated canvas by Rubens. They are all nearly nude, pinked and bronzed by the sun. The women have decked themselves with garlands of pale green seaweed, glistening wet, and the Munich-opera bridegroom is blowing on a great conch shell. His father-in-law, the tank manufacturer, has his portable radio, which is still transmitting a shortwave broadcast about the Battle of Britain, now at its climax.*]

HILDA [*capering, astride her rubber horse*]: Horsey, horsey, horsey!

HERR FAHRENKOPF [*ecstatically*]: London is burning, the heart of London's on fire! (WOLFGANG *turns a handspring on to the verandah and walks on his hands a few paces, then tumbles over with a great whoop.* MAXINE *laughs delightedly with the Germans.*] Beer, beer, beer!

FRAU FAHRENKOPF: Tonight champagne!

[*The euphoric horseplay and shouting continue as they gambol around the turn of the verandah.* SHANNON *has come on to the porch.* MAXINE's *laughter dies out a little sadly, with envy.*]

SHANNON: You're turning this place into the Mexican Berchtesgaden, Maxine honey?

MAXINE: I told you to wash that sand off. [*Shouts for beer from the Germans draw her around the verandah corner.*]

HANNAH: Mr Shannon, do you happen to know the Casa de Huéspedes, or anything about it, I mean? [SHANNON *stares at her somewhat blankly.*] We are, uh, thinking of . . . *moving* there tomorrow. Do you, uh, recommend it?

SHANNON: I recommend it along with the Black Hole of Calcutta and the Siberian salt-mines.

HANNAH [*nodding reflectively*]: I suspected as much. Mr Shannon, in your touring party, do you think there might be anyone interested in my watercolours? Or in my character sketches?

SHANNON: I doubt it. I doubt that they're corny enough to please my ladies. *Oh-oh! Great Caesar's ghost.* . . .
   [*This exclamation is prompted by the shrill, approaching call of his name.* CHARLOTTE *appears from the rear, coming from the hotel annex, and rushes like a teen-age Medea towards the verandah.* SHANNON *ducks into his cubicle, slamming the door so quickly that a corner of the mosquito netting is caught and sticks out, flirtatiously.* CHARLOTTE *rushes on to the verandah.*]

CHARLOTTE: *Larry!*

HANNAH: Are you looking for someone, dear?

CHARLOTTE: Yeah, the man conducting our tour, Larry Shannon.

HANNAH: Oh, Mr Shannon. I think he went down to the beach.

CHARLOTTE: I just now saw him coming up from the beach.
   [*She is tense and trembling, and her eyes keep darting up and down the verandah.*]

HANNAH: Oh. Well. . . . But . . .

CHARLOTTE: Larry? Larry! [*Her shouts startle the rain-forest birds into a clamorous moment.*]

HANNAH: Would you like to leave a message for him, dear?

CHARLOTTE: No. I'm staying right here till he comes out of wherever he's hiding.

HANNAH: Why don't you just sit down, dear. I'm an artist, a painter. I was just sorting out my watercolours and sketches in this portfolio, and look what I've come across. [*She selects a sketch and holds it up.*]

SHANNON [*from inside his cubicle*]: Oh, God!

CHARLOTTE [*darting to the cubicle*]: Larry, let me in there!

[*She beats on the door of the cubicle as* HERR FAHRENKOPF *comes around the verandah with his portable radio. He is bug-eyed with excitement over the news broadcast in German.*]

HANNAH: Guten abend.

[HERR FAHRENKOPF *jerks his head with a toothy grin, raising a hand for silence.* HANNAH *nods agreeably and approaches him with her portfolio of drawings. He maintains the grin as she displays one picture after another.* HANNAH *is uncertain whether the grin is for the pictures or the news broadcast. He stares at the pictures, jerking his head from time to time. It is rather like the pantomime of showing lantern slides.*]

CHARLOTTE [*suddenly crying out again*]: Larry, open this door and let me in! I know you're in there, Larry!

HERR FAHRENKOPF: Silence, please, for one moment! This is a recording of Der Führer addressing the Reichstag just ... [*He glances at his wristwatch*] ... eight hours ago, to-day, transmitted by Deutsches Nachrichtenbüro to Mexico City. Please! Quiet, bitte!

[*A human voice like a mad dog's bark emerges from the static momentarily.* CHARLOTTE *goes on pounding on Shannon's door.* HANNAH *suggests in pantomime that they go to the back verandah, but* HERR FAHRENKOPF *despairs of hearing that broadcast. As he rises to leave, the light catches his polished glasses so that he appears for a moment to have electric light bulbs in his forehead. Then he ducks his head in a genial little bow and goes out beyond the verandah, where he performs some muscle-flexing movements of a formalized nature, like the preliminary stances of Japanese Suma wrestlers.*]

HANNAH: May I show you my work on the other verandah?

[HANNAH *has started to follow Herr Fahrenkopf with her portfolio, but the sketches fall out, and she stops to gather them from the floor with the sad, preoccupied air of a lonely child picking flowers.* SHANNON'S *head slowly, furtively, appears through the window of his cubicle. He draws quickly back as* CHARLOTTE *darts that way, stepping on Hannah's spilt sketches.* HANNAH *utters a soft cry of protest, which is drowned by* CHARLOTTE'S *renewed clamour.*]

CHARLOTTE: Larry, Larry, Judy's looking for me. Let me come in, Larry, before she finds me here!

SHANNON: You can't come in. Stop shouting and I'll come out.

CHARLOTTE: All right, come out.

SHANNON: Stand back from the door so I *can*.

[*She moves a little aside and he emerges from his cubicle like a man entering a place of execution. He leans against the wall, mopping the sweat off his face with a handkerchief.*]

SHANNON: How does Miss Fellowes know what happened that night? Did you tell her?

CHARLOTTE: I didn't tell her; she guessed.

SHANNON: Guessing isn't knowing. If she is just guessing, that means she doesn't know – I mean if you're not lying, if you didn't tell her.

[HANNAH *has finished picking up her drawings and moves quietly over to the far side of the verandah.*]

CHARLOTTE: Don't talk to me like that.

SHANNON: Don't complicate my life now, please, for God's sake; don't complicate my life now.

CHARLOTTE: Why have you changed like this?

SHANNON: I have a fever. Don't complicate me . . . fever.

CHARLOTTE: You act like you hated me now.

SHANNON: You're going to get me kicked out of Blake Tours, Charlotte.

CHARLOTTE: Judy is, not me.

SHANNON: Why did you sing 'I Love You Truly' at me?

CHARLOTTE: Because I do love you truly!

SHANNON: Honey girl, don't you know that nothing worse could happen to a girl in your, your . . . unstable condition . . . than to get emotionally mixed up with a man in my unstable condition, huh?

CHARLOTTE: No, no, no I –

SHANNON [*cutting through*]: Two unstable conditions can set a whole world on fire, can blow it up, past repair, and that is just as true between two people as it's true between . . .

CHARLOTTE: All I know is you've got to marry me, Larry, after what happened between us in Mexico City!

SHANNON: A man in my condition can't marry; it isn't

decent or legal. He's lucky if he can even hold on to his job. [*He keeps catching hold of her hands and plucking them off his shoulders.*] I'm almost out of my mind. Can't you see that, honey?

CHARLOTTE: I don't believe you don't love me.

SHANNON: Honey, it's almost impossible for anybody to believe they're not loved by someone they believe they love, but, honey, I love *nobody*. I'm like that; it isn't my fault. When I brought you home that night I told you good night in the hall, just kissed you on the cheek like the little girl that you are, but the instant I opened my door, you rushed into my room and I couldn't get you out of it, not even when I, oh God, tried to scare you out of it by, oh God, don't you remember?

[MISS FELLOWES' *voice is heard from back of the hotel calling,* 'Charlotte!']

CHARLOTTE: Yes, I remember that after making love to me, you hit me, Larry, you struck me in the face, and you twisted my arm to make me kneel on the floor and pray with you for forgiveness.

SHANNON: I do that, I do that always when I, when ... I don't have a dime left in my nervous emotional bank account – I can't write a cheque on it, now.

CHARLOTTE: Larry, let me help you!

MISS FELLOWES [*approaching*]: Charlotte, Charlotte, Charlie!

CHARLOTTE: Help me and let me help you!

SHANNON: The helpless can't help the helpless!

CHARLOTTE: Let me in. Judy's coming!

SHANNON: Let me go. Go away!

[*He thrusts her violently back and rushes into his cubicle, slamming and bolting the door – though the gauze netting is left sticking out. As* MISS FELLOWES *charges on to the verandah,* CHARLOTTE *runs into the next cubicle, and* HANNAH *moves over from where she has been watching and meets her in the centre.*]

MISS FELLOWES: Shannon, Shannon! Where are you?

HANNAH: I think Mr Shannon has gone down to the beach.

MISS FELLOWES: Was Charlotte Goodall with him? A young blonde girl in our party – was she with him?

HANNAH: No, nobody was with him; he was completely alone.

MISS FELLOWES: I heard a door slam.

HANNAH: That was mine.

MISS FELLOWES [*pointing to the door with the gauze sticking out*]: Is this yours?

HANNAH: Yes, mine. I rushed out to catch the sunset.

[*At this moment* MISS FELLOWES *hears* CHARLOTTE *sobbing in Hannah's cubicle. She throws the door open.*]

MISS FELLOWES: Charlotte! Come out of there, Charlie! [*She has seized Charlotte by the wrist.*] What's your word worth – nothing? You promised you'd stay away from him! [CHARLOTTE *frees her arm, sobbing bitterly.* MISS FELLOWES *seizes her again, tighter, and starts dragging her away.*] I have talked to your father about this man by long-distance and he's getting out a warrant for his arrest, if he dare try coming back to the States after this!

CHARLOTTE: I don't care.

MISS FELLOWES: I do! I'm responsible for you.

CHARLOTTE: I don't want to go back to Texas.

MISS FELLOWES: Yes, you do! And you will!

[*She takes Charlotte firmly by the arm and drags her away behind the hotel.* HANNAH *comes out of her cubicle, where she had gone when* MISS FELLOWES *pulled Charlotte out of it.*]

SHANNON [*from his cubicle*]: Ah, God. . . .

[HANNAH *crosses to his cubicle and knocks by the door.*]

HANNAH: The coast is clear now, Mr Shannon.

[SHANNON *does not answer or appear. She sets down her portfolio to pick up Nonno's white linen suit, which she had pressed and hung on the verandah. She crosses to his cubicle with it, and calls in.*]

HANNAH: Nonno? It's almost time for supper! There's going to be a lovely, stormy sunset in a few minutes.

NONNO [*from within*]: Coming!

HANNAH: So is Christmas, Nonno.

NONNO: So is the Fourth of July!

HANNAH: We're past the Fourth of July. Hallowe'en comes next and then Thanksgiving. I hope you'll come forth sooner. [*She lifts the gauze net over his cubicle door.*] Here's your suit, I've pressed it. [*She enters the cubicle.*]

NONNO: It's mighty dark in here, Hannah.

HANNAH: I'll turn the light on for you.

[SHANNON *comes out of his cubicle, like the survivor of a plane crash, bringing out with him several pieces of his clerical garb. The black heavy silk bib is loosely fastened about his panting, sweating chest. He hangs over it a heavy gold cross with an amethyst centre and attempts to fasten on a starched round collar. Now* HANNAH *comes back out of Nonno's cubicle, adjusting the flowing silk tie which goes with her 'artist' costume. For a moment they both face front, adjusting their two outfits. They are like two actors in a play which is about to fold on the road, preparing gravely for a performance which may be the last one.*]

HANNAH [*glancing at Shannon*]: Are you planning to conduct church services of some kind here tonight, Mr Shannon?

SHANNON: Goddamit, please help me with this! [*He means the round collar.*]

HANNAH [*crossing behind him*]: If you're not going to conduct a church service, why get into that uncomfortable outfit?

SHANNON: Because I've been accused of being defrocked and of lying about it, that's why. I want to show the ladies that I'm still a clocked – *frocked!* – minister of the . . .

HANNAH: Isn't that lovely gold cross enough to convince the ladies?

SHANNON: No; they know I redeemed it from a Mexico City pawnshop, and they suspect that that's where I got it in the first place.

HANNAH: Hold still just a minute. [*She is behind him, trying to fasten the collar.*] There now; let's hope it stays on. The buttonhole is so frayed I'm afraid that it won't hold the button. [*Her fear is instantly confirmed: the button pops out.*]

SHANNON: Where'd it go?

HANNAH: Here, right under. . . .

[*She picks it up.* SHANNON *rips the collar off, crumples it and hurls it off the verandah. Then he falls into the hammock, panting and twisting.* HANNAH *quietly opens her sketch-pad and begins to sketch him. He doesn't at first notice what she is doing.*]

HANNAH [*as she sketches*]: How long have you been inactive in the, uh, Church, Mr Shannon?

SHANNON: What's that got to do with the price of rice in China?

HANNAH [*gently*]: Nothing.

SHANNON: What's it got to do with the price of coffee beans in Brazil?

HANNAH: I retract the question. With apologies.

SHANNON: To answer your question politely, I have been inactive in the Church for all but one year since I was ordained a minister of the Church.

HANNAH [*sketching rapidly and moving forward a bit to see his face better*]: Well, that's quite a sabbatical, Mr Shannon.

SHANNON: Yeah, that's ... quite a ... sabbatical.

[NONNO's *voice is heard from his cubicle repeating a line of poetry several times.*]

SHANNON: Is your grandfather talking to himself in there?

HANNAH: No; he composes out loud. He has to commit his lines to memory because he can't see to write them or read them.

SHANNON: Sounds like he's stuck on one line.

HANNAH: Yes. I'm afraid his memory is failing. Memory failure is his greatest dread. [*She says this almost coolly, as if it didn't matter.*]

SHANNON: Are you drawing me?

HANNAH: Trying to. You're a very difficult subject. When the Mexican painter Siqueiros did his portrait of the American poet Hart Crane he had to paint him with closed eyes because he couldn't paint his eyes open – there was too much suffering in them and he couldn't paint it.

SHANNON: Sorry, but I'm not going to close my eyes for you. I'm hypnotizing myself – at least trying to – by looking at the light on the orange tree ... leaves.

HANNAH: That's all right. I can paint your eyes open.

SHANNON: I had one parish one year and then I wasn't defrocked, but I was ... locked out of my church.

HANNAH: Oh ... Why did they lock you out of it?

SHANNON: Fornication and heresy ... in the same week.

HANNAH [*sketching rapidly*]: What were the circumstances of the ... uh ... first offence?

SHANNON: Yeah, the fornication came first, preceded the

heresy by several days. A very young Sunday-school teacher asked to see me privately in my study. A pretty little thing – no chance in the world – only child, and both of her parents were spinsters, almost identical spinsters wearing clothes of the opposite sexes. Fooling some of the people some of the time, but not me – none of the time. . . . [*He is pacing the verandah with gathering agitation, and the all-inclusive mockery that his guilt produces.*] Well, she declared herself to me – wildly.

HANNAH: A declaration of love?

SHANNON: Don't make *fun* of me, honey!

HANNAH: I wasn't.

SHANNON: The natural, or unnatural, attraction of one . . . lunatic for . . . another . . . that's all it was. I was the god-damnedest prig in those days that even you could imagine. I said, let's kneel down together and pray, and we did; we knelt down, but all of a sudden the kneeling position turned to a reclining position on the rug of my study and . . . When we got up? I struck her. Yes, I did, I struck her in the face and called her a damned little tramp. So she ran home. I heard the next day she'd cut herself with her father's straight-blade razor. Yeah, the paternal spinster shaved.

HANNAH: Fatally?

SHANNON: Just broke the skin surface enough to bleed a little but it made a scandal.

HANNAH: Yes, I can imagine that it . . . provoked some comment.

SHANNON: That it did, it did that. [*He pauses a moment in his fierce pacing as if the recollection still appalled him.*] So the next Sunday when I climbed into the pulpit and looked down over all of those smug, disapproving, accusing faces up-lifted, I had an impulse to shake them – so I shook them. I had a prepared sermon – meek, apologetic – I threw it away, tossed it into the chancel. Look here, I said, I shouted, I'm tired of conducting services in praise and worship of a senile delinquent – yeah, that's what I said, I shouted! All your Western theologies, the whole mythology of them, are based on the concept of God as a *senile delinquent*, by God, I

will not and cannot continue to conduct services in praise
and worship of this, this . . . this . . .

HANNAH [*quietly*]: Senile delinquent?

SHANNON: Yeah, this angry, petulant old man. I mean He's
represented like a bad-tempered childish old, old, sick,
peevish man – I mean like the sort of old man in a nursing-
home that's putting together a jigsaw puzzle and can't put it
together and gets furious at it and kicks over the table.
Yes, I tell you they *do* that, all our theologies do it – accuse
God of being a cruel, senile delinquent, blaming the world
and brutally punishing all He created for His own faults in
construction, and then, ha-ha, yeah – a thunderstorm broke
that Sunday. . . .

HANNAH: You mean *outside* the church?

SHANNON: Yep; it was wilder than I was! And out they slithered, they slithered out of their pews to their shiny black
cockroach sedans, ha-ha, and I shouted after them, hell, I
even followed them halfway out of the church, shouting
after them as they . . . [*He stops with a gasp for breath.*]

HANNAH: Slithered out?

SHANNON: I shouted after them, go on, go home and close
your house windows, all your windows and doors, against
the truth about God!

HANNAH: Oh, my heavens. Which is just what they did –
poor things.

SHANNON: Miss Jelkes honey, Pleasant Valley, Virginia, was
an exclusive suburb of a large city and these poor things
were not poor – materially speaking.

HANNAH [*smiling a bit*]: What was the, uh, upshot of
it?

SHANNON: Upshot of it? Well, I wasn't defrocked. I was just
locked out of the church in Pleasant Valley, Virginia, and
put in a nice little private asylum to recuperate from a
complete nervous breakdown, as they preferred to regard
it, and then, and then I . . . I entered my present line – tours
of God's world conducted by a minister of God with a
cross and a round collar to prove it. Collecting evidence!

HANNAH: Evidence of what, Mr Shannon?

SHANNON [*a touch shyly now*]: My personal idea of God, not as a senile delinquent, but as a . . .

HANNAH: Incomplete sentence.

SHANNON: It's going to storm tonight – a terrific electric storm. Then you will see the Reverend T. Lawrence Shannon's conception of God Almighty paying a visit to the world He created. I want to go back to the Church and preach the gospel of God as Lightning and Thunder . . . and also stray dogs vivisected and . . . and . . . and. . . . [*He points out suddenly towards the sea.*] That's him! There he is now! [*He is pointing out at a blaze, a majestic apocalypse of gold light, shafting the sky as the sun drops into the Pacific.*] His oblivious majesty – and *here I am* on this . . . dilapidated verandah of a cheap hotel, out of season, in a country caught and destroyed in its flesh and corrupted in its spirit by its gold-hungry Conquistadors that bore the flag of the Inquisition along with the Cross of Christ. Yes . . . and . . . [*There is a pause.*]

HANNAH: Mr Shannon . . . ?

SHANNON: Yes . . . ?

HANNAH [*smiling a little*]: I have a strong feeling you will go back to the Church with this evidence you've been collecting, but when you do and it's a black Sunday morning, look out over the congregation, over the smug, complacent faces for a few old, very old faces, looking up at you, as you begin your sermon, with eyes like a piercing cry for something to still look up to, something to still believe in. And then I think you'll not shout what you say you shouted that black Sunday in Pleasant Valley, Virginia. I think you will throw away the violent, furious sermon, you'll toss *it* into the chancel, and talk about . . . no, maybe talk about . . . nothing . . . just . . .

SHANNON: What?

HANNAH: Lead them beside still waters because you know how badly they need the still waters, Mr Shannon.

[*There is a moment of silence between them.*]

SHANNON: Lemme see that thing. [*He seizes the sketch-pad from her and is visibly impressed by what he sees. There is another moment which is prolonged to HANNAH's embarrassment.*]

HANNAH: Where did you say the patrona put your party of ladies?

SHANNON: She had her ... Mexican concubines put their luggage in the annex.

HANNAH: Where is the annex?

SHANNON: Right down the hill back of here, but all of my ladies except the teen-age Medea and the older Medea have gone out in a glass-bottomed boat to observe the submarine marvels.

HANNAH: Well, when they come back to the annex they're going to observe my watercolours with some marvellous submarine prices marked on the mattings.

SHANNON: By God, you're a hustler, aren't you; you're a fantastic, cool hustler.

HANNAH: Yes, like *you*, Mr Shannon. [*She gently removes her sketch-pad from his grasp.*] Oh, Mr Shannon, if Nonno, Grandfather, comes out of his cell number 4 before I get back, will you please look out for him for me? I won't be longer than three shakes of a lively sheep's tail. [*She snatches up her portfolio and goes briskly off the verandah.*]

SHANNON: Fantastic, absolutely fantastic.

[*There is a windy sound in the rain forest and a flicker of gold light like a silent scattering of gold coins on the verandah; then the sound of shouting voices. The Mexican boys appear with a wildly agitated creature – a captive iguana tied up in a shirt. They crouch down by the cactus clumps that are growing below the verandah and hitch the iguana to a post with a piece of rope.*
MAXINE *is attracted by the commotion and appears on the verandah above them.*]

PEDRO: Tenemos fiesta!*

PANCHO: Comeremos bien.

PEDRO: Damela, damela! Yo la ataré.

PANCHO: *Yo* la cojí – *yo* la ataré!

PEDRO: Lo que vas a *hacer* es dejarla escapar.

MAXINE: Ammarla fuerte! Ole, ole! No la dejes escapar. Dejala moverse! [*To Shannon.*] They caught an iguana.

*We're going to have a feast! / We'll eat good. / Give it to me! I'll tie it up. / I caught it – *I'll* tie it up! / You'll only let it get away. / Tie it up tight! Ole, ole! Don't let it get away. Give it enough room!

SHANNON: I've noticed they did that, Maxine.

[*She is holding her drink deliberately close to him. The Germans have heard the commotion and crowd on to the verandah.* FRAU FAHRENKOPF *rushes over to Maxine.*]

FRAU FAHRENKOPF: What is it? What's going on? A snake? Did they catch a snake?

MAXINE: No. *Lizard.*

FRAU FAHRENKOPF [*with exaggerated revulsion*]: Ouuu ... *lizard!* [*She strikes a grotesque attitude of terror as if she were threatened by Jack the Ripper.*]

SHANNON [*to Maxine*]: You like iguana meat, don't you?

FRAU FAHRENKOPF: Eat? *Eat?* A big *lizard?*

MAXINE: Yep, they're mighty good eating – taste like white meat of chicken.

[FRAU FAHRENKOPF *rushes back to her family. They talk excitely in German about the iguana.*]

SHANNON: If you mean Mexican chicken, that's no recommendation. Mexican chickens are scavengers and they taste like what they scavenge.

MAXINE: Naw; I mean Texas chicken.

SHANNON [*dreamily*]: Texas ... Chicken ...

[*He paces restlessly down the verandah.* MAXINE *divides her attention between his lean figure, that seems incapable of stillness, and the wriggling bodies of the Mexican boys lying on their stomachs half under the verandah – as if she were mentally comparing two opposite attractions to her simple, sensual nature.* SHANNON *turns at the end of the verandah and sees her eyes fixed on him.*]

SHANNON: What is the sex of this iguana, Maxine?

MAXINE: Hah, who cares about the sex of an iguana ... [*He passes close by her.*] ... except another ... iguana?

SHANNON: Haven't you heard the limerick about iguanas? [*He removes her drink from her hand and it seems as if he might drink it, but he only sniffs it, with an expression of repugnance. She chuckles.*]

> There was a young gaucho named Bruno
> Who said about love, This I do know:
> Women are fine, and sheep are divine,
>   But iguanas are – *Numero Uno!*

[*On 'Numero Uno'* SHANNON *empties Maxine's drink over the railing, deliberately on to the humped, wriggling posterior of* PEDRO, *who springs up with angry protests.*]

PEDRO: Me cágo ... hijo de la ...

SHANNON: Qué? Qué?

MAXINE: Véte!

[SHANNON *laughs viciously. The iguana escapes and both boys rush shouting after it. One of them dives on it and recaptures it at the end of the jungle.*]

PANCHO: La iguana se escapé.

MAXINE: Cojela, cojela! La cojíste? So no la cojes, te moderá el culo. La cojíste?

PEDRO: La cojí.*

[*The boys wriggle back under the verandah with the iguana.*]

MAXINE [*returning to Shannon*]: I thought you were gonna break down and take a drink, Reverend.

SHANNON: Just the odour of liquor makes me feel nauseated.

MAXINE: You couldn't smell it if you got it *in* you. [*She touches his sweating forehead. He brushes her hand off like an insect.*] Hah! [*She crosses over to the liquor cart, and he looks after her with a sadistic grin.*]

SHANNON: Maxine honey, whoever told you that you look good in tight pants was not a sincere friend of yours.

[*He turns away. At the same instant, a crash and a hoarse, startled outcry are heard from Nonno's cubicle.*]

MAXINE: I knew it! I *knew* it! The old man's took a fall!

[SHANNON *rushes into the cubicle, followed by* MAXINE. *The light has been gradually, steadily dimming during the incident of the iguana's escape. There is, in effect, a division of scenes here, though it is accomplished without a blackout or curtain. As* SHANNON *and* MAXINE *enter Nonno's cubicle,* HERR FAHRENKOPF *appears on the now twilit verandah. He turns on an outsize light fixture that is suspended from overhead, a full pearly-moon of a light globe that gives an unearthly lustre to the scene. The great pearly globe is decorated by night insects, large but gossamer moths that have immolated themselves on its*]

---

*The iguana's escaped. / Get it, get it! Have you got it? If you don't, it'll bite your behind. Have you got it? / He's got it.

surface: the light through their wings gives them an opalescent colour, a touch of fantasy.

Now SHANNON *leads the old poet out of his cubicle, on to the facing verandah. The old man is impeccably dressed in snow-white linen with a black string tie. His leonine mane of hair gleams like silver as he passes under the globe.*]

NONNO: No bones broken. I'm made out of indiarubber!

SHANNON: A traveller-born falls down many times in his travels.

NONNO: Hannah? [*His vision and other senses have so far deteriorated that he thinks he is being led out by* HANNAH.] I'm pretty sure I'm going to finish it here.

SHANNON [*shouting, gently*]: I've got the same feeling, Grampa.

[MAXINE *follows them out of the cubicle.*]

NONNO: I've never been surer of anything in my life.

SHANNON [*gently and wryly*]: I've never been surer of anything in mine either.

[HERR FAHRENKOPF *has been listening with an expression of entrancement to his portable radio, held close to his ear, the sound unrealistically low. Now he turns it off and makes an excited speech.*]

HERR FAHRENKOPF: The London fires have spread all the way from the heart of London to the Channel coast! Goering, Field-Marshal Goering, calls it 'the new phase of conquest!' Super-fire-bombs! Each night!

[NONNO *catches only the excited tone of this announcement and interprets it as a request for a recitation. He strikes the floor with his cane, throws back his silver-maned head and begins the delivery in a grand, declamatory style.*]

NONNO: Youth must be wanton, youth must be quick,
       Dance to the candle while lasteth the wick,

       Youth must be foolish and ...

[NONNO *falters on the line, a look of confusion and fear on his face. The Germans are amused.* WOLFGANG *goes up to Nonno and shouts into his face.*]

WOLFGANG: Sir? What is your age? How old?

[HANNAH, *who has just returned to the verandah, rushes up to her grandfather and answers for him.*]

HANNAH: He is ninety-seven years *young*!

HERR FAHRENKOPF: How old?

HANNAH: Ninety-seven – almost a *century young*!

[HERR FAHRENKOPF *repeats this information to his beaming wife and Hilda in German.*]

NONNO [*cutting in on the Germans*]:

      Youth must be foolish and mirthful and blind,
      Gaze not before and glance not behind,

      Mark not ...

[*He falters again.*]

HANNAH [*prompting him, holding tightly on to his arm*]:

      Mark not the shadow that darkens the way –

[*They recite the next lines together.*]

      Regret not the glitter of any lost day,
      But laugh with no reason except the red wine,
      For youth must be youthful and foolish and blind!

[*The Germans are loudly amused.* WOLFGANG *applauds directly in the old poet's face.* NONNO *makes a little unsteady bow, leaning forward precariously on his cane.* SHANNON *takes a firm hold of his arm as* HANNAH *turns to the Germans, opening her portfolio of sketches and addressing Wolfgang.*]

HANNAH: Am I right in thinking you are on your honeymoon? [*There is no response, and she repeats the question in German while* FRAU FAHRENKOPF *laughs and nods vehemently.*] Habe ich recht dass Sie auf Ihrer Hochzeitsreise sind! Was für eine hübsche junge Braut! Ich mache Pastell-Skizzen ... darf ich, würden Sie mir erlauben ...? Würden Sie, bitte ... bitte. ...

[HERR FAHRENKOPF *bursts into a Nazi marching song and leads his party to the champagne bucket on the table at the left.* SHANNON *has steered Nonno to the other table.*]

NONNO [*exhilarated*]: Hannah! What was the take?

HANNAH [*embarrassed*]: Grandfather, sit down, please stop shouting!

NONNO: Hah? Did they cross your palm with silver or paper, Hannah?

HANNAH [*almost desperately*]: Nonno! No more shouting! Sit down at the table. It's time to *eat*!

SHANNON: Chow time, Grampa.

NONNO [*confused but still shouting*]: How much did they come across with?

HANNAH: Nonno! *Please!*

NONNO: Did they, did you ... sell 'em a ... watercolour?

HANNAH: No sale, Grandfather!

MAXINE: Hah!

[HANNAH *turns to Shannon, her usual composure shattered, or nearly so.*]

HANNAH: He won't sit down or stop shouting.

NONNO [*blinking and beaming with the grotesque suggestion of an old coquette*]: Hah? How rich did we strike it, Hannah?

SHANNON: *You* sit down, Miss Jelkes. [*He says it with gentle authority, to which she yields. He takes hold of the old man's forearm and places in his hand a crumpled Mexican bill.*] Sir? Sir? [*He is shouting.*] Five! Dollars! I'm putting it in your pocket.

HANNAH: We can't accept ... gratuities, Mr Shannon.

SHANNON: Hell, I gave him five pesos.

NONNO: Mighty good for one poem!

SHANNON: Sir? Sir? The *pecuniary rewards* of a *poem* are *grossly inferior* to its *merits, always!*

[*He is being fiercely, almost mockingly tender with the old man – a thing we are when the pathos of the old, the ancient, the dying is such a wound to our own (savagely beleaguered) nerves and sensibilities that this outside demand on us is beyond our collateral, our emotional reserve. This is as true of Hannah as it is of Shannon, of course. They have both overdrawn their reserves at this point of the encounter between them.*]

NONNO: Hah? Yes.... [*He is worn out now, but still shouting.*] We're going to clean up in this place!

SHANNON: You bet you're going to clean up here!

[MAXINE *utters her one-note bark of a laugh.* SHANNON *throws a hard roll at her. She wanders amiably back towards the German table.*]

NONNO [*tottering, panting, hanging on to Shannon's arm, thinking it is Hannah's*]: Is the, the ... dining-room ... crowded? [*He looks blindly about with wild surmise.*]

SHANNON: Yep, it's filled to capacity! There's a big crowd at the door! [*His voice doesn't penetrate the old man's deafness.*]

NONNO: If there's a cocktail lounge, Hannah, we ought to ...
work that ... first. Strike while the iron is hot, ho, ho, while
it's hot.... [*This is like a delirium – only as strong a woman as
Hannah could remain outwardly impassive.*]

HANNAH: He thinks you're me, Mr Shannon. Help him into
a chair. Please stay with him a minute. I ...

[*She moves away from the table and breathes as if she has just
been dragged up half-drowned from the sea.* SHANNON *eases
the old man into a chair. Almost at once* NONNO's *feverish
vitality collapses and he starts drifting back towards half-sleep.*]

SHANNON [*crossing to Hannah*]: What're you breathing like
that for?

HANNAH: Some people take a drink, some take a pill. I just
take a few deep breaths.

SHANNON: You're making too much out of this. It's a natural
thing in a man as old as Grampa.

HANNAH: I know, I know. He's had more than one of these
little 'cerebral accidents' as you call them, and all in the
last few months. He was amazing till lately. I had to show
his passport to prove that he was the oldest living and
practising poet on earth. We did well, we made expenses
and *more*! But ... when I saw he was failing, I tried to per-
suade him to go back to Nantucket, but he conducts our
tours. He said, 'No; *Mexico*!' So here we are on this windy
hilltop like a pair of scarecrows.... The bus from Mexico
City broke down at an altitude of 15,000 feet above sea-
level. That's when I think the latest cerebral incident happened. It isn't so much the loss of hearing and sight but the
... dimming out of the mind that I can't bear, because until
lately, just lately, his mind was amazingly clear. But yesterday? In Tasco? I spent nearly all we had left on the wheel-
chair for him and still he insisted that we go on with the trip
till we got to the sea, the ... cradle of life as he calls it....
[*She suddenly notices Nonno, sunk in his chair as if lifeless. She
draws a sharp breath, and goes quietly to him.*]

SHANNON [*to the Mexican boys*]: Servicio! Aqui! [*The force of
his order proves effective: they serve the fish course.*]

HANNAH: What a kind man you are. I don't know how to
thank you, Mr Shannon. I'm going to wake him up now.

Nonno! [*She claps her hands quietly at his ear. The old man rouses with a confused, breathless chuckle.*] Nonno, linen napkins. [*She removes a napkin from the pocket of her smock.*] I always carry one with me, you see, in case we run into paper napkins, as sometimes happens, you see. . . .

NONNO: Wonderful place here. . . . I hope it is à la carte, Hannah. I want a very light supper so I won't get sleepy. I'm going to work after supper. I'm going to finish it here.

HANNAH: Nonno? We've made a friend here. Nonno, this is the Reverend Mr Shannon.

NONNO [*struggling out of his confusion*]: Reverend?

HANNAH [*shouting to him*]: Mr Shannon's an Episcopal clergyman, Nonno.

NONNO: A man of God?

HANNAH: A man of God, on vacation.

NONNO: Hannah, tell him I'm too old to baptize and too young to bury, but on the market for marriage to a rich widow, fat, fair, and forty.

[NONNO *is delighted by all of his own little jokes. One can see him exchanging these pleasantries with the rocking-chair brigades of summer hotels at the turn of the century – and with professors' wives at little colleges in New England. But now it has become somewhat grotesque in a touching way, this desire to please, this playful manner, these venerable jokes.* SHANNON *goes along with it. The old man touches something in him which is outside of his concern with himself. This part of the scene, which is played in a 'scherzo' mood, has an accompanying windy obbligato on the hilltop – all through it we hear the wind from the sea gradually rising, sweeping up the hill through the rain forest, and there are fitful glimmers of lightning in the sky.*]

NONNO: But very few ladies ever go past forty if you believe 'em, ho, ho! Ask him to . . . give the blessing. Mexican food needs blessing.

SHANNON: Sir, you give the blessing. I'll be right with you. [*He has broken one of his shoe-laces.*]

NONNO: Tell him I will oblige him on one condition.

SHANNON: What condition, sir?

NONNO: That you'll keep my daughter company when I retire after dinner. I go to bed with the chickens and get up

with the roosters, ho, ho! So you're a man of God. A bene-
dict or a bachelor?

SHANNON: Bachelor, sir. No sane and civilized woman would
have me, Mr Coffin.

NONNO: What did he say, Hannah?

HANNAH [*embarrassed*]: Nonno, give the blessing.

NONNO [*not hearing this*]: I call her my daughter, but she's my
daughter's daughter. We've been in charge of each other
since she lost both her parents in the very first automobile
crash on the island of Nantucket.

HANNAH: Nonno, give the blessing.

NONNO: She isn't a modern flapper, she isn't modern and she
– doesn't flap, but she was brought up to be a wonderful
wife and mother. But . . . I'm a selfish old man, so I've kept
her all to myself.

HANNAH [*shouting in his ear*]: Nonno, Nonno, the blessing!

NONNO [*rising with an effort*]: Yes, the blessing. Bless this food
to our use, and ourselves to Thy service. Amen. [*He totters
back into his chair.*]

SHANNON: Amen.
   [NONNO's *mind starts drifting, his head drooping forward. He
   murmurs to himself.*]

SHANNON: How good is the old man's poetry?

HANNAH: My grandfather was a fairly well-known minor
poet before the First World War and for a little while after.

SHANNON: In the minor league, huh?

HANNAH: Yes, a minor league poet with a major league spirit.
I'm proud to be his granddaughter. . . . [*She draws a pack of
cigarettes from her pocket, then replaces it immediately without
taking a cigarette.*]

NONNO [*very confused*]: Hannah, it's too hot for . . . hot cereals
this . . . morning. . . . [*He shakes his head several times with a
rueful chuckle.*]

HANNAH: He's not quite back, you see; he thinks it's morning. [*She says this as if making an embarrassing admission, with
a quick, frightened smile at Shannon.*]

SHANNON: Fantastic – *fantastic*.

HANNAH: That word 'fantastic' seems to be your favourite
word, Mr Shannon.

SHANNON [*looking out gloomily from the verandah*]: Yeah, well, you know we – live on two levels, Miss Jelkes, the realistic level and the fantastic level, and which is the real one, really? ...

HANNAH: I would say both, Mr Shannon.

SHANNON: But when you live on the fantastic level as I have lately but have got to operate on the realistic level, that's when you're spooked, that's the spook.... [*This is said as if it were a private reflection.*] I thought I'd shake the spook here but conditions have changed here. I didn't know the patrona had turned to a widow, a sort of bright widow spider. [*He chuckles almost like Nonno.*]

   [MAXINE *has pushed one of those gay little brass-and-glass liquor carts around the corner of the verandah. It is laden with an ice bucket, coconuts and a variety of liquors. She hums gaily to herself as she pushes the cart close to the table.*]

MAXINE: Cocktails, anybody?

HANNAH: No, thank you, Mrs Faulk, I don't think we care for any.

SHANNON: People don't drink cocktails between the fish and the entrée, Maxine honey.

MAXINE: Grampa needs a toddy to wake him up. Old folks need a toddy to pick 'em up. [*She shouts into the old man's ear.*] Grampa! How about a toddy? [*Her hips are thrust out at Shannon.*]

SHANNON: Maxine, your ass – excuse me, Miss Jelkes – your hips, Maxine, are too fat for this verandah.

MAXINE: Hah! Mexicans like 'em, if I can judge by the pokes and pinches I get in the buses to town. And so do the Germans. Ev'ry time I go near Herr Fahrenkopf he gives me a pinch or a goose.

SHANNON: Then go near him again for another goose.

MAXINE: Hah! I'm mixing Grampa a Manhattan with two cherries in it so he'll live through dinner.

SHANNON: Go on back to your Nazis. I'll mix the Manhattan for him. [*He goes to the liquor cart.*]

MAXINE [*to Hannah*]: How about you, honey – a little soda with lime juice?

HANNAH: Nothing for me, thank you.

SHANNON: Don't make nervous people more nervous, Maxine.

MAXINE: You better let me mix that toddy for Grampa; you're making a mess of it, Shannon.

[*With a snort of fury, he thrusts the liquor cart like a battering ram at her belly. Some of the bottles fall off it; she thrusts it right back at him.*]

HANNAH: Mrs Faulk, Mr Shannon, this is childish; please stop it!

[*The Germans are attracted by the disturbance. They cluster around, laughing delightedly.* SHANNON *and* MAXINE *seize opposite ends of the rolling liquor cart and thrust it towards each other, both grinning fiercely as gladiators in mortal combat. The Germans shriek with laughter and chatter in German.*]

HANNAH: Mr Shannon, stop it! [*She appeals to the Germans.*] Bitte! Nehmen Sie die Spirituosen weg. Bitte, nehmen Sie die weg.

[SHANNON *has wrested the cart from Maxine and pushed it at the Germans. They scream delightedly. The cart crashes into the wall of the verandah.* SHANNON *leaps down the steps and runs into the foliage. Birds scream in the rain forest. Then sudden quiet returns to the verandah as the Germans go back to their own table.*]

MAXINE: Crazy, black Irish protestant son of a ... protestant!

HANNAH: Mrs Faulk, he's putting up a struggle not to drink.

MAXINE: Don't interfere. You're an interfering woman.

HANNAH: Mr Shannon is dangerously ... disturbed.

MAXINE: I know how to handle him, honey – you just met him today. Here's Grampa's Manhattan cocktail with two cherries in it.

HANNAH: Please don't call him Grampa.

MAXINE: Shannon calls him Grampa.

HANNAH [*taking the drink*]: He doesn't make it sound condescending, but you *do*. My grandfather is a gentleman in the true sense of the word; he is a *gentle man*.

MAXINE: What are you?

HANNAH: I am his granddaughter.

MAXINE: Is that all you are?

HANNAH: I think it's enough to be.

MAXINE: Yeah, but you're also a dead-beat, using that dying old man for a front to get in places without the cash to pay even one day in advance. Why, you're dragging him around with you like Mexican beggars carry around a sick baby to put the touch on the tourists.

HANNAH: I told you I had no money.

MAXINE: Yes, and I told you that I was a widow – recent. In such a financial hole they might as well have buried me with my husband.

[SHANNON *reappears from the jungle foliage, but remains unnoticed by Hannah and Maxine.*]

HANNAH [*with forced calm*]: Tomorrow morning, at daybreak, I will go in town. I will set up my easel in the plaza and peddle my watercolours and sketch tourists. I am not a weak person; my failure here isn't typical of me.

MAXINE: I'm not a weak person either.

HANNAH: No. By no means, no. Your strength is awe-inspiring.

MAXINE: You're goddam right about that, but how do you think you'll get to Acapulco without the cab-fare or even the bus-fare there?

HANNAH: I will go on shanks's mare, Mrs Faulk – islanders are good walkers. And if you doubt my word for it, if you really think I came here as a dead-beat, then I will put my grandfather back in his wheel-chair and push him back down this hill to the road and all the way back into town.

MAXINE: Ten miles, with a storm coming up?

HANNAH: Yes, I would – I will. [*She is dominating Maxine in this exchange. Both stand beside the table.* NONNO's *head is drooping back into sleep.*]

MAXINE: I wouldn't let you.

HANNAH: But you've made it clear that you don't want us to stay here for one night even.

MAXINE: The storm would blow that old man out of his wheel-chair like a dead leaf.

HANNAH: He would prefer that to staying where he's not welcome, and I would prefer it for him, and for myself, Mrs Faulk. [*She turns to the Mexican boys.*] Where is his wheel-chair? Where is my grandfather's wheel-chair?

[*This exchange has roused the old man. He struggles up from his chair, confused, strikes the floor with his cane and starts declaiming a poem.*]

NONNO: Love's an old remembered song
                A drunken fiddler plays,
                Stumbling crazily along

                Crooked alleyways.
                When his heart is mad with music
                He will play the –

HANNAH: Nonno, not now, Nonno! He thought someone asked for a poem. [*She gets him back into the chair.* HANNAH *and* MAXINE *are still unaware of Shannon.*]

MAXINE: Calm down, honey.

HANNAH: I'm perfectly calm, Mrs Faulk.

MAXINE: I'm *not*. That's the trouble.

HANNAH: I understand that, Mrs Faulk. You lost your husband just lately. I think you probably miss him more than you know.

MAXINE: No, the trouble is Shannon.

HANNAH: You mean his nervous state and his ...?

MAXINE: No, I just mean Shannon. I want you to lay off him honey. You're not for Shannon and Shannon isn't for you.

HANNAH: Mrs Faulk, I'm a New England spinster who is pushing forty.

MAXINE: I got the vibrations between you – I'm very good at catching vibrations between people – and there sure was a vibration between you and Shannon the moment you got here. That, just that, believe me, nothing but that has made this ... misunderstanding between us. So if you just don't mess with Shannon, you and your Grampa can stay on here as long as you want to, honey.

HANNAH: Oh, Mrs Faulk, do I look like a *vamp*?

MAXINE: They come in all types. I've had all types of them here.

        [SHANNON *comes over to the table.*]

SHANNON: Maxine, I told you don't make nervous people more nervous, but you wouldn't listen.

MAXINE: What you need is a drink.

SHANNON: Let me decide about that.

HANNAH: Won't you sit down with us, Mr Shannon, and eat something? Please. You'll feel better.

SHANNON: I'm not hungry right now.

HANNAH: Well, just sit down with us, won't you?

[SHANNON *sits down with Hannah.*]

MAXINE [*warningly to Hannah*]: O.K., O.K....

NONNO [*rousing a bit and mumbling*]: Wonderful ... wonderful place here.

[MAXINE *retires from the table and wheels the liquor cart over to the German party.*]

SHANNON: Would you have gone through with it?

HANNAH: Haven't you ever played poker, Mr Shannon?

SHANNON: You mean you were bluffing?

HANNAH: Let's say I was drawing to an inside straight. [*The wind rises and sweeps up the hill like a great waking sigh from the ocean.*] It *is* going to storm. I hope your ladies aren't still out in that, that ... glass-bottomed boat, observing the submarine ... marvels.

SHANNON: That's because you don't know these ladies. However they're back from the boat trip. They're down at the cantina dancing together to the juke-box and hatching new plots to get me kicked out of Blake Tours.

HANNAH: What would you do if you ...?

SHANNON: Got the sack? Go back to the Church or take the long swim to China. [HANNAH *removes a crumpled pack of cigarettes from her pocket. She discovers only two left in the pack and decides to save them for later. She returns the pack to her pocket.*] May I have one of your cigarettes, Miss Jelkes? [*She offers him the pack. He takes it from her and crumples it and throws it off the verandah.*] Never smoke those; they're made out of tobacco from cigarette stubs that beggars pick up off sidewalks and out of gutters in Mexico City. [*He produces a tin of English cigarettes.*] Have these – Benson and Hedges, imported, in an airtight tin, my luxury in my life.

HANNAH: Why – thank you, I will, since you have thrown mine away.

SHANNON: I'm going to tell you something about yourself.
You are a lady, a *real* one and a *great* one.

HANNAH: What have I done to merit that compliment from
you?

SHANNON: It isn't a compliment; it's just a report on what
I've noticed about you at a time when it's hard for me to
notice anything outside myself. You took out those
Mexican cigarettes, you found you just had two left, you
can't afford to buy a new pack of even that cheap brand, so
you put them away for later. Right?

HANNAH: Mercilessly accurate, Mr Shannon.

SHANNON: But when I asked you for one, you offered it to
me without a sign of reluctance.

HANNAH: Aren't you making a big point out of a small
matter?

SHANNON: Just the opposite, honey. I'm making a small
point out of a very large matter. [SHANNON *has put a
cigarette in his lips, but has no matches.* HANNAH *has some, and
she lights his cigarette for him.*] How'd you learn how to light
a match in the wind?

HANNAH: Oh, I've learned lots of useful things like that. I
wish I'd learned some *big* ones.

SHANNON: Such as what?

HANNAH: How to help you, Mr Shannon....

SHANNON: Now I know why I came here!

HANNAH: To meet someone who can light a match in the
wind?

SHANNON [*looking down at the table, his voice choking*]: To meet
someone who wants to *help* me, Miss Jelkes.... [*He makes a
quick, embarrassed turn in the chair, as if to avoid her seeing that
he has tears in his eyes. She regards him steadily and tenderly, as she
would her grandfather.*]

HANNAH: Has it been so long since anyone has wanted to
help you, or have you just ...

SHANNON: Have I – what?

HANNAH: Just been so much involved with a struggle in
yourself that you haven't noticed when people have wanted
to help you, the little they can? I know people torture each
other many times like devils, but sometimes they do see

and know each other, you know, and then, if they're decent, they do want to help each other all that they can. Now will you please help *me*? Take care of Nonno while I remove my watercolours from the annex verandah because the storm is coming up by leaps and bounds now.

[*He gives a quick, jerky nod, dropping his face briefly into the cup of his hands. She murmurs 'Thank you' and springs up, starting along the verandah. Halfway across, as the storm closes in upon the hilltop with a thunderclap and a sound of rain coming,* HANNAH *turns to look back at the table.* SHANNON *has risen and gone around the table to Nonno.*]

SHANNON: Grampa? Nonno? Let's get up before the rain hits us, Grampa.

NONNO: What? What?

[SHANNON *gets the old man out of his chair and shepherds him to the back of the verandah as* HANNAH *rushes towards the annex. The Mexican boys hastily clear the table, fold it up and lean it against the wall.* SHANNON *and* NONNO *turn and face towards the storm, like brave men facing a firing squad.* MAXINE *is excitely giving orders to the boys.*]

MAXINE: Pronto, pronto, muchachos! Pronto, pronto!* Llevaros todas las cosas! Pronto, pronto! Recoje los platos! Apurate con el mantel!

PEDRO: Nos estamos dando prisa!

PANCHO: Que el chubasco lave los platos!

[*The German party look on the storm as a Wagnerian climax. They rise from their table as the boys come to clear it, and start singing exultantly. The storm, with its white convulsions of light, is like a giant white bird attacking the hilltop of the Costa Verde.* HANNAH *reappears with her watercolours clutched against her chest.*]

SHANNON: Got them?

HANNAH: Yes, just in time. Here is your God, Mr Shannon.

SHANNON [*quietly*]: Yes, I see Him, I hear Him, I know Him. And if He doesn't know that I know Him, let Him strike me dead with a bolt of His lightning.

[*He moves away from the wall to the edge of the verandah as a*

---

*Hurry, hurry, boys! Pick everything up! Get the plates! Hurry with the table cloth! / We *are* hurrying! / Let the storm wash the plates!

*fine silver sheet of rain descends off the sloping roof, catching the
light and dimming the figures behind it. Now everything is silver,
delicately lustrous.* SHANNON *extends his hands under the
rainfall, turning them in it as if to cool them. Then he cups them
to catch the water in his palms and bathes his forehead with it.
The rainfall increases. The sound of the marimba band at the
beach cantina is brought up the hill by the wind.* SHANNON
*lowers his hands from his burning forehead and stretches them
out through the rain's silver sheet as if he were reaching for something outside and beyond himself. Then nothing is visible but these
reaching-out hands. A pure white flash of lightning reveals*
HANNAH *and* NONNO *against the wall, behind* SHANNON,
*and the electric globe suspended from the roof goes out, the power
extinguished by the storm. A clear shaft of light stays on Shannon's reaching-out hands till the stage curtain has fallen,
slowly.**]

INTERVAL

**Note:* In staging, the plastic elements should be restrained so that
they don't take precedence over the more important human values. It
should not seem like an 'effect curtain'. The faint, windy music of the
marimba band from the cantina should continue as the houselights are
brought up for the intermission.

ACT THREE

The verandah, several hours later. Cubicles numbers 3, 4, and 5 are dimly lighted within. We see HANNAH *in number 3, and* NONNO *in number 4.* SHANNON, *who has taken off his shirt, is seated at a table on the verandah, writing a letter to his Bishop. All but this table have been folded and stacked against the wall and* MAXINE *is putting the hammock back up which had been taken down for dinner. The electric power is still off and the cubicles are lighted by oil lamps. The sky has cleared completely, the moon is making for full and it bathes the scene in an almost garish silver which is intensified by the wetness from the recent rainstorm. Everything is drenched – there are pools of silver here and there on the floor of the verandah. At one side a smudge-pot is burning to repel the mosquitoes, which are particularly vicious after a tropical downpour when the wind is exhausted.*

> [SHANNON *is working feverishly on the letter to the Bishop, now and then slapping a mosquito on his bare torso. He is shiny with perspiration, still breathing like a spent runner, muttering to himself as he writes and sometimes suddenly drawing a loud deep breath and simultaneously throwing back his head to stare up wildly at the night sky.* HANNAH *is seated on a straight-back chair behind the mosquito-netting in her cubicle – very straight herself, holding a small book in her hands, but looking steadily over it at Shannon, like a guardian angel. Her hair has been let down.* NONNO *can be seen in his cubicle rocking back and forth on the edge of the narrow bed as he goes over and over his lines of his first new poem in 'twenty-some years' – which he knows is his last one.*
>
> *Now and then the sound of distant music drifts up from the beach cantina.*]

MAXINE: Workin' on your sermon for next Sunday, Rev'rend?

SHANNON: I'm writing a very important letter, Maxine. [*He means don't disturb me.*]

MAXINE: Who to, Shannon?

SHANNON: The Dean of the Divinity School at Sewanee.

[MAXINE *repeats* 'Sewanee' *to herself, tolerantly.*] Yes, and I'd appreciate it very much, Maxine honey, if you'd get Pedro or Pancho to drive into town with it tonight so it will go out first thing in the morning.

MAXINE: The kids took off in the station wagon already – for some cold beers and hot whores at the cantina.

SHANNON: 'Fred's dead' – he's lucky. . . .

MAXINE: Don't misunderstand me about Fred, baby. I miss him, but we'd not only stopped sleeping together, we'd stopped talking together except in grunts – no quarrels, no misunderstandings, but if we exchanged two grunts in the course of a day, it was a long conversation we'd had that day between us.

SHANNON: Fred knew when I was spooked – wouldn't have to tell him. He'd just look at me and say, 'Well, Shannon, you're spooked.'

MAXINE: Yeah, well, Fred and me'd reached the point of just grunting.

SHANNON: Maybe he thought you'd turned into a pig, Maxine.

MAXINE: Hah! You know damn well that Fred respected me, Shannon, like I did Fred. We just, well, you know . . . age difference. . . .

SHANNON: Well, you've got Pedro and Pancho.

MAXINE: Employees. They don't respect me enough. When you let employees get too free with you, personally, they stop respecting you, Shannon. And it's well, it's . . . humiliating – not to be . . . respected.

SHANNON: Then take more bus trips to town for the Mexican pokes and the pinches, or get Herr Fahrenkopf to 'respect' you, honey.

MAXINE: Hah! You kill me. I been thinking lately of selling out here and going back to the States, to Texas, and operating a tourist camp outside some live town like Houston or Dallas, on a highway, and renting out cabins to business executives wanting a comfortable little intimate little place to give a little after-hours' dictation to their cute little secretaries that can't type or write shorthand. Complimentary rum-cocos – bathrooms with bidets. I'll introduce the bidet to the States.

SHANNON: Does everything have to wind up on that level with you Maxine?

MAXINE: Yes and no, baby. I know the difference between loving someone and just sleeping with someone – even I know about that. [*He starts to rise.*] We've both reached a point where we've got to settle for something that works for us in our lives – even if it isn't on the highest kind of level.

SHANNON: I don't want to rot.

MAXINE: You wouldn't. I wouldn't let you! I know your psychological history. I remember one of your conversations on this verandah with Fred. You was explaining to him how your problems first started. You told him that Mama, your Mama, used to send you to bed before you was ready to sleep – so you practised the little boy's vice, you amused yourself with yourself. And once she caught you at it and whaled your backside with the backside of a hair-brush because she said she had to punish you for it because it made God mad as much as it did Mama, and she had to punish you for it so God wouldn't punish you for it harder than she would.

SHANNON: I was talking to Fred.

MAXINE: Yeah; but I heard it, all of it. You said you loved God and Mama and so you quit it to please them, but it was your secret pleasure and you harboured a secret resentment against Mama and God for making you give it up. And so you got back at God by preaching atheistical sermons and you got back at Mama by starting to lay young girls.

SHANNON: I have never delivered an atheistical sermon, and never would or could when I go back to the Church.

MAXINE: You're not going back to no Church. Did you mention the charge of statutory rape to the Divinity Dean?

SHANNON [*thrusting his chair back so vehemently that it topples over*]: Why don't you *let up* on me? You haven't let up on me since I got here this morning! *Let up on me!* Will you please *let up* on me?

MAXINE [*smiling serenely into his rage*]: Aw, baby....

SHANNON: What do you mean by 'aw baby'? What do you want out of me, Maxine honey?

MAXINE: Just to do this. [*She runs her fingers through his hair. He thrusts her hand away.*]

SHANNON: Ah, God. [*Words fail him. He shakes his head with a slight, helpless laugh and goes down the steps from the verandah.*]

MAXINE: The Chinaman in the kitchen says, 'No sweat.' ... 'No sweat.' He says that's all his philosophy. All the Chinese philosophy in three words, 'Mei yoo gaunchi' – which is Chinese for 'No sweat.' ... With your record and a charge of statutory rape hanging over you in Texas, how could you go to a church except to the Holy Rollers with some lively young female rollers and a bushel of hay on the church floor?

SHANNON: I'll drive into town in the bus to post this letter tonight. [*He has started towards the path. There are sounds below. He divides the masking foliage with his hands and looks down the hill.*]

MAXINE [*descending the steps from the verandah*]: Watch out for the spook; he's out there.

SHANNON: My ladies are up to something. They're all down there on the road, around the bus.

MAXINE: They're running out on you, Shannon.

[*She comes up beside him. He draws back and she looks down the hill. The light in number 3 cubicle comes on and* HANNAH *rises from the little table that she had cleared for letter-writing. She removes her Kabuki robe from a hook and puts it on as an actor puts on a costume in his dressing-room.* NONNO'S *cubicle is also lighted dimly. He sits on the edge of his cot, rocking slightly back and forth, uttering an indistinguishable mumble of lines from his poem.*]

MAXINE: Yeah. There's a little fat man down there that looks like Jake Latta to me. Yep, that's Jake, that's Latta. I reckon Blake Tours has sent him here to take over your party, Shannon. [SHANNON *looks out over the jungle and lights a cigarette with jerky fingers.*] Well, let him do it. No sweat! He's coming up here now. Want me to handle it for you?

SHANNON: I'll handle it for myself. You keep out of it, please.

[*He speaks with a desperate composure.* HANNAH *stands just behind the curtain of her cubicle, motionless as a painted figure, during the scene that follows.* JAKE LATTA *comes up the verandah steps, beaming genially.*]

LATTA: Hi there, Larry.

SHANNON: Hello, Jake. [*He folds his letter into an envelope.*] Mrs Faulk honey, this goes air special.

MAXINE: First you'd better address it.

SHANNON: Oh!

[SHANNON *laughs and snatches the letter back, fumbling in his pocket for an address book, his fingers shaking uncontrollably.* LATTA *winks at Maxine. She smiles tolerantly.*]

LATTA: How's our boy doin', Maxine?

MAXINE: He'd feel better if I could get him to take a drink.

LATTA: Can't you get a drink down him?

MAXINE: Nope; not even a rum-coco.

LATTA: Let's have a rum-coco, Larry.

SHANNON: You have a rum-coco, Jake. I have a party of ladies to take care of. And I've discovered that situations come up in this business that call for cold, sober judgement. How about you? Haven't you ever made that discovery, Jake? What're you doing here? Are you here with a party?

LATTA: I'm here to pick up your party, Larry boy.

SHANNON: That's interesting! On whose authority, Jake?

LATTA: Blake Tours wired me in Cuernavaca to pick up your party here and put them together with mine 'cause you'd had this little nervous upset of yours and ...

SHANNON: Show me the wire! Huh?

LATTA: The bus-driver says you took the ignition key to the bus.

SHANNON: That's right. I have the ignition key to the bus and I have this party and neither the bus or the party will pull out of here till I say so.

LATTA: Larry, you're a sick boy. Don't give me trouble.

SHANNON: What jail did they bail you out of, you fat zero?

LATTA: Let's have the bus key, Larry.

SHANNON: Where did they dig you up? You've got no party in Cuernavaca, you haven't been out with a party since 'thirty-seven.

LATTA: Just give me the bus key, Larry.

SHANNON: In a pig's snout – like yours!

LATTA: Where is the reverend's bedroom, Mrs Faulk?

SHANNON: The bus key is in my pocket. [*He slaps his pants*

pocket fiercely.] Here, right here, in my pocket! Want it? Try and get it, Fatso!

LATTA: What language for a reverend to use, Mrs Faulk. . . .

SHANNON [*holding up the key*]: See it? [*He thrusts it back into his pocket.*] Now go back wherever you crawled from. My party of ladies is staying here three more days because several of them are in no condition to travel, and neither – neither am I.

LATTA: They're getting in the bus now.

SHANNON: How are you going to start it?

LATTA: Larry, don't make me call the bus-driver up here to hold you down while I get that key away from you. You want to see the wire from Blake Tours? [*He produces the wire.*] Read it.

SHANNON: You sent that wire to yourself.

LATTA: From Houston?

SHANNON: You had it sent you from Houston. What's that prove? Why, Blake Tours was nothing, *nothing*! – till they got me. You think they'd let me go? – Ho, ho! Latta, it's caught up with you, Latta, all the whores and tequila have hit your brain now, Latta. [LATTA *shouts down the hill for the bus-driver.*] Don't you realize what I mean to Blake Tours? Haven't you seen the brochure in which they mention, they brag, that special parties are conducted by the Reverend T. Lawrence Shannon, D.D., noted world traveller, lecturer, son of a minister and grandson of a bishop, and the direct descendant of two colonial governors? [MISS FELLOWES *appears at the verandah steps.*] Miss Fellowes has read the brochure, she's memorized the brochure. She knows what it says about me.

MISS FELLOWES [*to Latta*]: Have you got the bus key?

LATTA: Bus-driver's going to get it away from him, lady. [*He lights a cigar with dirty, shaky fingers.*]

SHANNON: Ha-ha-ha-ha-ha! [*His laughter shakes him back against the verandah wall.*]

LATTA: He's gone. [*He touches his forehead.*]

SHANNON: Why, those ladies . . . have had . . . some of them, most of them if not all of them . . . for the first time in their lives the advantage of contact, social contact, with a gentleman born and bred, whom under no other circumstances they could have possibly met ... let alone be given the chance to insult and accuse and ...

MISS FELLOWES: Shannon! The girls are in the bus and we want to go now, so give up that key. Now!

[HANK, *the bus-driver, appears at the top of the path, whistling casually: he is not noticed at first.*]

SHANNON: If I didn't have a decent sense of responsibility to these parties I take out, I would gladly turn over your party – because I don't like your party – to this degenerate here, this Jake Latta of the gutter-rat Lattas. Yes, I would – I would surrender the bus key in my pocket, even to Latta, but I am not that irresponsible, no, I'm not, to the parties that I take out, regardless of the party's treatment of me. I still feel responsible for them till I get them back wherever I picked them up. [HANK *comes on to the verandah.*] Hi, Hank. Are you friend or foe?

HANK: Larry, I got to get that ignition key now so we can get moving down there.

SHANNON: Oh! Then *foe*! I'm disappointed, Hank. I thought you were friend, not foe. [HANK *puts a wrestler's armlock on* Shannon *and* LATTA *removes the bus key from his pocket.* HANNAH *raises a hand to her eyes.*] O.K., O.K., you've got the bus key. By force. I feel exonerated now of all responsibility. Take the bus and the ladies in it and go. Hey, Jake, did you know they had lesbians in Texas – without the dikes the plains of Texas would be engulfed by the Gulf. [*He nods his head violently towards* MISS FELLOWES, *who springs forward and slaps him.*] Thank you, Miss Fellowes. Latta, hold on a minute. I will not be stranded here. I've had unusual expenses on this trip. Right now I don't have my fare back to Houston or even to Mexico City. Now if there's any truth in your statement that Blake Tours have really authorized you to take over my party, then I am sure they have ... [*He draws a breath, almost gasping.*] ... I'm sure they must have given you something in the ... the nature of ... *severance* pay? Or at least enough to get me back to the States?

LATTA: I got no money for you.

SHANNON: I hate to question your word, but . . .

LATTA: We'll drive you back to Mexico City. You can sit up front with the driver.

SHANNON: *You* would do that, Latta. *I'd* find it *humiliating*. Now! Give me my severance pay!

LATTA: Blake Tours is having to refund those ladies half the price of the tour. That's your severance pay. And Miss Fellowes tells me you got plenty of money out of this young girl you seduced in . . .

SHANNON: Miss Fellowes, did you really make such a . . . ?

MISS FELLOWES: When Charlotte returned that night, she'd cashed two traveller's cheques.

SHANNON: After I had spent all my own cash.

MISS FELLOWES: On what? Whores in the filthy places you took her through?

SHANNON: Miss Charlotte cashed two ten-dollar traveller's cheques because I had spent all the cash I had on me. And I've never had to, I've certainly never desired to, have relations with whores.

MISS FELLOWES: You took her through ghastly places, such as . . .

SHANNON: I showed her what she wanted me to show her. Ask her! I showed her San Juan de Letran, I showed her Tenampa and some other places not listed in the Blake Tours brochure. I showed her more than the floating gardens at Xochimilco, Maximilian's Palace, and the mad Empress Carlotta's little homesick chapel, Our Lady of Guadalupe, the monument to Juarez, the relics of the Aztec civilization, the sword of Cortez, the head-dress of Montezuma. I showed her what she told me she wanted to see. Where is she? Where is Miss . . . oh, down there with the ladies. [*He leans over the rail and shouts down.*] Charlotte! Charlotte! [MISS FELLOWES *seizes his arm and thrusts him away from the verandah rail.*]

MISS FELLOWES: Don't you dare!

SHANNON: Dare what?

MISS FELLOWES: Call her, speak to her, go near her, you, you . . . filthy!

[MAXINE *reappears at the corner of the verandah; with the*

ceremonial rapidity of a cuckoo bursting from a clock to announce the hour. She just stands there with an incongruous grin, her big eyes unblinking, as if they were painted on her round beaming face. HANNAH *holds a gold-lacquered Japanese fan motionless but open in one hand; the other hand touches the netting at the cubicle door as if she were checking an impulse to rush to Shannon's defence. Her attitude has the style of a Kabuki dancer's pose.* SHANNON's *manner becomes courtly again.*]

SHANNON: Oh, all right, I won't. I only wanted her to confirm my story that I took her out that night at her request, not at my ... suggestion. All that I did was offer my services to her when *she* told *me* she'd like to see things not listed in the brochure, not usually witnessed by ordinary tourists, such as ...

MISS FELLOWES: Your hotel bedroom? Later? That too? She came back *flea*-bitten!

SHANNON: Oh, now, don't exaggerate, please. Nobody ever got any fleas off Shannon.

MISS FELLOWES: Her clothes had to be fumigated!

SHANNON: I understand your annoyance, but you are going too far when you try to make out that I gave Charlotte fleas. I don't deny that ...

MISS FELLOWES: Wait till they get my *report*!

SHANNON: I don't deny that it's possible to get flea-bites on a tour of inspection of what lies under the public surface of cities, off the grand boulevards, away from the night-clubs, even away from Diego Rivera's murals, but ...

MISS FELLOWES: Oh, preach that in a pulpit, Reverend Shannon-*de*-frocked!

SHANNON [*ominously*]: You've said that once too often. [*He seizes her arm.*] This time before witnesses. Miss Jelkes? Miss Jelkes!

[HANNAH *opens the curtain of her cubicle.*]

HANNAH: Yes, Mr Shannon, what is it?

SHANNON: You heard what this ...

MISS FELLOWES: Shannon! Take your hand off my arm!

SHANNON: Miss Jelkes, just tell me, did you hear what she ...

[*His voice stops oddly with a choked, sobbing sound. He runs at the wall and pounds it with his fists.*]

MISS FELLOWES: I spent this entire afternoon and over twenty dollars checking up on this impostor, with long-distance phone-calls.

HANNAH: Not impostor – you mustn't say things like that.

MISS FELLOWES: You were locked out of your church! – for atheism and seducing of girls!

SHANNON [*turning about*]: In front of God and witnesses, you are lying, lying!

LATTA: Miss Fellowes, I want you to know that Blake Tours was deceived about this character's background, and Blake Tours will see that he is blacklisted from now on at every travel agency in the States.

SHANNON: How about Africa, Asia, Australia? The whole world, Latta, God's world, has been the range of my travels. I haven't stuck to the schedules of the brochures and I've always allowed the ones that were willing to see, to *see*! – the underworlds of all places, and if they had hearts to be touched, feelings to feel with, I gave them a priceless chance to feel and be touched. And none will ever forget it, none of them, ever, never! [*The passion of his speech imposes a little stillness.*]

LATTA: Go on, lie back in your hammock; that's all you're good for, Shannon. [*He goes to the top of the path and shouts down the hill.*] O.K. Let's get cracking. Get that luggage strapped on top of the bus. We're moving! [*He starts down the hill with* MISS FELLOWES.]

NONNO [*incongruously, from his cubicle*]:
How calmly does the orange branch
Observe the sky begin to blanch . . .

[SHANNON *sucks in his breath with an abrupt, fierce sound. He rushes off the verandah and down the path towards the road.* HANNAH *calls after him, with a restraining gesture.* MAXINE *appears on the verandah. Then a great commotion commences below the hill, with shrieks of outrage and squeals of shocked laughter.*]

MAXINE [*rushes to the path*]: Shannon! Shannon! Get back up here, get back up here. Pedro, Pancho, traerme a Shannon. Que está haciendo allí? Oh, my God! Stop him, for God's sake, somebody stop him!

[SHANNON *returns, panting and spent. He is followed by* MAXINE.]

MAXINE: Shannon, go in your room and stay there until that party's gone.

SHANNON: Don't give me orders.

MAXINE: You do what I tell you to do or I'll have you removed – you know where.

SHANNON: Don't push me, don't pull at me, Maxine.

MAXINE: All right; do as I say.

SHANNON: Shannon obeys only Shannon.

MAXINE: You'll sing a different tune if they put you where they put you in 'thirty-six. Remember 'thirty-six, Shannon?

SHANNON: O.K., Maxine, just ... let me breathe alone, please. I won't go, but I will lie in the ... hammock.

MAXINE: Go into Fred's room where I can watch you.

SHANNON: Later, Maxine, not yet.

MAXINE: Why do you always come here to crack up, Shannon?

SHANNON: It's the hammock, Maxine, the hammock by the rain forest.

MAXINE: Shannon, go in your room and stay there until I get back. Oh, my God, the money. They haven't paid the mother-grabbin' bill. I got to go back down there and collect their goddam bill before they ... Pancho, vijilalo, entiendes? [*She rushes back down the hill, shouting* 'Hey! Just a minute down there!']

SHANNON: What did I do? [*He shakes his head, stunned.*] I don't know what I did.

[HANNAH *opens the screen of her cubicle, but doesn't come out. She is softly lighted so that she looks, again, like a medieval sculpture of a saint. Her pale gold hair catches the soft light. She has let it down and still holds the silver-backed brush with which she was brushing it.*]

SHANNON: God almighty, I ... what did I do? I don't know what I did. [*He turns to the Mexican boys, who have come back up the path.*] Que hice? Que hice?

[*There is breathless, spasmodic laughter from the boys as* PANCHO *informs him that he pissed on the ladies' luggage.*]

PANCHO: Tú measte en las maletas de las señoras!

[SHANNON *tries to laugh with the boys, while they bend double with amusement.* SHANNON'S *laughter dies out in little choked spasms. Down the hill,* MAXINE'S *voice is raised in angry altercation with* JAKE LATTA, MISS FELLOWES' *voice is lifted and then there is a general rhubarb, to which is added the roar of the bus motor.*]

SHANNON: There go my ladies, ha, ha! There go my ... [*He turns about to meet* HANNAH'S *grave, compassionate gaze. He tries to laugh again. She shakes her head with a slight restraining gesture and drops the curtain so that her softly luminous figure is seen as through a mist.*] ... ladies, the last of my – ha, ha! – ladies. [*He bends far over the verandah rail, then straightens violently and with an animal outcry begins to pull at the chain suspending the gold cross about his neck.* PANCHO *watches indifferently as the chain cuts the back of Shannon's neck.* HANNAH *rushes out to him.*]

HANNAH: Mr Shannon, stop that! You're cutting yourself doing that. That isn't necessary, so stop it! [*To Pancho.*] Agarrale las manos! [PANCHO *makes a half-hearted effort to comply, but* SHANNON *kicks at him and goes on with the furious self-laceration.*] Shannon, let me do it, let me take it off you. Can I take it off you? [*He drops his arms. She struggles with the clasp of the chain, but her fingers are too shaky to work it.*]

SHANNON: No, no, it won't come off, I'll have to break it off me.

HANNAH: No, no, wait – I've got it. [*She has now removed it.*]

SHANNON: Thanks. Keep it. Good-bye! [*He starts towards the path down to the beach.*]

HANNAH: Where are you going? What are you going to do?

SHANNON: I'm going swimming. I'm going to swim out to China!

HANNAH: No, no, not tonight, Shannon! Tomorrow ... tomorrow, Shannon!

[*But he divides the trumpet-flowered bushes and passes through them.* HANNAH *rushes after him, screaming for 'Mrs Faulk.'* MAXINE *can be heard shouting for the Mexican boys.*]

MAXINE: Muchachos, cojerlo! Atarlo! Está loco. Traerlo aqui. Catch him, he's crazy. Bring him back and tie him up!

[*In a few moments* SHANNON *is hauled back through the bushes and on to the verandah by* MAXINE *and the boys. They rope him into the hammock. His struggle is probably not much of a real struggle – histrionics mostly. But* HANNAH *stands wringing her hands by the steps as* SHANNON, *gasping for breath, is tied up.*]

HANNAH: The ropes are too tight on his chest!

MAXINE: No, they're not. He's acting, acting. He likes it! I know this black Irish bastard like nobody ever knowed him, so you keep out of it, honey. He cracks up like this so regular that you can set a calendar by it. Every eighteen months he does it, and twice he's done it here and I've had to pay for his medical care. Now I'm going to call in town to get a doctor to come out here and give him a knockout injection, and if he's not better tomorrow he's going into the Casa de Locos again, like he did the last time he cracked up on me!

[*There is a moment of silence.*]

SHANNON: Miss Jelkes?

HANNAH: Yes.

SHANNON: Where are you?

HANNAH: I'm right here behind you. Can I do anything for you?

SHANNON: Sit here where I can see you. Don't stop talking. I have to fight this panic.

[*There is a pause. She moves a chair beside his hammock. The Germans troop up from the beach. They are delighted by the drama that* SHANNON *has provided. In their scanty swim-suits they parade on to the verandah and gather about Shannon's captive figure as if they were looking at a funny animal in a zoo. Their talk is in German except when they speak directly to Shannon or Hannah. Their heavily handsome figures gleam with oily wetness and they keep chuckling lubriciously.*]

HANNAH: Please! Will you be so kind as to leave him alone?

[*They pretend not to understand her.* FRAU FAHRENKOPF *bends over Shannon in his hammock and speaks to him loudly and slowly in English.*]

FRAU FAHRENKOPF: Is this true you make pee-pee all over the suitcases of the ladies from Texas? Hah? Hah? You run

down there to the bus and right in front of the ladies you
pees all over the luggage of the ladies from Texas?

[HANNAH's *indignant protest is drowned in the Rabelaisian
laughter of the Germans.*]

HERR FAHRENKOPF: Thees is vunderbar, vunderbar! Hah?
Thees is a *epic gesture*! Hah? Thees is the way to demonstrate
to ladies that you are a American *gentleman*! Hah?

[*He turns to the others and makes a ribald comment. The two
women shriek with amusement,* HILDA *falling back into the
arms of* WOLFGANG, *who catches her with his hands over her
almost nude breasts.*]

HANNAH [*calling out*]: Mrs Faulk! Mrs Faulk! [*She rushes to the
verandah angle as* MAXINE *appears there.*] Will you please ask
these people to leave him alone. They're tormenting him
like an animal in a trap.

[*The Germans are already trooping around the verandah, laughing and capering gaily.*]

SHANNON [*suddenly, in a great shout*]: Regression to infantilism,
ha, ha, regression to infantilism.... The infantile protest,
ha, ha, ha, the infantile expression of rage at Mama and
rage at God and rage at the goddam crib, and rage at the
everything, rage at the ... everything ... Regression to
infantilism....

[*Now all have left but Hannah and Shannon.*]

SHANNON: Untie me.

HANNAH: Not yet.

SHANNON: I can't stand being tied up.

HANNAH: You'll have to stand it a while.

SHANNON: It makes me panicky.

HANNAH: I know.

SHANNON: A man can die of panic.

HANNAH: Not if he enjoys it as much as you, Mr Shannon.

[*She goes into her cubicle directly behind his hammock. The
cubicle is lighted and we see her removing a small teapot and a tin
of tea from her suitcase on the cot, then a little alcohol burner.
She comes back out with these articles.*]

SHANNON: What did you mean by that insulting remark?

HANNAH: What remark, Mr Shannon?

SHANNON: That I enjoy it.

HANNAH: Oh ... that.

SHANNON: Yes. That.

HANNAH: That wasn't meant as an insult, just an observation. I don't judge people; I draw them. That's all I do, just draw them, but in order to draw them I have to observe them, don't I?

SHANNON: And you've observed, you think you've observed, that I like being tied in this hammock, trussed up in it like a hog being hauled off to the slaughter-house, Miss Jelkes.

HANNAH: Who wouldn't like to suffer and atone for the sins of himself and the world if it could be done in a hammock with ropes instead of nails, on a hill that's so much lovelier than Golgotha, the Place of the Skull, Mr Shannon? There's something almost voluptuous in the way that you twist and groan in that hammock – no nails, no blood, no death. Isn't that a comparatively comfortable, almost voluptuous kind of crucifixion to suffer for the guilt of the world, Mr Shannon?

[*She strikes a match to light the alcohol burner. A pure blue jet of flame springs up to cast a flickering, rather unearthly glow on their section of the verandah. The glow is delicately refracted by the subtle, faded colours of her robe – a robe given to her by a Kabuki actor who posed for her in Japan.*]

SHANNON: Why have you turned against me all of a sudden, when I need you the most?

HANNAH: I haven't turned against you at all, Mr Shannon. I'm just attempting to give you a character sketch of yourself, in words instead of pastel crayons or charcoal.

SHANNON: You're certainly suddenly very sure of some New England spinsterish attitudes that I didn't know you had in you. I thought that you were an *emancipated* Puritan, Miss Jelkes.

HANNAH: Who is ... ever ... completely?

SHANNON: I thought you were sexless, but you've suddenly turned into a woman. Know how I know that? Because you, not me – not me – are taking pleasure in my tied-up condition. All women, whether they face it or not, want to see a man in a tied-up situation. They work at it all their lives, to get a man in a tied-up situation. Their lives are fulfilled, they're satisfied at last, when they get a man, or as many men as they can, in the tied-up situation. [HANNAH *leaves the alcohol burner and teapot and moves to the railing, where she grips a verandah post and draws a few deep breaths.*] You don't like this observation of you? The shoe's too tight for comfort when it's on your own foot, Miss Jelkes? Some deep breaths again – feeling panic?

HANNAH [*recovering and returning to the burner*]: I'd like to untie you right now, but let me wait till you've passed through your present disturbance. You're still indulging yourself in your ... your Passion Play performance. I can't help observing this self-indulgence in you.

SHANNON: What rotten indulgence?

HANNAH: Well, your busload of ladies from the female college in Texas. I don't like those ladies any more than you do, but after all, they did save up all year to make this Mexican tour, to stay in stuffy hotels and eat the food they're used to. They want to be at home away from home, but you ... you indulged yourself, Mr Shannon. You did conduct the tour as if it was just for you, for your own pleasure.

SHANNON: Hell, what pleasure – going through hell all the way?

HANNAH: Yes, but comforted, now and then, weren't you, by the little musical prodigy under the wing of the college vocal instructor?

SHANNON: Funny, ha-ha funny! Nantucket spinsters have their wry humour, don't they?

HANNAH: Yes, they do. They have to.

SHANNON [*becoming progressively quieter under the cool influence of her voice behind him*]: I can't see what you're up to, Miss Jelkes honey, but I'd almost swear you're making a pot of tea over there.

HANNAH: That is just what I'm doing.

SHANNON: Does this strike you as the right time for a tea party?

HANNAH: This isn't plain tea; this is poppy-seed tea.

SHANNON: Are you a slave to the poppy?

HANNAH: It's a mild, sedative drink that helps you get through nights that are hard for you to get through, and

I'm making it for my grandfather and myself as well as for you, Mr Shannon. Because, for all three of us, this won't be an easy night to get through. Can't you hear him in his cell number 4, mumbling over and over and over the lines of his new poem? It's like a blind man climbing a staircase that goes to nowhere, that just falls off into space, and I hate to say what it is. . . . [*She draws a few deep breaths behind him.*]

SHANNON: Put some hemlock in his poppy-seed tea tonight so he won't wake up tomorrow for the removal to the Casa de Huéspedes. Do that act of mercy. Put in the hemlock and I will consecrate it, turn it to God's blood. Hell, if you'll get me out of this hammock I'll serve it to him myself, I'll be your accomplice in this act of mercy. I'll say, 'Take and drink this, the blood of our –'

HANNAH: Stop it! Stop being childishly cruel! I can't stand for a person that I respect to talk and behave like a small, cruel boy, Mr Shannon.

SHANNON: What've you found to respect in me, Miss ... Thin-Standing-Up-Female-Buddha?

HANNAH: I respect a person that has had to fight and howl for his decency and his –

SHANNON: *What* decency?

HANNAH: Yes, for his decency and his bit of goodness, much more than I respect the lucky ones that just had theirs handed out to them at birth and never afterwards snatched from them by ... unbearable ... torments, I . . . .

SHANNON: You *respect* me?

HANNAH: I do.

SHANNON: But you just said that I'm taking pleasure in a ... voluptuous crucifixion without nails. A ... what? ... painless atonement for the –

HANNAH [*cutting in*]: Yes, but I think –

SHANNON: Untie me!

HANNAH: Soon, soon. Be patient.

SHANNON: Now!

HANNAH: Not quite yet, Mr Shannon. Not till I'm reasonably sure that you won't swim out to China, because, you see, I think you think of the ... 'the long swim to China' as another painless atonement. I mean I don't think you think you'd be intercepted by sharks and barracudas before you got far past the barrier reef. And I'm afraid you *would be*. It's as simple as that, if that is simple.

SHANNON: What's simple?

HANNAH: Nothing, except for simpletons, Mr Shannon.

SHANNON: Do you believe in people being tied up?

HANNAH: Only when they might take the long swim to China.

SHANNON: All right, Miss Thin-Standing-Up-Female-Buddha, just light a Benson and Hedges cigarette for me and put it in my mouth and take it out when you hear me choking on it – if that doesn't seem to you like another bit of voluptuous self-crucifixion.

HANNAH [*looking about the verandah*]: I will, but ... where did I put them?

SHANNON: I have a pack of my own in my pocket.

HANNAH: Which pocket?

SHANNON: I don't know which pocket, you'll have to frisk me for it. [*She pats his jacket pocket.*]

HANNAH: They're not in your coat-pocket.

SHANNON: Then look for them in my pants' pockets.

[*She hesitates to put her hand in his pants' pockets, for a moment.*
HANNAH *has always had a sort of fastidiousness, a reluctance, towards intimate physical contact. But after the momentary fastidious hesitation, she puts her hands in his pants' pocket and draws out the cigarette pack.*]

SHANNON: Now light it for me and put it in my mouth.

[*She complies with these directions. Almost at once he chokes and the cigarette is expelled.*]

HANNAH: You've dropped it on you – where is it?

SHANNON [*twisting and lunging about in the hammock*]: It's under me, under me, burning. Untie me, for God's sake, will you – it's burning me through my pants!

HANNAH: Raise your hips so I can –

SHANNON: I can't; the ropes are too tight. Untie me, untieeeee meeeeee!

HANNAH: I've found it. I've got it!

[*But* SHANNON's *shout has brought* MAXINE *out of her office. She rushes on to the verandah and sits on Shannon's legs.*]

MAXINE: Now hear this, you crazy black Irish mick, you!

You Protestant black Irish looney. I've called up Lopez, Doc Lopez. Remember him – the man in the dirty white jacket that come here the last time you cracked up here? And hauled you off to the Casa de Locos? Where they threw you into that cell with nothing in it but a bucket and straw and a water-pipe? That you crawled up the water-pipe? And dropped head-down on the floor and got a concussion? Yeah, and I told him you were back here to crack up again and if you didn't quiet down here tonight you should be hauled out in the morning.

SHANNON [*cutting in, with the honking sound of a panicky goose*]: Off, off, off, off, off!

HANNAH: Oh, Mrs Faulk, Mr Shannon won't quiet down till he's left alone in the hammock.

MAXINE: Then why don't *you* leave him alone?

HANNAH: I'm not sitting on him and he ... has to be cared for by someone.

MAXINE: And that someone is *you*?

HANNAH: A long time ago, Mrs Faulk, I had experience with someone in Mr Shannon's condition, so I know how necessary it is to let them be quiet for a while.

MAXINE: He wasn't quiet; he was shouting.

HANNAH: He will quiet down again. I'm preparing a sedative tea for him, Mrs Faulk.

MAXINE: Yeah, I see. Put it out. Nobody cooks here but the Chinaman in the kitchen.

HANNAH: This is just a little alcohol burner, a spirit lamp, Mrs Faulk.

MAXINE: I know what it is. It goes out! [*She blows out the flame under the burner.*]

SHANNON: Maxine honey? [*He speaks quietly now.*] Stop persecuting this lady. You can't intimidate her. A bitch is no match for a lady except in a brass bed, honey, and sometimes not even there.

[*The Germans are heard shouting for beer – a case of it to take down to the beach.*]

WOLFGANG: Eine Kiste Carta Blanca.

FRAU FAHRENKOPF: Wir haben genug gehabt ... vielleicht nicht.

HERR FAHRENKOPF: Nein! Niemals genug.

HILDA: Mutter du bist dick ... aber wir sind es nicht.

SHANNON: Maxine, you're neglecting your duties as a beer-hall waitress. [*His tone is deceptively gentle.*] They want a case of Carta Blanca to carry down to the beach, so give it to 'em ... and tonight, when the moon's gone down, if you'll let me out of this hammock, I'll try to imagine you as a ... as a nymph in her teens.

MAXINE: A fat lot of good you'd be in your present condition.

SHANNON: Don't be a sexual snob at your age, honey.

MAXINE: Hah! [*But the unflattering offer has pleased her realistically modest soul, so she goes back to the Germans.*]

SHANNON: Now let me try a bit of your poppy-seed tea, Miss Jelkes.

HANNAH: I ran out of sugar, but I had some ginger, some sugared ginger. [*She pours a cup of tea and sips it.*] Oh, it's not well brewed yet, but try to drink some now and the – [*she lights the burner again*] – the second cup will be better. [*She crouches by the hammock and presses the cup to his lips. He raises his head to sip it, but he gags and chokes.*]

SHANNON: *Caesar's ghost!* – it could be chased by the witches' brew from Macbeth.

HANNAH: Yes, I know; it's still bitter.

[*The Germans appear on the wing of the verandah and go trooping down to the beach for a beer festival and a moonlight swim. Even in the relative dark they have a luminous colour, an almost phosphorescent pink and gold colour of skin. They carry with them a case of Carta Blanca beer and the fantastically painted rubber horse. On their faces are smiles of euphoria as they move like a dream-image, starting to sing a marching song as they go.*]

SHANNON: Fiends out of hell with the ... voices of ... angels.

HANNAH: Yes, they call it 'the logic of contradictions', Mr Shannon.

SHANNON [*lunging suddenly forward and undoing the loosened ropes*]: Out! Free! Unassisted!

HANNAH: Yes, I never doubted that you could get loose, Mr Shannon.

SHANNON: Thanks for your help, anyhow.

HANNAH: Where are you going?
   [*He has crossed to the liquor cart.*]

SHANNON: Not far. To the liquor cart to make myself a rum-coco.

HANNAH: Oh. . . .

SHANNON [*at the liquor cart*]: Coconut? Check. Machete? Check. Rum? Double check! Ice? The ice bucket's empty. O.K., it's a night for warm drinks. Miss Jelkes? Would you care to have your complimentary rum-coco?

HANNAH: No thank you, Mr Shannon.

SHANNON: You don't mind me having mine?

HANNAH: Not at all, Mr Shannon.

SHANNON: You don't disapprove of this weakness, this self-indulgence?

HANNAH: Liquor isn't your problem, Mr Shannon.

SHANNON: What is my problem, Miss Jelkes?

HANNAH: The oldest one in the world – the need to believe in something or in someone – almost anyone – almost anything . . . something.

SHANNON: Your voice sounds hopeless about it.

HANNAH: No, I'm not hopeless about it. In fact, I've discovered something to believe in.

SHANNON: Something like . . . God?

HANNAH: No.

SHANNON: What?

HANNAH: Broken gates between people so they can reach each other, even if it's just for one night only.

SHANNON: One-night stands, huh?

HANNAH: One night . . . communication between them on a verandah outside their . . . separate cubicles, Mr Shannon.

SHANNON: You don't mean physically, do you?

HANNAH: No.

SHANNON: I didn't think so. Then what?

HANNAH: A little understanding exchanged between them, a wanting to help each other through nights like this.

SHANNON: Who was the someone you told the widow you'd helped long ago to get through a crack-up like this one I'm going through?

HANNAH: Oh . . . that. Myself.

SHANNON: You?

HANNAH: Yes. I can help you because I've been through what you are going through now. I had something like your spook – I just had a different name for him. I called him the blue devil, and ... oh ... we had quite a battle, quite a contest between us.

SHANNON: Which you obviously won.

HANNAH: I couldn't afford to lose.

SHANNON: How'd you beat your blue devil?

HANNAH: I showed him that I could endure him and I made him respect my endurance.

SHANNON: How?

HANNAH: Just by, just by ... enduring. Endurance is something that spooks and blue devils respect. And they respect all the tricks that panicky people use to outlast and outwit their panic.

SHANNON: Like poppy-seed tea?

HANNAH: Poppy-seed tea or rum-cocos or just a few deep breaths. Anything, everything, that we take to give them the slip, and so to keep on going.

SHANNON: To where?

HANNAH: To somewhere like this, perhaps. This verandah over the rain forest and the still-water beach, after long, difficult travels. And I don't mean just travels about the world, the earth's surface. I mean ... subterranean travels, the ... the journeys that the spooked and bedevilled people are forced to take through the ... the *unlighted* sides of their natures.

SHANNON: Don't tell me you have a dark side to your nature. [*He says this sardonically.*]

HANNAH: I'm sure I don't have to tell a man as experienced and knowledgeable as you, Mr Shannon, that everything has its shadowy side?

[*She glances up at him and observes that she doesn't have his attention. He is gazing tensely at something off the verandah. It is the kind of abstraction, not vague but fiercely concentrated, that occurs in madness. She turns to look where he's looking. She closes her eyes for a moment and draws a deep breath, then goes on speaking in a voice like a hypnotist's, as if the words didn't*] *matter, since he is not listening to her so much as to the tone and the cadence of her voice.*]

HANNAH: Everything in the whole solar system has a shadowy side to it except the sun itself – the sun is the single exception. You're not listening, are you?

SHANNON [*as if replying to her*]: The spook is in the rain forest. [*He suddenly hurls his coconut shell with great violence off the verandah creating a commotion among the jungle birds.*] Good shot – it caught him right on the kisser and his teeth flew out like popcorn from a popper.

HANNAH: Has he gone off – to the dentist?

SHANNON: He's retreated a little way away for a little while, but when I buzz for my breakfast tomorrow, he'll bring it in to me with a grin that'll curdle the milk in the coffee and he'll stink like a ... gringo drunk in a Mexican jail who's slept all night in his vomit.

HANNAH: If you wake up before I'm out, I'll bring your coffee in to you ... if you call me.

SHANNON [*his attention returns to her*]: No, you'll be gone, God help me.

HANNAH: Maybe and maybe not. I might think of something tomorrow to placate the widow.

SHANNON: The widow's implacable, honey.

HANNAH: I think I'll think of something because I have to. I can't let Nonno be moved to the Casa de Huéspedes, Mr Shannon. Not any more than I could let you take the long swim out to China. You know that. Not if I can prevent it, and when I have to be resourceful, I can be very resourceful.

SHANNON: How'd you get over your crack-up?

HANNAH: I never cracked up, I couldn't afford to. Of course, I nearly did once. I was young once, Mr Shannon, but I was one of those people who can be young without really having their youth, and not to have your youth when you are young is naturally very disturbing. But I was lucky. My work, this occupational therapy that I gave myself – painting and doing quick character sketches – made me look out of myself, not in, and gradually, at the far end of the tunnel that I was struggling out of I began to see this faint, very

faint grey light – the light of the world outside me – and I
kept climbing towards it. I had to.

SHANNON: Did it stay a grey light?

HANNAH: No, no, it turned white.

SHANNON: Only white, never gold?

HANNAH: No, it stayed only white, but white is a very good
light to see at the end of a long black tunnel you thought
would be never ending, that only God or Death could put
a stop to, especially when you ... since I was ... far from
sure about God.

SHANNON: You're still unsure about him?

HANNAH: Not as unsure as I was. You see, in my profession I
have to look hard and close at human faces in order to catch
something in them before they get restless and call out,
'Waiter, the check, we're leaving'. Of course sometimes, a
few times, I just see blobs of wet dough that pass for human
faces, with bits of jelly for eyes. Then I cue in Nonno to
give a recitation, because I can't draw such faces. But those
aren't the usual faces, I don't think they're even real. Most
time I *do* see something, and I can catch it – I *can*, like I
caught something in your face when I sketched you this
afternoon with your eyes open. Are you still listening to
me? [*He crouches beside her chair, looking up at her intently.*] In
Shanghai, Shannon, there is a place that's called the House
for the Dying – the old and penniless dying, whose younger,
penniless living children and grandchildren take them there
for them to get through with their dying on pallets, on straw
mats. The first time I went there it shocked me, I ran away
from it. But I came back later and I saw that their children
and grandchildren and the custodians of the place had put
little comforts beside their death-pallets, little flowers and
opium candies and religious emblems. That made me able
to stay to draw their dying faces. Sometimes only their eyes
were still alive, but, Mr Shannon, those eyes of the penniless dying with those last little comforts beside them, I tell
you, Mr Shannon, those eyes looked up with their last dim
life left in them as clear as the stars in the Southern Cross,
Mr Shannon. And now ... now I am going to say something to you that will sound like something that only the

spinster granddaughter of a minor romantic poet is likely to say.... Nothing I've ever seen has seemed as beautiful to me, not even the view from this verandah between the sky and the still-water beach, and lately ... lately my grandfather's eyes have looked up at me like that.... [*She rises abruptly and crosses to the front of the verandah.*] Tell me, what is that sound I keep hearing down there?

SHANNON: There's a marimba band at the cantina on the beach.

HANNAH: I don't mean that, I mean that scraping, scuffling sound that I keep hearing under the verandah.

SHANNON: Oh, that. The Mexican boys that work here have caught an iguana and tied it up under the verandah, hitched it to a post, and naturally, of course, it's trying to scramble away. But it's got to the end of its rope, and get any further it cannot. Ha-ha – that's it. [*He quotes from Nonno's poem:* 'And still the orange,' etc.] Do you have any life of your own – besides your watercolours and sketches and your travels with Grampa?

HANNAH: We make a home for each other, my grandfather and I. Do you know what I mean by a home? I don't mean a regular home. I mean I don't mean what other people mean when they speak of a home, because I don't regard a home as a ... well, as a place, a building ... a house ... of wood, bricks, stone. I think of a home as being a thing that two people have between them in which each can ... well, nest – rest – live in, emotionally speaking. Does that make any sense to you, Mr Shannon?

SHANNON: Yeah, complete. But ...

HANNAH: Another incomplete sentence.

SHANNON: We better leave it that way. I might've said something to hurt you.

HANNAH: I'm not thin-skinned, Mr Shannon.

SHANNON: No, well, then, I'll say it.... [*He moves to the liquor cart.*] When a bird builds a nest to rest in and live in, it doesn't build it in a ... a falling-down tree.

HANNAH: I'm not a bird, Mr Shannon.

SHANNON: I was making an analogy, Miss Jelkes.

HANNAH: I thought you were making yourself another rum-coco, Mr Shannon.

SHANNON: Both. When a bird builds a nest, it builds it with an eye for the ... the relative permanence of the location, and also for the purpose of mating and propagating its species.

HANNAH: I still say that I'm not a bird, Mr Shannon, I'm a human being and when a member of that fantastic species builds a nest in the heart of another, the question of permanence isn't the first or even the last thing that's considered ... necessarily? ... always? Nonno and I have been continuously reminded of the impermanence of things lately. We go back to an hotel where we've been many times before and it isn't there any more. It's been demolished and there's one of those glassy, brassy new ones. Or if the old one's still there, the manager of the Maître D who always welcomed us back so cordially before has been replaced by someone new who looks at us with suspicion.

SHANNON: Yeah, but you still had each other.

HANNAH: Yes. We did.

SHANNON: But when the old gentleman goes?

HANNAH: Yes?

SHANNON: What will you do? Stop?

HANNAH: Stop or go on ... probably go on.

SHANNON: Alone? Checking into hotels alone, eating alone at tables for one in a corner, the tables waiters call aces?

HANNAH: Thank you for your sympathy, Mr Shannon, but in my profession I'm obliged to make quick contacts with strangers who turn to friends very quickly.

SHANNON: Customers aren't friends.

HANNAH: They turn to friends, if they're friendly.

SHANNON: Yeah, but how will it seem to be travelling alone after so many years of travelling with ...

HANNAH: I will know how it feels when I feel it – and don't say alone as if nobody had ever gone on alone. For instance, you.

SHANNON: I've always travelled with train-loads, plane-loads and bus-loads of tourists.

HANNAH: That doesn't mean you're still not really alone.

SHANNON: I never fail to make an intimate connexion with someone in my parties.

HANNAH: Yes, the youngest young lady, and I was on the verandah this afternoon when the latest of these young ladies gave a demonstration of how lonely the intimate connexion has always been for you. The episode in the cold, inhuman hotel room, Mr Shannon, for which you despise the lady almost as much as you despise yourself. Afterwards you are so polite to the lady that I'm sure it must chill her to the bone, the scrupulous little attentions that you pay her in return for your little enjoyment of her. The gentleman-of-Virginia act that you put on for her, your noblesse oblige treatment of her.... Oh no, Mr Shannon, don't kid yourself that you ever travel with someone. You have always travelled alone except for your spook, as you call it. He's your travelling companion. Nothing, nobody else has travelled with you.

SHANNON: Thank you for your sympathy, Miss Jelkes.

HANNAH: You're welcome, Mr Shannon. And now I think I had better warm up the poppy-seed tea for Nonno. Only a good night's sleep could make it possible for him to go on from here tomorrow.

SHANNON: Yes, well, if the conversation is over – I think I'll go down for a swim now.

HANNAH: To China?

SHANNON: No, not to China, just to the little island out here with the sleepy bar on it ... called the Cantina Serena.

HANNAH: Why?

SHANNON: Because I'm not a nice drunk and I was about to ask you a not nice question.

HANNAH: Ask it. There's no set limit on questions here tonight.

SHANNON: And no set limits on answers?

HANNAH: None I can think of between you and me, Mr Shannon.

SHANNON: That I will take you up on.

HANNAH: Do.

SHANNON: It's a bargain.

HANNAH: Only do lie back down in the hammock and drink a full cup of poppy-seed tea this time. It's warmer now and the sugared ginger will make it easier to get down.

SHANNON: All right. The question is this: have you never had in your life any kind of a love life? [HANNAH *stiffens for a moment.*] I thought you said there was no limit set on questions.

HANNAH: We'll make a bargain – I will answer your question *after* you've had a full cup of the poppy-seed tea so you'll be able to get the good night's sleep you need, too. It's fairly warm now and the sugared ginger's made it much more – [*she sips the cup*] – palatable.

SHANNON: You think I'm going to drift into dreamland so you can welch on the bargain? [*He accepts the cup from her.*]

HANNAH: I'm not a welcher on bargains. Drink it all. All. *All!*

SHANNON [*with a disgusted grimace as he drains the cup*]: Great Caesar's ghost! [*He tosses the cup off the verandah and falls into the hammock, chuckling.*] The Oriental idea of a Mickey Finn, huh? Sit down where I can see you, Miss Jelkes, honey. [*She sits down in a straight-back chair, some distance from the hammock.*] Where I can *see* you! I don't have an X-ray eye in the back of my head, Miss Jelkes. [*She moves the chair alongside the hammock.*] Further, further, up further. [*She complies.*] There now. Answer the question now, Miss Jelkes honey.

HANNAH: Would you mind repeating the question?

SHANNON [*slowly, with emphasis*]: Have you never had in all your life and your travels any experience, any encounter with what Larry-the-crackpot Shannon thinks of as a love life?

HANNAH: There are ... worse things than chastity, Mr Shannon.

SHANNON: Yeah, lunacy and death are both a little worse, *maybe*! But chastity isn't a thing that a beautiful woman or an attractive man falls into like a booby trap or an overgrown gopher hole, is it? [*There is a pause.*] I still think you are welching on the bargain and I ... [*He starts out of the hammock.*]

HANNAH: Mr Shannon, this night is just as hard for me to get through as it is for you to get through. But it's you that are welching on the bargain; you're not staying in the ham-

mock. Lie back down in the hammock. Now. Yes. Yes, I
have had two experiences, well, encounters, with ...

SHANNON: *Two,* did you say?

HANNAH: Yes, I said two. And I wasn't exaggerating and
don't you say 'fantastic' before I've told you both stories.
When I was sixteen, your favourite age, Mr Shannon, each
Saturday afternoon my grandfather Nonno would give me
thirty cents, my allowance, my pay for my secretarial and
housekeeping duties. Twenty-five cents for admission to
the Saturday matinée at the Nantucket movie theatre and
five cents extra for a bag of popcorn, Mr Shannon. I'd sit at
the almost empty back of the movie theatre so that the popcorn munching wouldn't disturb the other movie patrons.
Well ... one afternoon a young man sat down beside me
and pushed his ... knee against mine and ... I moved over
two seats, but he moved over beside me and continued this
... pressure! I jumped up and screamed, Mr Shannon. He
was arrested for molesting a minor.

SHANNON: Is he still in the Nantucket jail?

HANNAH: No. I got him out. I told the police that it was a
Clara Bow picture – it *was* a Clara Bow picture – and I was
just over-excited.

SHANNON: Fantastic.

HANNAH: Yes, very! The second experience is much more
recent, only two years ago, when Nonno and I were operating at the Raffles Hotel in Singapore, and doing very well
there, making expenses and more. One evening in the Palm
Court of the Raffles we met this middle-aged, sort of non-
descript Australian salesman. You know – plump, bald-
spotted, with a bad attempt at speaking with an upper-class
accent and terribly over-friendly. He was alone and looked
lonely. Grandfather said him a poem and I did a quick
character sketch that was shamelessly flattering of him. He
paid me more than my usual asking price and gave my
grandfather five Malayan dollars, yes, and he even pur-
chased one of my watercolours. Then it was Nonno's bed-
time. The Aussie salesman asked me out in a sampan with
him. Well, he'd been so generous ... I accepted. I did, I
accepted. Grandfather went up to bed and I went out in the

sampan with this ladies' underwear salesman. I noticed that he became more and more . . .

SHANNON: What?

HANNAH: Well . . . *agitated* . . . as the afterglow of the sunset faded out on the water. [*She laughs with a delicate sadness.*] Well, finally, eventually, he leaned towards me . . . we were vis-à-vis in the sampan . . . and he looked intensely, passionately into my eyes. [*She laughs again.*] And he said to me: 'Miss Jelkes? Will you do me a favour? Will you do something for me?' 'What?' said I. 'Well,' said he, 'if I turn my back, if I look the other way, will you take off some piece of your clothes and let me hold it, just hold it?'

SHANNON: Fantastic!

HANNAH: Then he said, 'It will just take a few seconds.' 'Just a few seconds for what?' I asked him. [*She gives the same laugh again.*] He didn't say for what, but . . .

SHANNON: His satisfaction?

HANNAH: Yes.

SHANNON: What did you do – in a situation like that?

HANNAH: I . . . gratified his request, I did! And he kept his promise. He did keep his back turned till I said ready and threw him . . . the part of my clothes.

SHANNON: What did he do with it?

HANNAH: He didn't move, except to seize the article he'd requested. I looked the other way while his satisfaction took place.

SHANNON: Watch out for commercial travellers in the Far East. Is that the moral, Miss Jelkes honey?

HANNAH: Oh, no, the moral is Oriental. Accept whatever situation you cannot improve.

SHANNON: 'When it's inevitable, lean back and enjoy it' – is that it?

HANNAH: He'd bought a watercolour. The incident was embarrassing, not violent. I left and returned unmolested. Oh, and the funniest part of all is that when we got back to the Raffles Hotel, he took the piece of apparel out of his pocket like a bashful boy producing an apple for his schoolteacher and tried to slip it into my hand in the elevator. I wouldn't accept it. I whispered, 'Oh, please keep it, Mr

Willoughby!' He'd paid the asking price for my water-colour and somehow the little experience had been rather touching. I mean it was so *lonely*, out there in the sampan with violet streaks in the sky and this little middle-aged Australian making sounds like he was dying of asthma! And the planet Venus coming serenely out of a fair-weather cloud, over the Straits of Malacca. . . .

SHANNON: And that experience . . . you call that a . . .

HANNAH: A love experience? Yes. I do call it one.

[*He regards her with incredulity, peering into her face so closely that she is embarrassed and becomes defensive.*]

SHANNON: That, that . . . sad, dirty little episode, you call it a . . .?

HANNAH [*cutting in sharply*]: Sad it certainly was – for the odd little man – but why do you call it 'dirty'?

SHANNON: How did you feel when you went into your bed-room?

HANNAH: Confused, I . . . a little confused, I suppose. . . . I'd known about loneliness – but not that degree or . . . depth of it.

SHANNON: You mean it didn't *disgust* you?

HANNAH: Nothing human disgusts me unless it's unkind, violent. And I told you how gentle he was – apologetic, shy, and really very, well, *delicate* about it. However, I do grant you it was on the rather fantastic level.

SHANNON: You're . . .

HANNAH: I am *what*? 'Fantastic'?

[*While they have been talking,* NONNO'S *voice has been heard now and then, mumbling, from his cubicle. Suddenly it becomes loud and clear.*]

NONNO: And finally the broken stem,
  The plummeting to earth and then. . . .

[*His voice subsides to its mumble.* SHANNON, *standing behind Hannah, places his hand on her throat.*]

HANNAH: What is that for? Are you about to strangle me, Mr Shannon?

SHANNON: You can't stand to be touched?

HANNAH: Save it for the widow. It isn't for me.

SHANNON: Yes, you're right. [*He removes his hand.*] I could do it with Mrs Faulk, the inconsolable widow, but I couldn't with you.

HANNAH [*dryly and lightly*]: Spinster's loss, widow's gain, Mr Shannon.

SHANNON: Or widow's loss, spinster's gain. Anyhow it sounds like some old parlour game in a Virginia or Nantucket Island parlour. But . . . I wonder something. . . .

HANNAH: What do you wonder?

SHANNON: If we couldn't . . . *travel* together, I mean just *travel* together?

HANNAH: Could we? In your opinion?

SHANNON: Why not? I don't see why not.

HANNAH: I think the impracticality of the idea will appear much clearer to you in the morning, Mr Shannon. [*She folds her dimly gold-lacquered fan and rises from her chair.*] Morning can always be counted on to bring us back to a more realistic level. . . . Good night, Mr Shannon. I have to pack before I'm too tired to.

SHANNON: Don't leave me out here alone yet.

HANNAH: I have to pack now so I can get up at daybreak and try my luck in the plaza.

SHANNON: You won't sell a watercolour or sketch in that blazing hot plaza tomorrow. Miss Jelkes honey, I don't think you're operating on the realistic level.

HANNAH: Would I be if I thought we could travel together?

SHANNON: I still don't see why we couldn't.

HANNAH: Mr Shannon, you're not well enough to travel anywhere with anybody right now. Does that sound cruel of me?

SHANNON: You mean that I'm stuck here for good? Winding up with the . . . inconsolable widow?

HANNAH: We all wind up with something or with someone, and if it's someone instead of just something, we're lucky, perhaps . . . unusually lucky. [*She starts to enter her cubicle, then turns to him again in the doorway.*] Oh, and tomorrow . . . [*She touches her forehead, as if a little confused as well as exhausted.*]

SHANNON: What about tomorrow?

HANNAH [*with difficulty*]: I think it might be better, tomorrow, if we avoid showing any particular interest in each other, because Mrs Faulk is a morbidly jealous woman.

SHANNON: *Is* she?

HANNAH: Yes; she seems to have misunderstood our ... sympathetic interest in each other. So I think we'd better avoid any more long talks on the verandah. I mean till she's thoroughly reassured it might be better if we just say good morning or good night to each other.

SHANNON: We don't even have to say that.

HANNAH: I will, but you don't have to answer.

SHANNON [*savagely*]: How about wall-tappings between us by way of communication? You know, like convicts in separate cells communicate with each other by tapping on the walls of the cells? One tap: I'm here. Two taps: are you there? Three taps: yes, I am. Four taps: that's good, we're together. *Christ!* ... Here, take this. [*He snatches the gold cross from his pocket.*] Take my gold cross and hock it; it's 22-carat gold.

HANNAH: What do you, what are you ... ?

SHANNON: There's a fine amethyst in it; it'll pay your travel expenses back to the States.

HANNAH: Mr Shannon, you're making no sense at all now.

SHANNON: Neither are you, Miss Jelkes, talking about tomorrow, and ...

HANNAH: All I was saying was ...

SHANNON: You won't *be* here tomorrow! Had you forgotten you won't be here tomorrow?

HANNAH [*with a slight, shocked laugh*]: Yes, I *had*, I'd *forgotten*!

SHANNON: The widow wants you out and out you'll go, even if you sell your watercolours like hot cakes to the pariah dogs in the plaza. [*He stares at her, shaking his head hopelessly.*]

HANNAH: I suppose you're right, Mr Shannon. I must be too tired to think or I've contracted your fever. . . . It had actually slipped my mind for a moment that –

NONNO [*abruptly, from his cubicle*]: Hannah!

HANNAH [*rushing to his door*]: Yes; what is it, Nonno? [*He doesn't hear her and repeats her name louder.*] Here I am, I'm here.

NONNO: Don't come in yet, but stay where I can call you.

HANNAH: Yes, I'll *hear* you, Nonno. [*She turns towards Shannon, drawing a deep breath.*]

SHANNON: Listen, if you don't take this gold cross that I never want on me again, I'm going to pitch it off the verandah at the spook in the rain forest. [*He raises an arm to throw it, but she catches his arm to restrain him.*]

HANNAH: All right, Mr Shannon, I'll take it. I'll hold it for you.

SHANNON: Hock it, honey, you've got to.

HANNAH: Well, if I do, I'll mail the pawn ticket to you so you can redeem it, because you'll want it again, when you've gotten over your fever. [*She moves blindly down the verandah and starts to enter the wrong cubicle.*]

SHANNON: That isn't your cell; you went past it. [*His voice is gentle again.*]

HANNAH: I did. I'm sorry. I've never been this tired in all my life. [*She turns to face him again. He stares into her face. She looks blindly out, past him.*] Never! [*There is a slight pause.*] What did you say is making that constant, dry, scuffling sound beneath the verandah?

SHANNON: I told you.

HANNAH: I didn't hear you.

SHANNON: I'll get my flashlight. I'll show you. [*He lurches rapidly into his cubicle and back out with a flashlight.*] It's an iguana. I'll show you. . . . See? The iguana? At the end of its rope? Trying to go on past the end of its goddam rope? Like *you*! Like *me*! Like Grampa with his last poem!

[*In the pause which follows singing is heard from the beach.*]

HANNAH: What is a – what – iguana?

SHANNON: It's a kind of lizard – a big one, a giant one. The Mexican kids caught it and tied it up.

HANNAH: Why did they tie it up?

SHANNON: Because that's what they do. They tie them up and fatten them up and then eat them up, when they're ready for eating. They're a delicacy. Taste like white meat of chicken. At least the Mexicans think so. And also the kids, the Mexican kids, have a lot of fun with them, poking out their eyes with sticks and burning their tails with matches. You know? Fun? Like that?

HANNAH: Mr Shannon, please go down and cut it loose!

SHANNON: I can't do that.

HANNAH: Why can't you?

SHANNON: Mrs Faulk wants to eat it. I've got to please Mrs Faulk. I am at her mercy. I am at her disposal.

HANNAH: I don't understand. I mean I don't understand how anyone could eat a big lizard.

SHANNON: Don't be so critical. If you got hungry enough you'd eat it too. You'd be surprised what people will eat if hungry. There's a lot of hungry people still in the world. Many have died of starvation, but a lot are still living and hungry, believe you me, if you will take my word for it. Why, when I was conducting a party of – *ladies*? – yes, ladies . . . through a country that shall be nameless but in this world, we were passing by rubberneck bus along a tropical coast when we saw a great mound of . . . well, the smell was unpleasant. One of my ladies said, 'Oh, Larry, what is that?' My name being Lawrence, the most familiar ladies sometimes call me Larry. I didn't use the four-letter word for what the great mound was. I didn't think it was necessary to say it. Then she noticed, and I noticed too, a pair of very old natives of this nameless country, practically naked except for a few filthy rags, creeping and crawling about this mound of . . . and . . . occasionally stopping to pick something out of it, and pop it into their mouths. What? Bits of undigested . . . food particles, Miss Jelkes. [*There is silence for a moment. She makes a gagging sound in her throat and rushes the length of the verandah to the wooden steps and disappears for a while.* SHANNON *continues, to himself and the moon.*] Now why did I tell her that? Because it's true? That's no reason to tell her, because it's true. Yeah. Because it's true was a good reason not to tell her. Except . . . I think I first *faced* it in that nameless country. The gradual, rapid, natural, unnatural – predestined, accidental – cracking up and going to pieces of young Mr T. Lawrence Shannon, yes, still *young* Mr T. Lawrence Shannon, by which rapid-slow process . . . his final tour of ladies through tropical countries. . . . Why did I say 'tropical'? Hell! Yes! It's always been tropical

countries I took ladies through. Does that, does that –
huh? – signify something, I wonder? Maybe. Fast decay
is a thing of hot climates, steamy, hot, wet climates, and I
run back to them like a. . . . Incomplete sentence. . . .
Always seducing a lady or two, or three or four or five
ladies in the party, but really ravaging her first by pointing
out to her the – what? – horrors? Yes, horrors! – of the
tropical country being conducted a tour through. My . . .
brain's going out now, like a failing – power. . . . So I stay
here, I reckon, and live off la patrona for the rest of my
life. Well, she's old enough to predecease me. She could
check out of here first, and I imagine that after a couple of
years of having to satisfy her I might be prepared for the
shock of her passing on. . . . Cruelty . . . pity. What is it?
. . . Don't know, all I know is. . . .

HANNAH [*from below the verandah*]: You're talking to yourself.

SHANNON: No. To you. I knew you could hear me out there,
but not being able to see you I could say it easier, you
know . . .

NONNO: A chronicle no longer gold,
            A bargaining with mist and mould. . . .

HANNAH [*coming back on to the verandah*]: I took a closer look
at the iguana down there.

SHANNON: You did? How did you like it? Charming?
Attractive?

HANNAH: No; it's not an attractive creature. Nevertheless,
I think it should be cut loose.

SHANNON: Iguanas have been known to bite their tails off
when they're tied up by their tails.

HANNAH: This one is tied by its throat. It can't bite its own
head off to escape from the end of the rope, Mr Shannon.
Can you look at me and tell me truthfully that you don't
know it's able to feel pain and panic?

SHANNON: You mean it's one of God's creatures?

HANNAH: If you want to put it that way, yes, it is. Mr Shannon, will you please cut it loose, set it free? Because if you
don't I will.

SHANNON: Can you look at *me* and tell *me* truthfully that this reptilian creature, tied up down there, doesn't mostly disturb you because of its parallel situation to your Grampa's dying-out effort to finish one last poem, Miss Jelkes?

HANNAH: Yes, I . . .

SHANNON: Never mind completing that sentence. We'll play God tonight like kids play house with old broken crates and boxes. All right? Now Shannon is going to go down there with his machete and cut the damn lizard loose so it can run back to its bushes because God won't do it and we are going to play God here.

HANNAH: I knew you'd do that. And I thank you.

[SHANNON *goes down the two steps from the verandah with the machete. He crouches beside the cactus that hides the iguana and cuts the rope with a quick, hard stroke of the machete. He turns to look after its flight, as the low, excited mumble in cubicle 3 grows louder. Then* NONNO'S *voice turns to a sudden shout.*]

NONNO: *Hannah! Hannah!* [*She rushes to him as he wheels himself out of his cubicle on to the verandah.*]

HANNAH: Grandfather! What is it?

NONNO: I! believe! it! is! *finished!* Quick, before I forget it – pencil, paper! Quick! please! Ready?

HANNAH: Yes. All ready, Grandfather.

NONNO [*in a loud, exalted voice*]:

How calmly does the orange branch
Observe the sky begin to blanch
Without a cry, without a prayer,
With no betrayal of despair.

Sometime while night obscures the tree
The zenith of its life will be
Gone past forever, and from thence
A second history will commence.

A chronicle no longer gold,
A bargaining with mist and mould,
And finally the broken stem
The plummeting to earth; and then

An intercourse not well designed
For beings of a golden kind
Whose native green must arch above
The earth's obscene, corrupting love.

And still the ripe fruit and the branch
Observe the sky begin to blanch
Without a cry, without a prayer,
With no betrayal of despair.

O Courage, could you not as well
Select a second place to dwell,
Not only in that golden tree
But in the frightened heart of me?

Have you got it?

HANNAH: Yes!

NONNO: All of it?

HANNAH: Every word of it.

NONNO: It is *finished*?

HANNAH: Yes.

NONNO: Oh! God! Finally finished?

HANNAH: Yes, finally finished. [*She is crying. The singing voices flow up from the beach.*]

NONNO: After waiting so long!

HANNAH: Yes, we waited so long.

NONNO: And it's good! It is *good*?

HANNAH: It's – it's . . . .

NONNO: What?

HANNAH: Beautiful, Grandfather! [*She springs up, a fist to her mouth.*] Oh, Grandfather, I am so happy for you. Thank you for writing such a lovely poem! It was worth the long wait. Can you sleep now, Grandfather?

NONNO: You'll have it typewritten tomorrow?

HANNAH: Yes. I'll have it typed up and send it off to *Harper's*.

NONNO: Hah? I didn't hear that, Hannah.

HANNAH [*shouting*]: I'll have it typed up tomorrow, and mail it to *Harper's* tomorrow! They've been waiting for it a long time, too! You know!

NONNO: Yes; I'd like to pray now.

HANNAH: Good night. Sleep now, Grandfather. You've finished your loveliest poem.

NONNO [*faintly, drifting off*]: Yes, thanks and praise . . .

[MAXINE *comes around the front of the verandah, followed by* PEDRO *playing a harmonica softly. She is prepared for a night swim, a vividly striped towel thrown over her shoulders. It is apparent that the night's progress has mellowed her spirit: her face wears a faint smile which is suggestive of those cool, impersonal, all-comprehending smiles on the carved heads of Egyptian or Oriental deities. Bearing a rum-coco, she approaches the hammock, discovers it empty, the ropes on the floor, and calls softly to Pedro.*]

MAXINE: Shannon ha escapado! [PEDRO *goes on playing dreamily. She throws back her head and shouts.*] Shannon! [*The call is echoed by the hill beyond.* PEDRO *advances a few steps and points under the verandah.*]

PEDRO: Miré. Allé 'hasta Shannon.

[SHANNON *comes into view from below the verandah, the severed rope and machete dangling from his hands.*]

MAXINE: What are you doing down there, Shannon?

SHANNON: I cut loose one of God's creatures at the end of the rope.

[HANNAH, *who has stood motionless with closed eyes behind the wicker chair, goes quietly towards the cubicles and out of the moon's glare.*]

MAXINE [*tolerantly*]: What'd you do that for, Shannon?

SHANNON: So that one of God's creatures could scramble home safe and free. . . . . A little act of grace, Maxine.

MAXINE [*smiling a bit more definitely*]: C'mon up here, Shannon. I want to talk to you.

SHANNON [*starting to climb on to the verandah, as* MAXINE *rattles the ice in the coconut shell*]: What d'ya want to talk about, Widow Faulk?

MAXINE: Let's go down and swim in that liquid moon-light.

SHANNON: Where did you pick up that poetic expression? [MAXINE *glances back at* PEDRO *and dismisses him with* 'Vamos.' *He leaves with a shrug, the harmonica fading out.*]

MAXINE: Shannon, I want you to stay with me.

SHANNON [*taking the rum-coco from her*]: You want a drinking companion?

MAXINE: No, I just want you to stay here, because I'm alone here now and I need somebody to help me manage the place.

[HANNAH *strikes a match for a cigarette.*]

SHANNON [*looking towards her*]: I want to remember that face. I won't see it again.

MAXINE: Let's go down to the beach.

SHANNON: I can make it down the hill, but not back up.

MAXINE: I'll get you back up the hill. [*They have started off now, towards the path down through the rain forest.*] I've got five more years, maybe ten, to make this place attractive to the male clientele, the middle-aged ones at least. And you can take care of the women that are with them. That's what you can do, you know that, Shannon.

[*He chuckles happily. They are now on the path,* MAXINE *half leading, half supporting him. Their voices fade as* HANNAH *goes into Nonno's cubicle and comes back with a shawl, her cigarette left inside. She pauses between the door and the wicker chair and speaks to herself and the sky.*]

HANNAH: Oh, God, can't we stop now? Finally? Please let us. It's so quiet here, now.

[*She starts to put the shawl about Nonno, but at the same moment his head drops to one side. With a soft intake of breath, she extends a hand before his mouth to see if he is still breathing. He isn't. In a panicky moment, she looks right and left for someone to call to. There's no one. Then she bends to press her head to the crown of Nonno's and the curtain starts to descend.*]

THE END

Nazi Marching Song

Heute wollen wir ein Liedlein singen,
Trinken wollen wir den kühlen Wein;
Und die Gläser sollen dazu klingen,
Denn es muss, es muss geschieden sein.

Gib' mir deine Hand,
Deine weisse Hand,
Leb' wohl, mein Schatz, leb' wohl, mein Schatz,
Lebe wohl, lebe wohl,
Denn wir fahren. Boom! Boom!
Denn wir fahren. Boom! Boom!
Denn wir fahren gegen Engeland. Boom! Boom!

Let's sing a little song today,
And drink some cool wine;
The glasses should be ringing
Since we must, we must part.

Give me your hand,
Your white hand,
Farewell, my love, farewell,
Farewell, farewell,
Since we're going –
Since we're going –
Since we're going against England.

MORE ABOUT PENGUINS
AND PELICANS

For further information about books available from Penguins please write to Dept EP, Penguin Books Ltd, Harmondsworth, Middlesex UB7 0DA.

In the U.S.A.: For a complete list of books available from Penguins in the United States write to Dept CS, Penguin Books, 625 Madison Avenue, New York, New York 10022.

In Canada: For a complete list of books available from Penguins in Canada write to Penguin Books Canada Ltd, 2801 John Street, Markham, Ontario L3R 1B4.

In Australia: For a complete list of books available from Penguins in Australia write to the Marketing Department, Penguin Books Australia Ltd, P.O. Box 257, Ringwood, Victoria 3134.

A selection of anthologies in Penguin Plays

CLASSIC IRISH DRAMA

Introduced by W. A. Armstrong

Yeat's *The Countess Cathleen* tells of two merchants who traffic in men's souls, and of how the Countess sells her own rather than see her people starve.

Synge's *The Playboy of the Western World* is about a peasant boy who thinks he has killed his father and so becomes a hero – until his murdered father reappears.

O'Casey's *Cock-a-doodle Dandy*, which the author considered his best play, is a satire directed against superstition, avarice and priestly authority.

ABSURD DRAMA

Introduced by Martin Esslin

Containing Ionesco's first full-length play, *Amédée*, and three short plays: Adamov's *Professo V Taranne*, Arrabal's *The Two Executioners*, and Edward Albee's *The Zoo Story*.

THREE EUROPEAN PLAYS

Introduced and Edited by E. Martin Browne

In his ebullient comedy *Ring Round the Moon*, Anouilh draws vivid and entertaining portraits of human idiosyncrasies – with a total disregard for accepted moral values. Ugo Betti's reputation now rivals that of Pirandello; his concern with morality and religion is demonstrated in *The Queen and the Rebels*, a political drama of our own times written in the classical tradition. Sartre's *In Camera* involves three of life's victims who come to recognize that 'hell is other people'.

Arts and Entertainments in Penguins

Charlton Heston

THE ACTOR'S LIFE: THE JOURNALS 1956–1976

'Here, better than any book I have read, is the feeling of what it is like to be a filmstar ... a goldmine' – *Daily Telegraph*

Charlton Heston remembers it all, from the cold-water flat in a New York slum to the top of the greatest show on earth – Hollywood.

Richard Buckle

NIJINSKY

'The best biography of a dancer in the language' – *Lincoln Kirstein*

In the history of ballet the legend of Nijinsky surpasses them all. A slight as a snowflake, as strong as steel, this was the greatest dancer, the greatest mime artist, the most revolutionary choreographer the stage has known.

John Heilpern

CONFERENCE OF THE BIRDS

Peter Brook and his international troupe of actors left their base in Paris to journey through the Sahara in search of new forms of theatre. 'A beautifully detailed and evocatively written account of people embroiled in a genuine search for new values ... the closest thing yet written to an explanation of the phenomenon of Peter Brook' – Charles Marowitz in the *Sunday Times*